THE BEST TEST PREPARATION FOR THE

GRE

GRADUATE

RECORD

EXAMINATION

IN

MATHEMATICS

Om Prakash Agrawal, Ph.D.
Mathematics Instructor
University of Kansas, Lawrence, Kansas

Thomas E. Elsner, Ph.D.
Professor of Mathematics
GMI Engineering and Management Institute, Flint, Michigan

John S. Robertson, Ph.D.
Associate Professor of Mathematics
United States Military Academy, West Point, New York

J. Terry Wilson, Ph.D.
Chairperson of Mathematics Department
San Jacinto College, Pasadena, Texas

Research and Education Association
61 Ethel Road West
Piscataway, New Jersey 08854

The Best Test Preparation for the
GRADUATE RECORD EXAMINATION
(GRE) IN MATHEMATICS

REVISED PRINTING 1993

Printed in the United States of America

Library of Congress Catalog Card Number 88-90713

International Standard Book Number 0-87891-637-7

Research & Education Association
61 Ethel Road West
Piscataway, New Jersey 08854

REA supports the effort to conserve and
protect environmental resources by
printing on recycled papers.

CONTENTS

PREFACE   v

ABOUT THE TEST   v

SCORING THE TEST   vii

GRE MATH STUDY SCHEDULE   ix

GRE MATH TEST I
    Answer Sheet Form I   1
    Test I   2
    Answer Key   27
    Detailed Explanations of Answers   28

GRE MATH TEST II

    Answer Sheet Form II   61
    Test II   62
    Answer Key   86
    Detailed Explanations of Answers   87

GRE MATH TEST III

    Answer Sheet Form III   107
    Test III   108
    Answer Key   132
    Detailed Explanations of Answers   133

GRE MATH TEST IV

    Answer Sheet Form IV   165
    Test IV   166
    Answer Key   191
    Detailed Explanations of Answers   192

GRE MATH TEST V

    Answer Sheet Form V   210
    Test V   211
    Answer Key   236
    Detailed Explanations of Answers   237

GRE MATH TEST VI

    Answer Sheet Form VI   265
    Test VI   266
    Answer Key   294
    Detailed Explanations of Answers   295

PREFACE

This book provides an accurate and complete representation of the Graduate Record Examination in Mathematics. The six practice exams provided are based on the most recently administered Graduate Record Examinations in Mathematics. Each test is two hours and fifty minutes in length and includes every type of question that can be expected on the actual exam. Following each exam is an answer key complete with detailed explanations designed to clarify the material to the student. By completing all six exams and studying the explanations which follow, students can discover their strengths and weaknesses and thereby become well prepared for the actual exam.

ABOUT THE TEST

The Graduate Record Examination in Mathematics is offered four times a year by the Educational Testing Service, under the direction of the Graduate Record Examinations Board. Applicants for graduate school submit GRE test results together with other undergraduate records as part of the highly competitive admission process to graduate school.

The questions on the test are composed by a committee of specialists who are selected from various undergraduate and graduate faculties. This test consists of approximately 66 multiple-choice questions. Some questions are grouped together under a particular diagram and/or graph. Emphasis is placed on the following major areas of mathematics:

I. Analysis (50%)
   A. Trigonometry
   B. Coordinate Geometry
   C. Introductory Differential Equations
   D. Introductory Real Variable Theory
   E. Elementary Topology of the Line, Plane, 3-space, and n-space
   F. Riemann and Elementary Lebesgue Integration

II. Algebra (25%)
   A. Elementary

B. Linear
 — matrices
 — linear transformations
 — characteristic polynomials
 — eigenvectors
 — other
C. Abstract
 — elementary theory of groups, rings, and fields
 — number theory

III. Miscellaneous (25%)
  A. Probability and Statistics
  B. Set Theory
  C. Logic
  D. Combinatorial Analysis
  E. Topology
  F. Numerical Analysis
  G. Computer Programming
  H. Application of Mathematical Models to Real Life Situations

The topics described above are not exhaustive. The questions test beyond simple recall of information. They determine the students' understanding of fundamental concepts and their ability to apply these concepts to specific situations. Due to the wide diversity of coursework in undergraduate mathematics, not all the material that a student may have studied will be presented on the exam. The questions are based on the courses of study most commonly offered in an undergradute mathematics curriculum.

SCORING THE TEST

Each correct answer receives one "raw score" point, each incorrect answer deducts 1/4 of a point, and any omissions should not be counted. Use the formula below to calculate your raw score.

$$\underline{\qquad} \; - \; (\quad \times \; 1/4 \;) = \underline{\qquad}$$

number
right

number
wrong - DO NOT INCLUDE
UNANSWERED QUESTIONS

raw
score
(round to nearest whole number)

By using the conversion table on page *viii*, the raw score can be converted to a scaled score, and a percentile ranking can be determined. Your scaled score is what is sent to the colleges, and your estimated percentile rank indicates your rank compared to other students who have taken the exam. For example, if you raw score is 46, then according to the conversion table your scaled score would be 850 and your percentile rank would be 77, meaning that you scored better than 77% of the students taking the GRE Mathematics.

While taking these practice tests, it is helpful to observe the same conditions that will be encountered during the actual test administration.

• Work in a quiet place, free from distractions and interruptions.

• Do not use any reference materials, calculators, or slide rules since these items are not allowed for use during the test.

• Work straight through the test. Extra time and short breaks do not occur during the actual exam.

• Time yourself accurately, if possible with a watch or clock alarm. Looking up to check the time will act as a distraction (note: watches with alarms are not permitted at the testing center.)

• Since incorrect answers are penalized 1/4 of a point each, and unanswered questions are not counted, it is not a good idea to guess. However, if you are able to eliminate one or more of the answers, guessing may be to your advantage statistically (that is, the odds of choosing the right answer improve.)

GRE MATHEMATICS
SCORE CONVERSION TABLE

RAW SCORE	SCALED SCORE	PERCENTILE RANK	RAW SCORE	SCALED SCORE	PERCENTILE RANK
60-66	990	95	29	680	44
59	980	94	28	670	42
58	970	93	27	660	40
57	960	92	26	650	38
56	950	91	25	640	35
55	940	90	24	630	33
54	930	88	23	620	31
53	920	87	22	610	29
52	910	86	21	600	27
51	900	85	20	590	25
50	890	83	19	580	23
49	880	81	18	570	21
48	870	80	17	560	19
47	860	78	16	550	18
46	850	77	15	540	16
45	840	75	14	530	15
44	830	74	13	520	14
43	820	73	12	510	12
42	810	71	11	500	11
41	800	69	10	490	10
40	790	67	09	480	08
39	780	65	08	470	07
38	770	63	07	460	06
37	760	61	06	450	05
36	750	59	05	440	04
35	740	57	04	430	04
34	730	55	03	420	03
33	720	53	02	410	03
32	710	51	01	400	02
31	700	48	00	400	02
30	690	46			

GRE MATH STUDY SCHEDULE

The following is a suggested six week study schedule for the Graduate Record Examination in Mathematics. In order for this schedule to benefit you the most, it is necessary that you follow the study activities carefully. You may want to condense or expand this schedule depending on how soon you will be taking the actual GRE Math. Set aside time each week, and work straight through the activity without rushing. By following a structured schedule, you will be sure to complete an adequate amount of studying, and you will be confident and prepared on the day of the actual exam.

Week 1: Acquaint yourself with the GRE Math by reading the Preface and About the Test. Take Test 1 as a diagnostic test in order to determine your strengths and weaknesses. After checking the answer key and the explanations, make a note of the questions that were difficult. Review the specific field of difficulty by using the appropriate textbooks, notes, etc., to prepare to take Test 2.

Week 2: Take Test 2. Read through all the detailed explanations carefully (not just those for your incorrect answers), and make a note of any sections that were difficult for you, or any questions that were still unclear after reading the explanations. Use sources of information, such as textbooks, notes, or course materials, to review those areas that need clarification.

Week 3: Take Test 3. Read through all the detailed explanations carefully (not just those for your incorrect answers), and make a note of any sections that were difficult for you, or any questions that were still unclear after reading the explanations. Use sources of information, such as textbooks, notes, or course materials, to review those areas that need clarification.

Week 4: Take Test 4. Read through all the detailed explanations carefully (not just those for your incorrect answers), and make a note of any sections that were difficult for you, or any questions that were still unclear after reading the explanations. Use sources of information, such as textbooks, notes, or course materials, to review those areas that need clarification.

Week 5: Take Test 5. Read through all the detailed explanations carefully (not just those for your incorrect answers), and make a note of any sections that were difficult for you, or any questions that were still unclear after reading the explanations. Use sources of information, such as textbooks, notes, or course materials, to review those areas that need clarification.

Week 6: Take Test 6. Read through all the detailed explanations carefully (not just those for your incorrect answers), and make a note of any sections that were difficult for you, or any questions that were still unclear after reading the explanations.

Compare your progress between the exams. Note any sections where you were able to improve your score, and sections where your score remained the same or declined. Allow yourself extra study time for those areas that require added attention.

GRE

MATH TEST

TEST I

THE GRADUATE RECORD EXAMINATION

MATH TEST

ANSWER SHEET

1. Ⓐ Ⓑ Ⓒ Ⓓ Ⓔ
2. Ⓐ Ⓑ Ⓒ Ⓓ Ⓔ
3. Ⓐ Ⓑ Ⓒ Ⓓ Ⓔ
4. Ⓐ Ⓑ Ⓒ Ⓓ Ⓔ
5. Ⓐ Ⓑ Ⓒ Ⓓ Ⓔ
6. Ⓐ Ⓑ Ⓒ Ⓓ Ⓔ
7. Ⓐ Ⓑ Ⓒ Ⓓ Ⓔ
8. Ⓐ Ⓑ Ⓒ Ⓓ Ⓔ
9. Ⓐ Ⓑ Ⓒ Ⓓ Ⓔ
10. Ⓐ Ⓑ Ⓒ Ⓓ Ⓔ
11. Ⓐ Ⓑ Ⓒ Ⓓ Ⓔ
12. Ⓐ Ⓑ Ⓒ Ⓓ Ⓔ
13. Ⓐ Ⓑ Ⓒ Ⓓ Ⓔ
14. Ⓐ Ⓑ Ⓒ Ⓓ Ⓔ
15. Ⓐ Ⓑ Ⓒ Ⓓ Ⓔ
16. Ⓐ Ⓑ Ⓒ Ⓓ Ⓔ
17. Ⓐ Ⓑ Ⓒ Ⓓ Ⓔ
18. Ⓐ Ⓑ Ⓒ Ⓓ Ⓔ
19. Ⓐ Ⓑ Ⓒ Ⓓ Ⓔ
20. Ⓐ Ⓑ Ⓒ Ⓓ Ⓔ
21. Ⓐ Ⓑ Ⓒ Ⓓ Ⓔ
22. Ⓐ Ⓑ Ⓒ Ⓓ Ⓔ

23. Ⓐ Ⓑ Ⓒ Ⓓ Ⓔ
24. Ⓐ Ⓑ Ⓒ Ⓓ Ⓔ
25. Ⓐ Ⓑ Ⓒ Ⓓ Ⓔ
26. Ⓐ Ⓑ Ⓒ Ⓓ Ⓔ
27. Ⓐ Ⓑ Ⓒ Ⓓ Ⓔ
28. Ⓐ Ⓑ Ⓒ Ⓓ Ⓔ
29. Ⓐ Ⓑ Ⓒ Ⓓ Ⓔ
30. Ⓐ Ⓑ Ⓒ Ⓓ Ⓔ
31. Ⓐ Ⓑ Ⓒ Ⓓ Ⓔ
32. Ⓐ Ⓑ Ⓒ Ⓓ Ⓔ
33. Ⓐ Ⓑ Ⓒ Ⓓ Ⓔ
34. Ⓐ Ⓑ Ⓒ Ⓓ Ⓔ
35. Ⓐ Ⓑ Ⓒ Ⓓ Ⓔ
36. Ⓐ Ⓑ Ⓒ Ⓓ Ⓔ
37. Ⓐ Ⓑ Ⓒ Ⓓ Ⓔ
38. Ⓐ Ⓑ Ⓒ Ⓓ Ⓔ
39. Ⓐ Ⓑ Ⓒ Ⓓ Ⓔ
40. Ⓐ Ⓑ Ⓒ Ⓓ Ⓔ
41. Ⓐ Ⓑ Ⓒ Ⓓ Ⓔ
42. Ⓐ Ⓑ Ⓒ Ⓓ Ⓔ
43. Ⓐ Ⓑ Ⓒ Ⓓ Ⓔ
44. Ⓐ Ⓑ Ⓒ Ⓓ Ⓔ

45. Ⓐ Ⓑ Ⓒ Ⓓ Ⓔ
46. Ⓐ Ⓑ Ⓒ Ⓓ Ⓔ
47. Ⓐ Ⓑ Ⓒ Ⓓ Ⓔ
48. Ⓐ Ⓑ Ⓒ Ⓓ Ⓔ
49. Ⓐ Ⓑ Ⓒ Ⓓ Ⓔ
50. Ⓐ Ⓑ Ⓒ Ⓓ Ⓔ
51. Ⓐ Ⓑ Ⓒ Ⓓ Ⓔ
52. Ⓐ Ⓑ Ⓒ Ⓓ Ⓔ
53. Ⓐ Ⓑ Ⓒ Ⓓ Ⓔ
54. Ⓐ Ⓑ Ⓒ Ⓓ Ⓔ
55. Ⓐ Ⓑ Ⓒ Ⓓ Ⓔ
56. Ⓐ Ⓑ Ⓒ Ⓓ Ⓔ
57. Ⓐ Ⓑ Ⓒ Ⓓ Ⓔ
58. Ⓐ Ⓑ Ⓒ Ⓓ Ⓔ
59. Ⓐ Ⓑ Ⓒ Ⓓ Ⓔ
60. Ⓐ Ⓑ Ⓒ Ⓓ Ⓔ
61. Ⓐ Ⓑ Ⓒ Ⓓ Ⓔ
62. Ⓐ Ⓑ Ⓒ Ⓓ Ⓔ
63. Ⓐ Ⓑ Ⓒ Ⓓ Ⓔ
64. Ⓐ Ⓑ Ⓒ Ⓓ Ⓔ
65. Ⓐ Ⓑ Ⓒ Ⓓ Ⓔ
66. Ⓐ Ⓑ Ⓒ Ⓓ Ⓔ

GRE MATHEMATICS
TEST I

TIME: 2 hours and 50 minutes
66 Questions

DIRECTIONS: Choose the best answer for each question and mark the letter of your selection on the corresponding answer sheet.

1.   The graph of the arccosine function is the graph of the arcsine function

(A)   translated horizontally $\pi / 2$ units to the right

(B)   first reflected in the horizontal axis and then translated vertically $\pi / 2$ units upward

(C)   first translated horizontally $\pi / 2$ units to the left and then reflected in the horizontal axis

(D)   first translated vertically $\pi / 2$ units downward and then reflected in the vertical axis

(E)   translated horizontally $\pi / 2$ units to the left

2.   If $f(x) = e^x - e^{-x}$, then $[f'(x)]^2 - [f(x)]^2$ equals

(A)   4   (B) $4e^{-2x}$

(C) $2e^{-x}$

(E) $2e^x$

(D) 2

3. The domain of $f(x) = \dfrac{\sqrt[3]{x+2}}{x-6}$ is given by

(A) $(6, +\infty)$

(D) $[-2, +\infty) \setminus \{6\}$

(B) $[-2, +\infty)$

(E) $R \setminus \{6\}$

(C) $R \setminus \{-2, 6\}$

4. Let $M = \begin{bmatrix} 1 & 2 \\ 3 & 9 \end{bmatrix}$. The determinant of the adjoint of M is

(A) 9

(D) 18

(B) 6

(E) 3

(C) 27

5. The number of generators of a cyclic group of order 8 is

(A) 6

(D) 2

(B) 4

(E) 1

(C) 3

6. An integrating factor for the ordinary differential equation

$$\frac{-2y}{x} \, dx + (x^2 y \cos y + 1) \, dy = 0 \quad \text{is}$$

(A) 1

(D) $-2x$

(B) $\dfrac{-2}{x}$

(E) x^2

(C) $\dfrac{1}{x^2}$

7. Assuming convergence, find $x = \sqrt{3 + \sqrt{3 + \sqrt{3 + \ldots}}}$

(A) $\dfrac{1}{2}(\sqrt{5} + 1)$

(B) $\dfrac{1}{2}(\sqrt{13} - 1)$

(C) $\dfrac{1}{2}(\sqrt{5} - 1)$

(D) $\dfrac{1}{2}(\sqrt{13} + 1)$

(E) $\dfrac{1}{2}(\sqrt{13} - \sqrt{5})$

8. Let x be a random variable possessing the probability density function

$$f(x) = \begin{cases} cx & x \in [0, 10] \\ 0 & \text{otherwise} \end{cases}$$

where $c \in R$. The probability that x is an element of $[1, 2]$ is

(A) $\dfrac{1}{100}$

(B) $\dfrac{3}{100}$

4

(C) $\dfrac{5}{100}$

(E) $\dfrac{9}{100}$

(D) $\dfrac{7}{100}$

9.   Let the random variable X have the probability density function

$$f(x) = \begin{cases} 1 - \dfrac{x}{2} & x \in (0, 2) \\ 0 & \text{otherwise} \end{cases}$$

The expected value of the random variable X^2 is

(A) $\dfrac{1}{3}$

(D) $\dfrac{1}{6}$

(B) $\dfrac{5}{6}$

(E) $\dfrac{2}{3}$

(C) $\dfrac{1}{2}$

10.   Find the number of solutions of the set of all algebraic equations of height two.

(A) 0

(D) 3

(B) 1

(E) 4

(C) 2

11. Define a metric on $R^2 = R \times R$ by $d[(x_1, y_1); (x_2, y_2)]$ $= |x_2 - x_1| + |y_2 - y_1|$. The unit ball $d[(0, 0); (x, y)] < 1$ is

(A) the interior of a circle with center $(0, 0)$ and radius 1

(B) $(0, 0)$

(C) the interior of a square with vertices $(-1, 1), (1, 1), (1, -1)$ and $(-1, -1)$

(D) the interior of a square with vertices $(-1, 0), (0, 1), (1, 0)$ and $(0, -1)$

(E) the interior of a triangle with vertices $(-1, -1), (0, \sqrt{3})$, and $(1, -1)$

12. Which of the following is **not** equal to $f(x) = \dfrac{x + 1}{x - 1}$ when both are defined?

(A) $-f(x^{-1})$

(B) $[f(-x)]^{-1}$

(C) $f^{-1}(x)$

(D) $f^{-1}(x^{-1})$

(E) $\frac{1}{2}[f^{-1}(x) - f(x^{-1})]$

13. Let $M = \begin{bmatrix} 6 & 10 \\ -2 & -3 \end{bmatrix}$. The trace of M^5 equals

(A) 27

(B) 3^5

6

(C) 5^3 (E) 33

(D) $6^5 + (-3)^5$

14.   The degree of the minimum polynomial satisfied by a nonscalar, 8 by 8, idempotent matrix M is

(A) 4   (D) 3

(B) 2   (E) 6

(C) 8

15.   Find the incidence matrix for the graph:

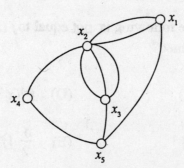

(A) $\begin{bmatrix} 0 & 1 & 0 & 0 & 1 \\ 1 & 0 & 1 & 1 & 0 \\ 0 & 1 & 0 & 0 & 1 \\ 0 & 1 & 0 & 0 & 1 \\ 1 & 0 & 1 & 1 & 0 \end{bmatrix}$ (B) $\begin{bmatrix} 1 & 2 & 1 & 1 & 1 \\ 2 & 1 & 3 & 1 & 1 \\ 1 & 3 & 1 & 1 & 1 \\ 1 & 1 & 1 & 1 & 1 \\ 1 & 1 & 1 & 1 & 1 \end{bmatrix}$

(C) $$\begin{bmatrix} 0 & 2 & 0 & 0 & 1 \\ 2 & 0 & 3 & 1 & 0 \\ 0 & 3 & 0 & 0 & 1 \\ 0 & 1 & 0 & 0 & 1 \\ 1 & 0 & 1 & 1 & 0 \end{bmatrix}$$

(D) $$\begin{bmatrix} 1 & 2 & 0 & 0 & 1 \\ 2 & 1 & 3 & 1 & 0 \\ 0 & 3 & 1 & 0 & 1 \\ 0 & 1 & 0 & 1 & 1 \\ 1 & 0 & 1 & 1 & 1 \end{bmatrix}$$

(E) $$\begin{bmatrix} 1 & 1 & 0 & 0 & 1 \\ 1 & 1 & 1 & 1 & 0 \\ 0 & 1 & 1 & 0 & 1 \\ 0 & 1 & 0 & 1 & 1 \\ 1 & 0 & 1 & 1 & 1 \end{bmatrix}$$

16.   The fixed point(s) of the Mobius transformation
$w(z) = \dfrac{z-2}{z-1}$ is (are)

(A) $1 \pm \sqrt{3}$ (D) $1 \pm i$

(B) $1 \pm 2i$ (E) $-1 \pm \sqrt{2}\, i$

(C) $2i$

17.   The sum of the 9th roots of unity is

(A) 0   (D) 10

(B) 1   (E) $1 + i$

(C) 9

18. Let x , y , z represent Boolean variables. Which of the following is not a Boolean function?

(A) $f(x, y) = x\sqrt{y}$

(B) $f(x, y, z) = \max\ \{x, y, z\}$

(C) $f(x, y) = x^2 + y - xy$

(D) $f(x, y, z) = x + y + z - xy - yz$

(E) $f(x, y, z) = xyz$

19. What is the maximum perimeter of all rectangles that can be inscribed in $\dfrac{x^2}{a^2} + \dfrac{y^2}{b^2} = 1$?

(A) $4\sqrt{a^2 + b^2}$ (D) $a^2 + b^2$

(B) $\dfrac{8}{\sqrt{a^2 + b^2}}$ (E) $2(a^2 + b^2)$

(C) $2\sqrt{a^2 + b^2}$

20. Which of the following is a topological property?

(A) boundedness

(B) being a Cauchy sequence

(C) completeness

(D) being an accumulation (limit) point

(E) length

21. The value of $I = \oint_c \dfrac{\cos z}{z(z - \pi)}\, dz$ where C is the circle
$|z - 1| = 2$ is

(A) 0

(D) $-4i$

(B) $2i$

(E) $4i$

(C) $-2i$

22. Let $p(x)$, $q(x)$, and $r(x)$ be open statements relative to the set
S. Then $\sim (\exists x \in S)\,[(p(x) \lor q(x)) \land r(x)]$ is equivalent to

(A) $(\forall x \in S)\,\{[(\sim p(x)) \lor (\sim q(x))] \lor [\sim r(x)]\}$

(B) $(\forall x \in S)\,\{[(\sim p(x)) \land (\sim q(x))] \lor [\sim r(x)]\}$

(C) $(\forall x \in S)\,\{[(\sim p(x)) \land (\sim q(x))] \lor [r(x)]\}$

(D) $(\forall x \in S)\,\{[(\sim p(x)) \lor (\sim q(x))] \land [\sim r(x)]\}$

(E) $(\forall x \in S)\,\{[(\sim p(x)) \lor (\sim q(x))] \land [r(x)]\}$

23. Let $x_n = \dfrac{n^n}{n!}$ for $n = 1, 2, 3, \ldots$. Then $\displaystyle\lim_{n \to +\infty} \dfrac{x_{n+1}}{x_n}$ equals

(A) $\sqrt{e}$

(D) e^2

(B) e

(E) e^{-1}

(C) $\sqrt{e^3}$

24. The derivative of $f(x) = \displaystyle\int_x^0 \dfrac{\cos xt}{t}\, dt$ is

(A) $-\dfrac{\cos 2x^2}{x}$

(D) $-\dfrac{\sin 2x^2}{x}$

(B) $\dfrac{1}{x}[1 + 2 \cos x^2]$

(E) $\dfrac{\cos x^2}{x}$

(C) $\dfrac{1}{x}[1 + 2 \sin x^2]$

25. The maximum value of the directional derivative on the surface $z = f(x, y) = xe^{xy} + y \cos x$ at $P(0, 1)$ is

(A) 1

(D) $\sqrt{4}$

(B) $\sqrt{2}$

(E) $\sqrt{5}$

(C) $\sqrt{3}$

26. The number of ordered partitions of the positive integer 5 is

(A) 20

(B) 18

(C) 16

(D) 14

(E) 12

27. The Wronskian of $f_1(x) = x^2 \sin x$ and $f_2(x) = x^2 \cos x$ is

(A) x^2

(B) $-x^2$

(C) x^4

(D) $-x^4$

(E) $2x^4$

28. Given the linear second-order difference equation

$$y_{k+2} - y_{k+1} - 2y_k = 0 \; ; \; k = 0,1,2,\ldots$$

$$y_0 = 9 \; ; \; y_1 = -12$$

find y_6.

(A) -54

(B) 64

(C) -32

(D) 27

(E) 54

29. Which of the following numbers is divisible by 9?

(A) 7224466

(D) 5224466

(B) 9224466

(E) 1224466

(C) 3224466

30. The inflection point for $f(x) = \dfrac{\ln x}{x}$ occurs at $x =$

(A) $\sqrt{e}$

(D) e^{-1}

(B) e

(E) $\sqrt{e^{-1}}$

(C) $\sqrt{e^3}$

31. The dimension of the null space of

$$M = \begin{bmatrix} 1 & 2 & -1 & 0 \\ 3 & 2 & 0 & 1 \\ 1 & 2 & 0 & 2 \\ -1 & 0 & 1 & 3 \end{bmatrix}$$

is:

(A) 2

(D) 3

(B) 1

(E) 0

(C) 4

32.   Find the radical of the commutative ring Z_8 .

(A) Z_8

(D) $\{0, 2, 4\}$

(B) $\{0\}$

(E) $\{0, 2\}$

(C) $\{0, 2, 4, 6\}$

33.   Which of the following is equivalent to $\sin^3 x \cos^2 x$?

(A) $\frac{1}{16} [2 \sin x - \sin 3x - 2 \sin 5x]$

(B) $\frac{1}{16} [\sin x - 2 \sin 3x - \sin 5x]$

(C) $\frac{1}{16} [2 \sin x - \sin 3x - \sin 5x]$

(D) $\frac{1}{16} [2 \sin x + \sin 3x - \sin 5x]$

(E) $\frac{1}{16} [\sin x + \sin 3x - \sin 5x]$

34.   The absolute maximum of $f(x) = \cos 2x - 2 \cos x$ on $[0, 2\pi]$ occurs at $x =$

(A) $\frac{\pi}{3}$

(D) $\frac{5\pi}{3}$

(B) $\frac{\pi}{2}$

(E) $\frac{3\pi}{4}$

(C) π

35. The eigenvalue which corresponds to the eigenvector

$\begin{bmatrix} 3 \\ 2 \end{bmatrix}$ for $M = \begin{bmatrix} 1 & -3 \\ -2 & 2 \end{bmatrix}$ is

(A) 1

(D) -4

(B) 4

(E) 2

(C) -1

36. Evaluate the sum $\sum\limits_{n=1}^{m} \arctan\left(\dfrac{1}{n^2 + n + 1}\right)$

(A) $m^2 + 1$

(B) $\dfrac{1}{m^2 + m}$

(C) $\cot(m + 1) - \dfrac{1}{m^2 + 1}$

(D) $\arctan(m + 1) - \dfrac{\pi}{4}$

(E) $(-1)^m \sin(m + 1) + \tan m$

37. The conjugates of an element are the other roots of the irreducible polynomial of which the given element is a root. The conjugates of $\sqrt{\sqrt{3} + 1}$ over the field of rational numbers are

(A) $\sqrt{\sqrt{3} + 1}$, $\sqrt{\sqrt{3} - 1}$

15

(B) $\sqrt{\sqrt{3}+1}$, $-\sqrt{\sqrt{3}+1}$

(C) $\pm\sqrt{1+\sqrt{3}}$, $\pm\sqrt{1-\sqrt{3}}$

(D) $\pm\sqrt{\sqrt{3}+1}$, $\pm\sqrt{\sqrt{3}-1}$

(E) $\sqrt{\sqrt{3}+1}$, $-\sqrt{\sqrt{3}-1}$

38. The smallest positive integer n for which the inequality $2^n > n^2$ is true for $\{n, n+1, \ldots\}$ is

(A) 1   (D) 4

(B) 2   (E) 5

(C) 3

39. Consider the two player (P_1, P_2) game G with payoff matrix

$$P_1 \begin{array}{c} P_2 \\ \begin{bmatrix} 1 & -1 \\ 2 & 3 \end{bmatrix} \end{array}$$

The minimax value of G is

(A) $\dfrac{5}{3}$ (D) 5

(B) 1   (E) 0

(C) $\dfrac{3}{2}$

16

40. The first Newton approximation x_1 for a zero of $f(x) = x^3 - 2x$ with initial approximation $x_0 = 2$ is

(A) $\dfrac{12}{5}$ (D) $\dfrac{6}{5}$

(B) 2 (E) $\dfrac{7}{5}$

(C) $\dfrac{8}{5}$

41. The value of $\displaystyle\int_1^4 |x - 2|\, dx$ is

(A) 3 (D) $\dfrac{3}{2}$

(B) $\dfrac{5}{2}$ (E) $\dfrac{7}{2}$

(C) 2

42. A Sylow 3-subgroup of a group of order 72 has order

(A) 3 (D) 27

(B) 9 (E) 36

(C) 18

43. Which of the following sets, together with the given binary operation *, does $\underline{not}$ form a group?

Note: Z = integers
Q = rationals
R = reals
C = complex numbers

(A) $G = \{a + b\sqrt{2} \in R\backslash\{0\} \mid a,b \in Q\}$
*: usual multiplication of real numbers

(B) $G = \{a + bi\sqrt{2} \in C\backslash\{0\} \mid a,b \in Q\}$
*: usual multiplication of complex numbers

(C) $G = \{\sqrt[3]{a} \in R \mid a \in Z\}$
*: for $a,b \in G$, $\sqrt[3]{a} * \sqrt[3]{b} = \sqrt[3]{a+b}$

(D) $G = R\backslash\{0\}$
*: for $a,b \in G$, $a * b = |a|\,b$

(E) $G = \{z \in C \mid |z| = 1\}$
*: usual multiplication of complex numbers

44. Let $M = \begin{bmatrix} 2 & 4 \\ 1 & 2 \end{bmatrix}$. Then $M^6 = kM$ for $k =$

(A) 2^6 (D) 2^{12}

(B) 2^8 (E) 2^{14}

(C) 2^{10}

45. From a group of 15 mathematics graduate school applicants, 10 are selected at random. Let P be the probability that 4 of the 5 applicants who would make the best graduate students are included in the 10 selected. Which of the following statements is true?

(A) $0 \leq P \leq \frac{1}{5}$

(D) $\frac{3}{5} < P \leq \frac{4}{5}$

(B) $\frac{1}{5} < P \leq \frac{2}{5}$

(E) $\frac{4}{5} < P \leq 1$

(C) $\frac{2}{5} < P \leq \frac{3}{5}$

46. The equation $r = 2 \sin \theta - \cos \theta$ in rectangular coordinates is given by

(A) $x^2 + y^2 + x - 2y = 0$

(B) $x^2 - x + 2y = 0$

(C) $x^2 + y^2 + 2x - y = 0$

(D) $x^2 - y^2 - x + 2y = 0$

(E) $y^2 - x^2 - x + 2y = 0$

47. The decimal $2.0259\overline{259}$ is equivalent to which of the following?

(A) $\dfrac{20237}{9990}$

(B) $\dfrac{547}{270}$

19

(C) $\dfrac{20239}{9999}$ (D) $\dfrac{747}{370}$

(E) $\dfrac{737}{380}$

48. The general term of the Maclaurin series for xe^{-x^2} is

(A) $\dfrac{(-1)^n\, x^{2n}}{(n+1)!}$ (D) $\dfrac{(-1)^n\, x^{2n+1}}{n!}$

(B) $\dfrac{(-1)^{n+1}\, x^{2n+1}}{n!}$ (E) $\dfrac{(-1)^{n+1}\, x^{2n}}{n!}$

(C) $\dfrac{(-1)^n\, x^{2n+1}}{(n+1)!}$

49. The solution set for the inequality $x - \dfrac{3}{x} > 2$ is given by

(A) $(0, +\infty)$ (D) $(-\infty, 0) \cup (3, +\infty)$

(B) $(3, +\infty)$ (E) $(-\infty, 3)$

(C) $(-1, 0) \cup (3, +\infty)$

50. The volume (in cubic units) generated by rotating the region defined by the curves
$$y = x$$
$$y = 2\sqrt{x}$$
around the x-axis is

(A) $\dfrac{16\pi}{5}$ (B) $\dfrac{32\pi}{15}$

20

(C) $\dfrac{16\pi}{3}$ (D) $\dfrac{32\pi}{3}$

(E) π

51. Let A and B be subsets of U and denote the complement of subset X of U by X^c. Find $[[A \cap (A \cap B^c)] \cap B]^c$.

(A) B^c (D) U

(B) A^c (E) $\varnothing$

(C) $A \cup B^c$

52. The cross product $\vec{u} \times \vec{v}$ of the vectors

$$\vec{u} = 2\vec{i} - \vec{j} + 3\vec{k}$$
$$\vec{v} = \vec{i} + 2\vec{j} - \vec{k}$$

is given by

(A) $7\vec{i} + \vec{j} + 3\vec{k}$ (D) $-5\vec{i} + 5\vec{j} + 5\vec{k}$

(B) $5\vec{i} + 5\vec{j} + 3\vec{k}$ (E) $7\vec{i} - \vec{j}$

(C) -3

21

53. Find the number of left cosets of the cyclic subgroup generated by $(1, 1)$ of $Z_2 \times Z_4$ where Z_n denotes the cyclic group of $\{0, 1, 2, \ldots, n-1\}$ under addition modulo n.

(A) 1 (D) 6

(B) 2 (E) 8

(C) 4

54. Up to isomorphism, how many abelian groups are there of order 36?

(A) 1 (D) 12

(B) 4 (E) 18

(C) 9

55. If $i = \sqrt{-1}$, then $\sum_{j=0}^{10} (-i)^j$ is

(A) i (D) $1 + i$

(B) -1 (E) $1 - i$

(C) $-i$

56. The set of gaussian integers, $R = \{a+ib\,|\,a,b\in Z(\text{integers})\}$, is a commutative subring of the complex numbers. An element $u = e+id$ in R is a unit of R if there exists $V\in R$ such that $uv = 1$. The unit(s) of R is (are)

(A) ± 1 (D) $\pm 1,\ \pm i$

(B) $\pm i$ (E) 1

(C) $1, i$

57. The number of solutions (equivalence classes) of the congruence $3x + 11 \equiv 20 \pmod{12}$ is:

(A) no solutions   (D) 4

(B) 1   (E) 6

(C) 3

58. Let R be the region defined by
$$y = x - 1; \quad x = 1; \quad y = -x + 3$$
Find the maximum value of $f(x, y) = -2x + 3y$ on R.

(A) –2   (D) 4

(B) 1   (E) –1

(C) 2

59. If $|x|$ is large, then $f(x) = \dfrac{x^5 - x^4 + x^3 + x}{x^3 - 1}$ is approximately

(A) $x^2 + x$ (D) $x^2 + 1$

(B) $x^2 - x + 1$ (E) $x^2 - x$

(C) x^2

60. The number of vertices of an ordinary polyhedron with 12 faces and 17 edges is

(A) 7 (D) 9

(B) 5 (E) 13

(C) 11

61. Let T be a linear transformation of the plane such that $T(1, 1) = (-1, 1)$ and $T(2, 3) = (1, 2)$. Then $T(2, 4)$ equals

(A) $(4, 2)$ (D) $(2, 4)$

(B) $(2, -4)$ (E) $(-3, 2)$

(C) $(3, -2)$

24

62. The function $f(z) = \sin x \cosh y + v(x, y)i$ is analytic for $v(x, y)$ equal to

(A) $\cos x \cosh y$

(D) $\sin x \sinh y$

(B) $\cos x \sinh y$

(E) $\sin y \cosh x$

(C) $- \sin y \cosh x$

63. Let T represent a nonsingular linear transformation from E^n into E^n. Which of the following is not true?

(A) Null space of $T = \{0\}$

(B) T is one-to-one

(C) Dimension of null space is zero: $\operatorname{Dim} N(T) = 0$

(D) Dimension of range space is n: $\operatorname{Dim} R(T) = n$

(E) $\operatorname{Dim} N(T^{-1}) = \operatorname{Dim} R(T)$

64. Find the value of the sum: $1 + \dfrac{2}{3} + \dfrac{4}{9} + \dfrac{8}{27} + \ldots$

(A) $\dfrac{11}{3}$

(D) 3

(B) $\dfrac{5}{2}$

(E) ∞

(C) 2

65. The circles

$$c_1: x^2 + y^2 + 2ax + 2by + c = 0$$

$$c_2: x^2 + y^2 + 2a'x + 2b'y + c' = 0$$

are orthogonal if

(A) $2aa' + 2bb' = c + c'$

(B) $a + a' + b + b' = cc'$

(C) $aa' - bb' = c - c'$

(D) $2aa' - 2bb' = c - c'$

(E) $a + b + c = a' + b' + c'$

66. The inverse of the matrix $M = \begin{bmatrix} 2 & 1 & 3 \\ 0 & -1 & 2 \\ 4 & 3 & 1 \end{bmatrix}$ is the matrix

$$M^{-1} = \frac{1}{6} \begin{bmatrix} -7 & 8 & a \\ 8 & -10 & -4 \\ 4 & b & -2 \end{bmatrix} \text{ where}$$

(A) $a = 5 ; b = -2$ (D) $a = 2 ; b = -3$

(B) $a = 3 ; b = 2$ (E) $a = 2 ; b = 3$

(C) $a = 1 ; b = -3$

26

GRE MATHEMATICS
TEST I

ANSWER KEY

1.	B	23.	B	45.	B
2.	A	24.	A	46.	A
3.	E	25.	B	47.	B
4.	E	26.	C	48.	D
5.	B	27.	D	49.	C
6.	C	28.	A	50.	D
7.	D	29.	C	51.	D
8.	B	30.	C	52.	D
9	E	31.	B	53.	B
10.	B	32.	C	54.	B
11.	D	33.	D	55.	C
12.	D	34.	C	56.	D
13.	E	35.	C	57.	C
14.	B	36.	D	58.	D
15.	C	37.	C	59.	B
16.	D	38.	E	60.	A
17.	A	39.	A	61.	A
18.	D	40.	C	62.	B
19.	A	41.	B	63.	E
20.	D	42.	B	64.	D
21.	C	43.	D	65.	A
22.	B	44.	C	66.	A

GRE MATHEMATICS
TEST I

DETAILED EXPLANATIONS
OF ANSWERS

1.   (B)
    Whereas the fundamental identity for the trigonometric functions is $\sin^2 x + \cos^2 x = 1$, the fundamental identity for the inverse trigonometric functions is $\arcsin x + \arccos x = \pi/2$. Thus $\arccos x = \pi/2 - \arcsin x$. The curve of $\arcsin x$ reflected in the horizontal axis will represent the curve of $-\arcsin x$. Adding $\pi/2$ is geometrically equivalent to translating the curve vertically $\pi/2$ units upward.

2.   (A)
    Since $f'(x) = e^x + e^{-x}$, we have

$$[f'(x)]^2 - [f(x)]^2 = [e^x + e^{-x}]^2 - [e^x - e^{-x}]^2$$

$$= e^{2x} + 2 + e^{-2x} - e^{2x} + 2 - e^{-2x}$$

$$= 4$$

Using the identities

$$f(x) = 2\sinh x, \ f'(x) = 2\cosh x, \text{ and } \cosh^2 x - \sinh^2 x = 1,$$

we also have

$$[f'(x)]^2 - [f(x)]^2 = [2\cosh x]^2 - [2\sinh x]^2$$

$$= 4.$$

3.   (E)

The numerator is defined for all real numbers since it contains a cube root. The denominator is defined and nonzero except for $x = 6$. So, the domain is $R\backslash\{6\}$.

4.   (E)

The determinant of M, denoted $|M|$, is given by

$$|M| = \begin{vmatrix} 1 & 2 \\ 3 & 9 \end{vmatrix} = 3.$$

For an $n \times n$ nonsingular matrix M, we have $M^{-1} = |M|^{-1}$ adj (M) and $|M^{-1}| = |M|^{-1}$ so that

$$|M^{-1}| = | \; |M|^{-1} \text{ adj }(M) \; |$$

$$|M|^{-1} = (\; |M|^{-1})^n \; |\text{ adj }(M) \; |$$

$$|\text{ adj }(M)\; | = |M|^{n-1}$$

Since $|M| = 3$, $|\text{ adj }(M)| = |M|^{2-1} = 3$.

5.   (B)

Let g be any generator of a cyclic group G of order 8. The generators of G are of the form g^r where r is relatively prime to 8 (that is, the greatest common divisor of r and 8 is 1). The positive integers less than 8 and relatively prime to 8 are 1, 3, 5, 7. Therefore the four generators of G are g^1, g^3, g^5, and g^7.

6. (C)

An integrating factor for an ordinary differential equation of the form $M\,dx + N\,dy = 0$ is a function of the form $J(x, y)$ such that $JM\,dx + JN\,dy = 0$ is exact, that is,

$$\frac{\partial(JM)}{\partial y} = \frac{\partial(JN)}{\partial x}.$$

The given equation is not exact since

$$\frac{\partial M}{\partial y} - \frac{\partial N}{\partial x} = \frac{-2}{x} - 2xy \cos y$$

$$= \frac{-2}{x}\,(1 + x^2 y \cos y)$$

$$\neq 0$$

but since $r(x) = \dfrac{1}{N}\left(\dfrac{\partial M}{\partial y} - \dfrac{\partial N}{\partial x}\right) = \dfrac{-2}{x}$ is a function of x, an integrating factor is given by

$$J(x) = e^{\int r(x)\,dx}$$

$$= e^{-\int \frac{2}{x}\,dx}$$

$$= e^{-2 \ln x}$$

$$= \frac{1}{x^2}.$$

7. (D)

We have $x = \sqrt{3 + x}$ or $x^2 = 3 + x$ so that $x^2 - x - 3 = 0$.

Using the quadratic formula, we obtain $x = \dfrac{1 \pm \sqrt{13}}{2}$.

We choose the positive square root, obtaining $x = \dfrac{1 + \sqrt{13}}{2}$ since x is positive.

8.　　(B)

In order for $f(x)$ to be a valid probability density function

$$\int_{-\infty}^{+\infty} f(x)\ dx = 1.$$

Thus, $1 = \int_0^{10} cx\ dx = 50c$ so that $c = \dfrac{1}{50}$.

The probability that x is in $[1, 2]$, denoted $P\ (1 \le x \le 2)$, is given by

$$P(1 \le x \le 2) = \int_1^2 \frac{x}{50}\ dx = \frac{1}{50}\left[\frac{x^2}{2}\right]_1^2 = \frac{3}{100}.$$

The graph of the probability density function is shown below.

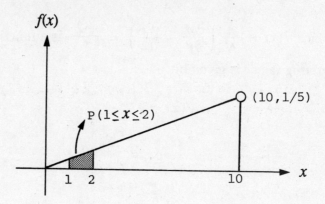

9.　　(E)

The expected value of a function $g(x)$ of a random variable X, denoted $E[g(X)]$, is defined by

$$E[g(X)] = \int_{-\infty}^{+\infty} g(x)\ f(x)\ dx$$

where $f(x)$ is the probability function for X. We have

$$E[X^2] = \int_{-\infty}^{\infty} X^2 f(x)dx = \int_0^2 X^2\left(1 - \frac{x}{2}\right)\ dx$$

$$= \left[\frac{x^3}{3} - \frac{x^4}{8}\right]_0^2$$

$$= \frac{2}{3}.$$

10.   (B)

An algebraic equation is of the form

$$a_N x^N + a_{N-1} x^{N-1} + \ldots + a_1 x + a_0 = 0$$

where N is a positive integer and $a_N, \ldots a_0$ are integers. $(a_N \neq 0)$. The height h is defined by $h = N + |a_N| + \ldots + |a_0|$. For $h = 2$, we have $N = 1, |a_1| = 1$, and $|a_0| = 0$. This implies that $a_1 = \pm 1$ so that $x = 0$. Note that there are no other possibilities except for $N = 1$. We see that if $N = 0$ then the equation is of degree 0 and is of the form $a_0 = 0$, which is unacceptable, as we require $a_N \neq 0$. If $N = 2$, on the other hand, we obtain $h = 2 = N + 0 + 0 + \ldots + 0$, so $a_2 = 0 = a_1 = a_0$ which is again unacceptable.

11.   (D)

A point (x, y) is in the unit ball if and only if $|x| + |y| < 1$. The boundary consists of the following lines:

a) $x \geq 0; \; y \geq 0: \quad x + y = 1$

b) $x \geq 0; \; y \leq 0: \quad x - y = 1$

c) $x \leq 0; \; y \geq 0: \quad -x + y = 1$

d) $x \leq 0; \; y \leq 0: \quad -x - y = 1$

These lines intersect at $(-1, 0)$, $(0, 1)$, $(1, 0)$, and $(0, -1)$.

12.   (D)

Trying the given solutions:

$$-f(x^{-1}) = -\left(\frac{\frac{1}{x} + 1}{\frac{1}{x} - 1} \right) = \frac{x + 1}{x - 1} = f(x)$$

32

and $[f(-x)]^{-1} = \left[\dfrac{-x+1}{-x-1}\right]^{-1} = \dfrac{-x-1}{-x+1} = \dfrac{x+1}{x-1} = f(x)$.

But if we solve $\ y = f(x) = \dfrac{x+1}{x-1}\ $ for x:

$$y(x-1) = x+1$$

$$xy - x = y + 1$$

$$x = \dfrac{y+1}{y-1}$$

Thus $f^{-1}(x) = f(x)$. However,

$$f^{-1}(x^{-1}) = \dfrac{x^{-1}+1}{x^{-1}-1}$$

$$= \dfrac{1+x}{1-x}$$

$$= -f(x)$$

13.   (E)

Let $\lambda_1, \lambda_2, \ldots \lambda_n$ be the eigenvalues of an $n \times n$ matrix M. The trace of M, denoted $tr(M)$, equals $\displaystyle\sum_{k=1}^{n} \lambda_k$. If p is a positive integer, then $tr(M^p)$ equals $\displaystyle\sum_{k=1}^{n} \lambda_k^p$. The eigenvalues of M are given by

$$\begin{vmatrix} 6-\lambda & 10 \\ -2 & -3-\lambda \end{vmatrix} = 0$$

which implies

$$-18 - 6\lambda + 3\lambda + \lambda^2 + 20 = 0$$

$$(\lambda - 1)(\lambda - 2) = 0$$

$$\lambda = 1,2$$

Thus $tr(M^5) = 1^5 + 2^5 = 33$.

14.   (B)

The Cayley-Hamilton theorem guarantees that M will satisfy a polynomial of degree 8. However, since M is idempotent $M^2 = M$ or $M^2 - M = 0$. Thus M satisfies $p(x) = x^2 - x$. Assuming that M satisfies a linear polynomial (degree 1) equation $\hat{p}(x) = a_1 x + a_0 = 0$ implies that M is a scalar matrix, i.e.,

$$a_1 M + a_0 I_8 = 0$$

$$M = -\frac{a_0}{a_1} I_8 ,$$

which contradicts the fact that M is nonscalar.

15.   (C)

The incidence matrix for the graph G is a 5×5 matrix whose (i,j) entry equals the number of edges connecting x_i and x_j. Thus the matrix of G is given by

$$\begin{bmatrix} 0 & 2 & 0 & 0 & 1 \\ 2 & 0 & 3 & 1 & 0 \\ 0 & 3 & 0 & 0 & 1 \\ 0 & 1 & 0 & 0 & 1 \\ 1 & 0 & 1 & 1 & 0 \end{bmatrix}$$

16.   (D)

A fixed point z must satisfy $z = w(z) = \dfrac{z-2}{z-1}$ which implies $z^2 - z = z - 2$. The solutions of $z^2 - 2z + 2 = 0$ are given by

$$z = \frac{2 \pm \sqrt{4 - 4(1)(2)}}{2} = 1 \pm i .$$

34

17. (A)

The nth roots of unity are solutions of the polynomial equation $x^n - 1 = 0$. For $n > 1$ and a leading coefficient of 1, the sum of the roots of a polynomial is equal to the negative of the coefficient of the x^{n-1} term. Hence the sum of the nth roots of unity $(n > 1)$ is zero. For another demonstration of this fact, let $1, \alpha, \ldots, \alpha^{n-1}$ denote the nth roots of unity $(n > 1)$. Then

$$1 + \alpha + \ldots + \alpha^{n-1} = \frac{1 - \alpha^n}{1 - \alpha} = 0 \text{ since } \alpha^n = 1.$$

18. (D)

A Boolean variable is a variable whose value can be either 0 or 1. A Boolean function is a function whose variables (both independent and dependent) are Boolean variables. The function $f(x, y, z) = x + y + z - xy - xz$ is not a Boolean function since $f(1, 0, 1) = 2$.

19. (A)

The perimeter $P(x, y)$ for the rectangle shown in the figure below is $P(x, y) = 4x + 4y$. We want to maximize this quantity subject to the constraint

$$\varnothing(x, y) = \frac{x^2}{a^2} + \frac{y^2}{b^2} - 1 = 0.$$

Introducing a Lagrange multiplier λ, we must maximize $L(x, y) = P(x, y) + \lambda \varnothing(x, y)$. Taking the first order partial derivatives of $L(x, y)$ and setting them equal to zero yields

$$\frac{\partial L}{\partial x} = 4 + \lambda \frac{2x}{a^2} = 0$$

$$\frac{\partial L}{\partial y} = 4 + \lambda \frac{2y}{b^2} = 0.$$

Thus $\dfrac{2x}{a^2} = \dfrac{2y}{b^2}$. Substituting $y = \dfrac{b^2 x}{a^2}$ into $\dfrac{x^2}{a^2} + \dfrac{y^2}{b^2} = 1$

yields $\dfrac{x^2}{a^2} + \dfrac{b^4 x^2}{a^4 b^2} = 1$, so that $x = \dfrac{a^2}{\sqrt{a^2 + b^2}}$ and

$y = \dfrac{b^2}{\sqrt{a^2 + b^2}}$.

The maximum perimeter is $4\sqrt{a^2 + b^2}$.

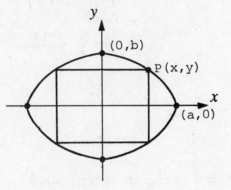

20.   (D)

A one-to-one bicontinuous function h from a topological space (X, τ) onto a topological space (X', τ') is called a homeomorphism. A property P of sets of a topological space (X, τ) is called topological if it is invariant under homeomorphisms. To see that the property of being an accumulation point is topological, let x be an accumulation point of a set $S \subseteq X$ and consider $h(x) \in h(S) \subseteq X'$. Let $D_{x'}$ be an open set in X' containing $h(x)$. Then $D_x = h^{-1}(D_{x'})$ is an open set if X containing x. Since x is an accumulation of point of S, there exists an $\bar{x} \in S \cap D_x$ such that $x \neq \bar{x}$. Thus $h(\bar{x}) = h(S) \cap D_{x'}$, distinct from $h(x)$, which implies that $h(x)$ is an accumulation point of $h(S)$.

21.   (C)

According to Cauchy's integral formula we have

$$f(a) = \frac{1}{2\pi i} \oint_C \frac{f(z)}{z - a}\, dz ,$$

where C is a closed contour which includes a, and f is analytic within and on C. Now, if we let

$$f(z) = \frac{(\cos z)}{(z - \pi)} ,$$

and $a = 0$, we will have

$$f(a) = f(0) = \frac{1}{2\pi i} \oint_C \frac{f(z)}{z} \, dz$$

$$= \frac{1}{2\pi i} \oint_C \frac{\cos z}{z - \pi} \, dz$$

$$= \frac{\cos 0}{0 - \pi}$$

$$= \frac{1}{-\pi}$$

$$\Rightarrow \oint_C \frac{\cos z}{z - \pi} \, dz = \frac{-1}{\pi} (2\pi i)$$

$$= -2i$$

Note that we can use the Cauchy integral formula for the circle $C : |z - 1| = 2$ since it does not include the point $z = \pi$.

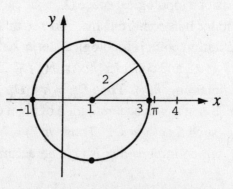

22.   (B)

Propositional algebra is similar to set algebra with union ($\cup$) replaced with disjunction ($\vee$), intersection ($\cap$) replaced with conjunction ($\wedge$) complementation (^{c}) replaced with negation ($\sim$), the universal set (Ω) replaced with tautology (1), and the empty set ($\emptyset$) replaced with absurdity (0). Also,

$$\sim(\forall x \in S)w(x) \Leftrightarrow (\exists x \in S)\,[\sim w(x)] \text{ and}$$

$$\sim(\exists x \in S)w(x) \Leftrightarrow (\forall x \in S)\,[\sim w(x)]$$

for an open statement $w(x)$ relative to S. We have

$$\sim(\exists x \in S)\,[(p(x) \vee q(x)) \wedge r(x)]$$

$$\Leftrightarrow (\forall x \in S)\,\{\sim[(p(x) \vee q(x)) \wedge r(x)]\}$$

$$\Leftrightarrow (\forall x \in S)\,\{[\sim(p(x) \vee q(x))] \vee [\sim r(x)]\}$$

$$\Leftrightarrow (\forall x \in S)\,\{[(\sim p(x)) \wedge (\sim q(x))] \vee [\sim r(x)]\}$$

23.   (B)
   We have

$$\lim_{n \to +\infty} \frac{x_{n+1}}{x_n} = \lim_{n \to +\infty} \frac{(n+1)^{n+1} n!}{(n+1)! \; n^n}$$

$$= \lim_{n \to +\infty} \frac{(n+1)^n (n+1) \, n!}{n^n \, (n+1)!}$$

$$= \lim_{n \to +\infty} \left(1 + \frac{1}{n}\right)^n$$

$$= e$$

24.   (A)
   By the chain rule, the derivative of a function defined by

$$\phi(x, a(x), b(x)) = \int_{a(x)}^{b(x)} g(x, t)\, dt$$

is given by

$$\frac{d\phi(x, a(x), b(x))}{dx} = \frac{\partial \phi}{\partial x} + \frac{\partial \phi}{\partial a} \frac{da(x)}{dx} + \frac{\partial \phi}{\partial b} \frac{db(x)}{dx}$$

$$= \int_{a(x)}^{b(x)} \frac{\partial g(x,t)}{dx} \, dt + g(x,b(x)) \frac{db(x)}{dx} - g(x,a(x)) \frac{da(x)}{dx} \, .$$

Note that in evaluating $\frac{\partial \varnothing}{\partial a}$ and $\frac{\partial \varnothing}{\partial b}$, a and b must be considered as independent variables. Therefore, before taking the derivative with respect to either a or b, we must replace $a(x)$ and $b(x)$ by a and b in the definition of $\varnothing(x, a(x) , b(x))$. Thus

$$\frac{df}{dx} = \int_x^0 \left[\frac{-t \, \sin xt}{t} \right] dt + 0 - \frac{\cos x^2}{x}$$

$$= \left[\frac{\cos xt}{x} \right]_x^0 - \frac{\cos x^2}{x}$$

$$= \frac{1}{x} - \frac{\cos x^2}{x} - \frac{\cos x^2}{x}$$

$$= \frac{1}{x} [1 - 2\cos x^2]$$

$$= -\frac{\cos 2x^2}{x} \, .$$

25.   (B)

The directional derivative of the function $P(x, y)$ along the path through (x, y) and parallel to the unit vector $\vec{u}$ is equal to $\frac{\partial f}{\partial u} = \nabla \vec{P} \cdot \vec{u}$. Therefore, since the values $|\nabla \vec{P}|$ and $|\vec{u}| = 1$ are constant, the directional derivative of $\frac{\partial f}{\partial u}$ is maximized when the angle between $\nabla \vec{P}$ and $\vec{u}$ is zero. Therefore, the maximum value of the directional derivative at $P(x, y)$ equals the magnitude of the gradient

$$\nabla f(x,y) = \frac{\partial f}{\partial x} i + \frac{\partial f}{\partial y} j$$

at $P(x, y)$. We have

$$\frac{\partial f}{\partial x} = xye^{xy} + e^{xy} - y\sin x \;\; ; \;\; \frac{\partial f(0,1)}{\partial x} = 1$$

$$\frac{\partial f}{\partial y} = x^2 e^{xy} + \cos x \;\;\;\;\;\; ; \;\; \frac{\partial f(0,1)}{\partial y} = 1$$

Thus $\vec{\nabla} f(0,1) = \vec{i} + \vec{j}$ so that $\left|\vec{\nabla} f(0,1)\right| = \sqrt{2}$.

26.   (C)

Let n and k represent positive integers with k satisfying $1 \le k \le n$. An ordered partition of n into k parts is a decomposition of n into the sum of k positive integers:

$$n = x_1 + x_2 + x_3 + \ldots + x_k.$$

For a fixed k, the number of ordered partitions of n into k parts is the number of distinct ways of placing $\bar{k} = k - 1$ identical markers in the $\bar{n} = n - 1$ spaces between a row of n ones. The first marker can be placed in $\bar{n}$ ways, the second in $\bar{n} - 1$ ways, ..., and the last marker in $\bar{n} - [\bar{k} - 1]$ ways. The number of ways is therefore $\bar{n}(\bar{n} - 1) \ldots (\bar{n} - \bar{k} + 1)$.

Since the markers are identical, in each way of placing them we can switch the markers around without changing the chosen spaces and still have the same way of placing. Therefore, each group of $k!$ ways of placing the k markers, as long as the spaces chosen are still the same, are actually identical. Hence we must divide the above result by $k!$ to arrive at the correct answer. That is, the number of distinct ways is:

$$\frac{\bar{n}(\bar{n} - 1) \ldots (\bar{n} - [\bar{k} - 1])}{\bar{k}!} = \frac{\bar{n}!}{\bar{k}!(\bar{n} - \bar{k})!}$$

$$= \binom{\bar{n}}{\bar{k}},$$

which is the binomial coefficient. Since we can have ordered partitions of 5 into 1, 2, 3, 4 or 5 parts (that is, we can decompose 5 as a sum of 1, 2, 3, 4 or 5 positive integers), the number of ordered partitions of 5 is

$$\sum_{k=0}^{4} \begin{bmatrix} 4 \\ k \end{bmatrix} = (1+1)^4 = 2^4 = 16.$$

27.　(D)

The Wronskian is given by

$$W(x) = \begin{vmatrix} f_1(x) & f_2(x) \\ f_1'(x) & f_2'(x) \end{vmatrix}$$

$$= \begin{vmatrix} x^2 \sin x & x^2 \cos x \\ 2x \sin x + x^2 \cos x & 2x \cos x - x^2 \sin x \end{vmatrix}$$

$$= 2x^3 \sin x \cos x - x^4 \sin^2 x - 2x^3 \sin x \cos x - x^4 \cos^2 x$$

$$= -x^4.$$

28.　(A)

Assuming a solution of the form $y_k = r^k$, we obtain

$$r^{k+2} - r^{k+1} - 2r^k = 0$$

$$r^k(r - 2)(r + 1) = 0$$

so that $r = -1, 2$. Hence

$$y_k = c_1(-1)^k + c_2 2^k$$

and since $y_0 = 9$ and $y_1 = -12$, we have

$$c_1 + c_2 = 9$$

$$-c_1 + 2c_2 = -12$$

This implies $c_1 = 10$ and $c_2 = -1$ which implies $y_k = 10(-1)^k - 2^k$. For $k = 6$, we obtain $y_6 = -54$. Note that in the general form of a second order homogeneous recursion equation, we have $y_{k+2} + Ay_{k+1} + By_k = 0$. The general form of the solution of this equation is $c_1 r_1^k + c_2 r_2^k = y_k$. To evaulate r_1 and r_2, we can insert the special solution r^k directly into the equation and get:

$$r^{k+2} + Ar^{k+1} + Br^k = 0$$

$$\Rightarrow r^k(r^2 + Ar + B) = 0$$

$$\Rightarrow r^2 + Ar + B = 0.$$

We observe that if this quadratic equation has 2 distinct roots, r_1 and r_2, then any expression of the form $c_1 r_1^k + c_2 r_2^k$ will be a solution to the equation, where c_1, c_2 are arbitrary constants, because of the linearity of the equation.

29.   (C)

Let N represent a positive integer and write N as

$$N = u_0 + 10u_1 + 10^2 u_2 + 10^3 u_3 + \ldots + 10^n u_n .$$

Recalling that $a \equiv b \pmod{c}$ means that $a - b$ is divisible by c, we have that $u_j 10^j \equiv u_j \pmod 9$ for $0 \leq j \leq n$. Thus $N \equiv u_0 + u_1 + \ldots + u_n \pmod 9$ which implies $N -$ (sum of digits of N) is divisible by 9. Therefore N is divisible by 9 if and only if the sum of its digits is divisible by 9. Since $(3 + 2 + 2 + 4 + 4 + 6 + 6)/9 = 3$, 3224466 is divisible by 9.

30.   (C)

The possible inflection points of f occur where $f''(x) = 0$ or where $f''(x)$ does not exist. We have

$$f'(x) = \frac{x\left(\frac{1}{x}\right) - \ln x}{x^2} = \frac{1 - \ln x}{x^2}$$

$$f''(x) = \frac{x^2\left(\frac{-1}{x}\right) - 2x(1 - \ln x)}{x^4} = \frac{2\ln x - 3}{x^3}$$

Setting $f''(x) = 0$ implies that $x = e^{3/2}$. There are no elements in the domain of $f(x)$ such that $f''(x)$ does not exist. The function f is concave downward on $(0, e^{3/2}]$ and concave upward on $[e^{3/2}, +\infty)$. Thus, there is an inflection point at $x = e^{3/2}$.

31. (B)

We first reduce M to echelon form using elementary row operations:

$$M \xrightarrow[\substack{-R_1 + R_2 \to R_2 \\ R_1 + R_2 \to R_3 \\ 2R_1 + R_4 \to R_4}]{} \begin{bmatrix} 1 & 2 & -1 & 0 \\ 0 & -4 & 3 & 1 \\ 0 & 0 & 1 & 2 \\ 0 & 4 & -1 & 3 \end{bmatrix}$$

$$\xrightarrow[R_3 \leftrightarrow R_4]{} \begin{bmatrix} 1 & 2 & -1 & 0 \\ 0 & -4 & 3 & 1 \\ 0 & 4 & -1 & 3 \\ 0 & 0 & 1 & 2 \end{bmatrix}$$

$$\xrightarrow[R_2 + R_3 \to R_3]{} \begin{bmatrix} 1 & 2 & -1 & 0 \\ 0 & -4 & 3 & 1 \\ 0 & 0 & 2 & 4 \\ 0 & 0 & 1 & 2 \end{bmatrix}$$

$$\xrightarrow[\substack{-R_2 \to R_2 \\ -\frac{1}{2}R_3 + R_4 \to R_4}]{} \begin{bmatrix} 1 & 2 & -1 & 0 \\ 0 & 4 & -3 & -1 \\ 0 & 0 & 2 & 4 \\ 0 & 0 & 0 & 0 \end{bmatrix}$$

$$\xrightarrow[\frac{1}{2}R_3 \to R_3]{} \begin{bmatrix} 1 & 2 & -1 & 0 \\ 0 & 4 & -3 & -1 \\ 0 & 0 & 1 & 2 \\ 0 & 0 & 0 & 0 \end{bmatrix} = M_e$$

Since M_e has three linearly independent row vectors, the rank of M is three. This implies that the null space has dimension $4 - 3 = 1$.

32.   (C)

For a ring R, the radical is the set of nilpotent elements of R, that is, the set $\{r \in R \mid r^n = 0 \text{ for some } n \in Z^+\}$. The powers of the elements of $Z_8 = \{0, 1, 2, 3, 4, 5, 6, 7\}$ are

$$0:\ 0, 0, 0, 0, \ldots$$
$$1:\ 1, 1, 1, 1, \ldots$$
$$2:\ 2, 4, 0, 0, \ldots$$
$$3:\ 3, 1, 3, 1, \ldots$$
$$4:\ 4, 0, 0, 0, \ldots$$
$$5:\ 5, 1, 5, 1, \ldots$$
$$6:\ 6, 4, 0, 0, \ldots$$
$$7:\ 7, 1, 7, 1, \ldots$$

Thus the radical of Z_8 is $\{0, 2, 4, 6\}$.

33.   (D)

Using the identities $\sin x = \dfrac{e^{ix} - e^{-ix}}{2i}$ and $\cos x = \dfrac{e^{ix} + e^{-ix}}{2}$, we obtain

$$\sin^3 x \cos^2 x = \left[\frac{e^{ix} - e^{-ix}}{2i}\right]^3 \left[\frac{e^{ix} + e^{-ix}}{2}\right]^2$$

$$= \frac{1}{-32i} \left[e^{2xi} - e^{-2xi}\right]^2 \left[e^{xi} - e^{-xi}\right]$$

$$= \frac{1}{-32i} \left[e^{4xi} - 2 + e^{-4xi}\right] \left[e^{xi} - e^{-xi}\right]$$

$$= \frac{1}{-32i} \left[e^{5xi} - 2e^{xi} + e^{-3xi} - e^{3xi} + 2e^{-xi} - e^{-5xi}\right]$$

$$= \frac{1}{16} \left[2 \sin x + \sin 3x - \sin 5x\right]$$

34.   (C)

Since f is continuous on $[0, 2\pi]$, an absolute maximum exists. It must occur at the endpoints $[(0, -1)\,;\, (2\pi, -1)]$ or at an interior point

44

where $f'(x) = 0$. Setting $f'(x) = -2\sin 2x + 2\sin x$ equal to zero implies $\sin x\,(1 - 2\cos x) = 0$, so that $x = \pi/3, \pi, 5\pi/3$. Since $f(\pi/3) = -3/2, f(\pi) = 3, f(5\pi/3) = -3/2, f(0) = -1$ and $f(2\pi) = -1$, the absolute maximum of f occurs at $x = \pi$.

35.   (C)

A number λ is called an eigenvalue for a matrix M if there exists a nonzero vector X such that $MX = \lambda X$. This implies that the determinant $|\lambda I - M| = 0$. Thus

$$\begin{vmatrix} \lambda - 1 & 3 \\ 2 & \lambda - 2 \end{vmatrix} = 0$$

$$\lambda^2 - 3\lambda - 4 = 0 \; ; \; \lambda = -1, 4$$

For $\lambda = -1$, $[\lambda I - M] X = 0$ yields

$$\begin{bmatrix} -2x_1 & + & 3x_2 \\ 2x_1 & - & 3x_2 \end{bmatrix} = \begin{bmatrix} 0 \\ 0 \end{bmatrix}$$

so that $2x_1 - 3x_2 = 0$. Therefore $\begin{bmatrix} 3 \\ 2 \end{bmatrix}$ is an eigenvector for $\lambda = -1$. The solution also follows from the fact that $\begin{bmatrix} 3 \\ 2 \end{bmatrix}$ is an eigenvector:

$$\lambda \begin{bmatrix} 3 \\ 2 \end{bmatrix} = \begin{bmatrix} 1 & -3 \\ -2 & 2 \end{bmatrix} \begin{bmatrix} 3 \\ 2 \end{bmatrix} = - \begin{bmatrix} 3 \\ 2 \end{bmatrix}$$

which implies $\lambda = -1$.

36.   (D)

We can rearrange each term in the sum as follows:

$$\frac{1}{n^2 + n + 1} = \frac{(n + 1) - n}{1 + n(n + 1)}.$$

Now if we define $\tan a_n = n$, then we will have

$$\frac{1}{n^2 + n + 1} = \frac{\tan a_{n+1} - \tan a_n}{1 + \tan a_n \tan a_{n+1}} = \tan(a_{n+1} - a_n).$$

So $\arctan\left(\frac{1}{n^2 + n + 1}\right) = \arctan(\tan(a_{n+1} - a_n)) = a_{n+1} - a_n$

So $\displaystyle\sum_{n=1}^{m} \arctan\left(\frac{1}{n^2 + n + 1}\right) = \sum_{n=1}^{m} (a_{n+1} - a_n)$

$$= (a_2 - a_1) + (a_3 - a_2) + \ldots + (a_{m+1} - a_m)$$

$$= a_{m+1} - a_1$$

$$= \arctan(m + 1) - \arctan 1$$

$$= \arctan(m + 1) - \frac{\pi}{4}$$

37. (C)

The conjugates of $\sqrt{\sqrt{3} + 1}$ consist of the set of all zeros of the irreducible polynomial of $\sqrt{\sqrt{3} + 1}$ over the rational numbers. We first determine a polynomial over the rationals for which $\sqrt{\sqrt{3} + 1}$ is a zero:

$$x = \sqrt{\sqrt{3} + 1}$$

$$x^2 = \sqrt{3} + 1$$

$$p(x) = x^4 - 2x^2 - 2$$

We now use the Eisenstein test to establish the irreducibility of $p(x) = x^4 + 2x^2 - 2$ over the rational numbers. Firstly, $p(x)$ is an element of the set of polynomials with integer coefficients. Secondly, $a_2 = 1 \equiv 0$ (mod 2), $a_1 = -2 \equiv 0$ (mod 2), $a_0 = -2 \equiv 0$ (mod 2^2). Therefore $p(x)$ is irreducible over the rational numbers. The conjugates of

$\sqrt{\sqrt{3} + 1}$ are the zeros of $p(x)$:

46

$$x^4 - 2x^2 - 2 = 0$$

$$x^2 = \frac{2 \pm \sqrt{4+8}}{2} = 1 \pm \sqrt{3}$$

$$x = \pm\sqrt{1+\sqrt{3}}, \pm\sqrt{1-\sqrt{3}}.$$

38. (E)

We have

$2^1 > 1^2$ is true

$2^2 > 2^2$ is false

$2^3 > 3^2$ is false

$2^4 > 4^2$ is false

$2^5 > 5^2$ is true

The inequality is true for $n = 5$. Assume $2^n > n^2$ for $n = k$. We will will show that $2^{k+1} > (k+1)^2$. Consider $f(x) = 2^x - 2x - 1$ so that $f'(x) = 2^x \ln 2 - 2$. We have $f(5) > 0$ and $f'(x) > 0$ for $x \in [5, +\infty)$ which implies $2^k > 2k + 1$ for $k \geq 5$. Since $2^k > k^2$, we have

$$2^k + 2^k > k^2 + 2k + 1$$

$$2^{k+1} > (k+1)^2.$$

39. (A)

For a nonstrictly determined two player (P_1, P_2) game G with payoff matrix M

$$P_1 \begin{array}{c} \quad\quad P_2 \\ \begin{bmatrix} a_{11} & a_{12} \\ a_{21} & a_{22} \end{bmatrix}, \end{array}$$

the minimax value v is given by $v = \dfrac{|M|}{d}$ where $d = (a_{11} + a_{22}) - (a_{12} + a_{21})$.

Thus $v = \dfrac{5}{(1+3)-(-1+2)} = \dfrac{5}{3}$. This game favors player P_1 to the extent that it will, on the average, pay him 5/3 units/game.

40.　　(C)

The first Newton approximation can be obtained from the formula

$$x_{n+1} = x_n - \frac{f(x_n)}{f'(x_n)}$$

with $n = 0$. Since $f'(x) = 3x^2 - 2$, we have

$$x_1 = x_0 - \frac{f(x_0)}{f'(x_0)} = 2 - \frac{4}{10} = \frac{8}{5}.$$

41.　　(B)

Note that $|x - 2| = \begin{cases} -(x-2) & \text{if } x \le 2 \\ (x-2) & \text{if } x > 2 \end{cases}$

Therefore

$$\int_1^4 |x-2|\, dx = -\int_1^2 (x-2)\, dx + \int_2^4 (x-2)\, dx$$

$$= -\left[\frac{x^2}{2} - 2x\right]_1^2 + \left[\frac{x^2}{2} - 2x\right]_2^4$$

$$= -\left[(2-4) - \left(\frac{1}{2} - 2\right)\right] + [(8-8) - (2-4)]$$

$$= \frac{5}{2}.$$

The graph of $|x - 2|$ on $[1, 4]$ is shown following.

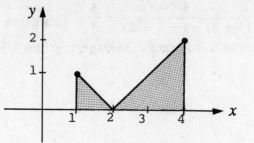

42.   (B)

For a group of order n, a Sylow p-subgroup has order p^k where k is the largest positive integer such that p^k divides n. Since $72 = 2^3\, 3^2$, a Sylow 3-subgroup has 9 elements.

43.   (D)

A set G, together with a binary operation * is called a group, denoted $(G, *)$, if

1) the binary operation * is associative; $f, g, h \in G$ implies $(f * g) * h = f * (g * h)$,

2) G contains an identity element: there exists $e \in G$ such that $e * g = g * e = g$ for all $g \in G$.

3) Each element of G has an inverse: if $g \in G$, there exists $g' \in G$ such that $g * g' = g' * g = e$.

The set $G = R\backslash\{0\}$ together with the binary operation $a * b = |a| b$ does not form a group. The number 1 is a "right" identity element, but it is not a "left" identity element:

1) $1 * b = b$ for all $b \in G$

2) $a * 1 \neq a$ for $a \in G$ when $a < 0$

44. (C)

We have

$$M^2 = \begin{bmatrix} 2 & 4 \\ 1 & 2 \end{bmatrix}^2 = \begin{bmatrix} 8 & 16 \\ 4 & 8 \end{bmatrix} = 4M$$

so that $M^6 = (4M)^3 = 4^3 M^2 M = 4^4 M M = 4^5 M$.

45. (B)

The total number of selections possible is the number of ways of selecting 10 graduate students from 15 applicants which is $\begin{bmatrix} 15 \\ 10 \end{bmatrix}$. Since the selection process was random, the probability of any selection is $\dfrac{1}{\begin{bmatrix} 15 \\ 10 \end{bmatrix}}$. We must determine the number of selections which include 4 of the 5 "best students." Firstly, 4 of the possible 10 people selected must be selected from the 5 "best students." This can be accomplished in $\begin{bmatrix} 5 \\ 4 \end{bmatrix}$ ways. The other $10 - 4 = 6$ people must come from the other $15 - 5 = 10$ applicants. This can be accomplished in $\begin{bmatrix} 10 \\ 6 \end{bmatrix}$ ways. Thus, there are $\begin{bmatrix} 5 \\ 4 \end{bmatrix}\begin{bmatrix} 10 \\ 6 \end{bmatrix}$ ways of selecting 4 of the 5 "best students." Hence, the probability of selecting 4 of the 5 "best students" is

$$\frac{\begin{bmatrix} 5 \\ 4 \end{bmatrix}\begin{bmatrix} 10 \\ 6 \end{bmatrix}}{\begin{bmatrix} 15 \\ 10 \end{bmatrix}} = \frac{5!}{4!\,1!}\ \frac{10!}{6!\,4!}\ \frac{10!\,5!}{15!} = \frac{50}{143}$$

50

46.   (A)

Since $r^2 = x^2 + y^2$, $\sin \theta = y/r$, and $\cos \theta = x/r$, we have

$r = 2y/r - x/r$

$r^2 = 2y - x$

$x^2 + y^2 + x - 2y = 0$

47.   (B)

Set $x = 0.0259\,\overline{259}$. Then $9990x = 10000x - 10x = 259.\overline{259}$
$- 0.\overline{259}$ so that

$$x = \frac{259}{9990} = \frac{7}{270}. \text{ Thus } 2.0259\,\overline{259} = \frac{547}{270}.$$

48.   (D)

The Maclaurin series for e^x is $1 + x + \dfrac{x^2}{2!} + \dfrac{x^3}{3!} + \ldots + \dfrac{x^n}{n!} + \ldots$.

Therefore

$$xe^{-x^2} = x\left[1 - x^2 + \frac{x^4}{2!} - \frac{x^6}{3!} + \frac{x^8}{4!} + \ldots + \frac{(-1)^n x^{2n}}{n!} + \ldots\right],$$

so that the general term is given by $\dfrac{(-1)^n x^{2n+1}}{n!}$.

49.   (C)

The solution set for the inequality is equivalent to finding where
the function

$$f(x) = x - \frac{3}{x} - 2 = \frac{(x-3)(x+1)}{x}$$

is positive. The figure below shows the x-axis subdivided into regions
where f is continuous and never zero; we always omit endpoints. Thus
f has the same sign throughout each subinterval; the signs are shown

below. The solution of the inequality is $(-1,0) \cup (3,+\infty)$.

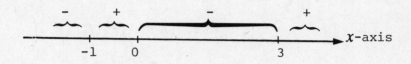

50.   (D)

The x-coordinates of the points of intersection of the curves are solutions of $x = 2\sqrt{x}$ which implies $x = 0,4$. The region is shown below. The volume generated is given by

$$\text{Volume} = \pi \int_0^4 \left[(2\sqrt{x})^2 - (x)^2 \right] dx$$

$$= \pi \left[2x^2 - \frac{x^3}{3} \right]_0^4$$

$$= \frac{32\pi}{3} .$$

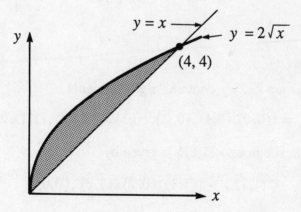

51.　(D)

Using the associative law for intersection, we can write:

$$[A \cap (A \cap B^c)] \cap B]^c = [A \cap A \cap B \cap B^c]^c$$

$$= [(A \cap A) \cap (B \cap B^c)]^c$$

$$= [A \cap (\emptyset)]^c$$

$$= \emptyset^c$$

$$= U.$$

52.　(D)

The cross product of $\vec{u} \times \vec{v}$ is equal to the determinant

$$\begin{vmatrix} \vec{i} & \vec{j} & \vec{k} \\ 2 & -1 & 3 \\ 1 & 2 & -1 \end{vmatrix} = (\vec{i} + 4\vec{k} + 3\vec{j}) - (-\vec{k} + 6\vec{i} - 2\vec{j})$$

$$= -5\vec{i} + 5\vec{j} + 5\vec{k}.$$

53.　(B)

The group $Z_2 \times Z_4$ contains eight elements

$$Z_2 \times Z_8 = \{(0,0),(0,1),(0,2),(0,3),(1,0),(1,1),(1,2),(1,3)\}$$

The cyclic subgroup <(1,1)> is given by

$$<(1,1)> = \{(1,1),(0,2),(1,3),(0,0)\}$$

Since

$$(0,1) + <(1,1)> = \{(1,2),(0,3),(1,0),(0,1)\}$$

there are two left cosets.

54. (B)

Let G be an abelian group with order n. Then G is isomorphic to the products of the form

$$Z_{(p_1{}^{n_1})} \times Z_{(p_2{}^{n_2})} \times \ldots \times Z_{(p_k{}^{n_k})},$$

Where the p_j's, not necessarily distinct, are the primes in the factorization of n and $(p_1{}^{n_1})(p_2{}^{n_2}) \ldots (p_k{}^{n_k}) = n$. Here Z_n denotes the cyclic group of $\{0, 1, 2, 3, 4, 5, 6, 7\}$ under addition modulo n. For $n = 36 = 2^2\, 3^2$, we have G isomorphic to

$$Z_4 \times Z_9 = Z_{(2^2)} \times Z_{(3^2)}$$

$$Z_2 \times Z_2 \times Z_9 = Z_{(2^1)} \times Z_{(1^1)} \times Z_{(3^2)}$$

$$Z_4 \times Z_3 \times Z_3 = Z_{(2^2)} \times Z_{(3^1)} \times Z_{(3^1)}$$

$$Z_2 \times Z_2 \times Z_3 \times Z_3 = Z_{(2^1)} \times Z_{(2^1)} \times Z_{(3^1)} \times Z_{(3^1)}.$$

55. (C)

The sum of $a + ar + ar^2 + \ldots + ar^{n-1} + \ldots$ is $\dfrac{a(1 - r^n)}{1 - r}$.
We have

$$\sum_{j=0}^{10} (-i)^j = 1 - i + i^2 - i^3 + \ldots + i^{10}$$

so that $a = 1$, $r = -i$, and $n = 11$. Thus

$$\sum_{j=0}^{10} (-i)^j = \frac{1 - (-i)^{11}}{1 + i} = \frac{1 + i}{1 - i} \frac{1 - i}{1 - i} = -i.$$

56. (D)

The number 1 is the identity element R. An element $u = a + ib$ in R is a unit if there exists $v = c + id$ in R such that $u\,v = 1$. If u is a unit, then $\bar{u} = a - ib$ is also a unit since $\overline{uv} = 1$. We have

$$1 = uv = \overline{uv} \Rightarrow 1 = uv(\overline{uv}) = (u\bar{u})(v\bar{v})$$

$$= |u|^2|v|^2 = (a^2 + b^2)(c^2 + d^2)$$

Since a, b, c, d are integers and $a^2 + b^2 \neq 0$, we know that $a^2 + b^2 = 1$. The solutions are $a = 0$, $b = \pm 1$ and $a = \pm 1$, $b = 0$ which implies that the units are $\pm 1, \pm i$.

57.   (C)
We have

$$3x + 11 \equiv 20 \pmod{12}$$
$$3x \equiv 9 \pmod{12}$$
$$x \equiv 3 \pmod{4}$$

The numbers in the set $\{..., -9, -5, -1, 3, 7, 11, 15, ...\}$ satisfy $3x + 11 \equiv 20 \pmod{12}$. Each of these numbers is in one of the following equivalence classes:

$$<3> \ = \{..., -9, 3, 15, 27, ...\}$$
$$<7> \ = \{..., -5, 7, 19, 31, ...\}$$
$$<11> = \{..., -1, 11, 23, 35, ...\}$$

58.   (D)
The region R is shown below. Since R is convex and $f(x, y)$ is linear, the maximum of f occurs at a corner point. We have

$$f(1,0) = -2$$
$$f(2,1) = -1$$
$$f(1,2) = \ \ 4.$$

Therefore the maximum is 4.

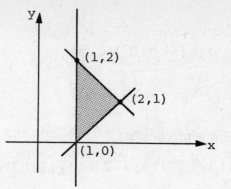

59.   (B)

We have

$$\begin{array}{r}
x^2 - x + 1 \\
\hline
x^3 - 1 \overline{\smash{\big)}\, x^5 - x^4 + x^3 + 0x^2 + x} \\
\end{array}$$

$$
\begin{array}{r}
x^5 \qquad\qquad\; - x^2 \\
\hline
-x^4 + x^3 + \; x^2 + x \\
-x^4 \qquad\qquad + x \\
\hline
x^3 + \; x^2 + x \\
x^3 \qquad\quad - 1 \\
\hline
x^2 + 1
\end{array}
$$

so that $\dfrac{x^5 - x^4 + x^3 + x}{x^3 - 1} = x^2 - x + 1 + \dfrac{x^2 + 1}{x^3 - 1}.$

As $|x| \to +\infty$, $\dfrac{x^2 + 1}{x^3 - 1} \to 0$ so that $f(x) \approx x^2 - x + 1$.

60.   (A)

Let F represent the number of faces, E the number of edges, and V the number of vertices of an ordinary polyhedron. Euler's theorem states that $F - E + V = 2$. Thus $12 - 17 + V = 2$ so that $V = 7$.

56

61.   (A)

We have $(2, 4) = a\,(1,1) + b\,(2,3)$ so that

$$2 = a + 2b$$
$$4 = a + 3b$$

Thus $b = 2$ and $a = -2$ which implies

$$T\,(2,4) = -2T\,(1,1) + 2T\,(2,3) = -2\,(-1,1) + 2(1,2) = (4,2).$$

62.   (B)

The function $f(z)$ is analytic if and only if the Cauchy-Riemann conditions are satisfied:

$$\frac{\partial u}{\partial x} = \frac{\partial v}{\partial y}$$

$$\frac{\partial u}{\partial y} = -\frac{\partial v}{\partial x}$$

Thus

$$\frac{\partial v}{\partial y} = \frac{\partial u}{\partial x} = \cos x \cosh y$$

and

$$\frac{\partial v}{\partial x} = -\frac{\partial u}{\partial y} = -\sin x \sinh y\ .$$

We have

$$v(x,y) = \int \frac{\partial u}{\partial x}\ dy = \int \cos x \cosh y\ dy = \cos x \sinh y + g(x)\ .$$

Also,

$$-\sin x \sinh y = \frac{\partial v}{\partial x} = -\sin x \sinh y + g'(x)\ ,$$

so that $g(x) = $ constant. Hence $v(x,y) = \cos x \sinh y + $ constant.

63.   (E)

A linear transformation T from E^n into E^n is called nonsingular if there exists a linear transformation T^I from E^n into E^n such that $T\,T^I$

$= T'T = I_n$, I_n being the identity transformation. The transformation T' is called the inverse of T and is denoted T^{-1}. Let $x, y \in E^n$ and assume $Tx = Ty$. Then $x = T^{-1} Tx = T^{-1} Ty = y$ so that T is one-to-one. If $Tx = 0$, then $x = 0$ since $T0 = 0$ and T is one-to-one. Thus the null space of $T = \{0\}$ and Dim $N(T) = 0$. The equation $n = $ Dim $N(T) + $ Dim $R(T)$ shows that $n = $ Dim $R(T)$. Reversing the roles of T and T^{-1} above shows that T^{-1} is one-to-one; $N(T^{-1}) = \{0\}$, and Dim $N(T^{-1}) = 0$. Thus Dim $N(T^{-1}) \neq $ Dim $R(T)$.

64.　　(D)

The given series is geometric, so its sum is $\dfrac{1}{1 - \dfrac{2}{3}} = 3$.

65.　　(A)

Two circles C_1 and C_2 are said to be orthogonal if they interesect at right angles. This means that at a point of intersection $P(\overline{x}, \overline{y})$ of C_1 and C_2, the radius r_1 of C_1 is tangent to C_2 at P and the radius of r_2 of C_2 is tangent to C_1 at P. Note that the centers of C_1 and C_2 are $(-a, -b)$ and $(-a', -b')$, respectively. The slope of the tangent line at the point of intersection $P(\overline{x}, \overline{y})$ is equal to the negative reciprocal of the slope through $(-a, -b)$ and $P(\overline{x}, \overline{y})$. It is also equal to the slope through the points $P(\overline{x}, \overline{y})$ and $(-a', -b')$. Thus

$$\frac{-1}{\dfrac{\overline{y} + b}{\overline{x} + a}} = \frac{\overline{y} + b'}{\overline{x} + a'}$$

$$-[\overline{x}^2 + (a + a')\overline{x} + aa'] = \overline{y}^2 + (b + b')\overline{y} + bb'.$$

Multiplying by 2 and rearranging terms,

$$\Rightarrow -[(\overline{x}^2 + 2a\overline{x} + \overline{y}^2 + 2b\overline{y}) + (\overline{x}^2 + 2a'\overline{x} + \overline{y}^2 + 2b'\overline{y})]$$

$$= 2aa' + 2bb'c$$

$$\Rightarrow c + c' = 2aa' + 2bb'$$

58

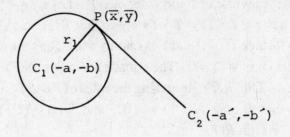

$P(\overline{x}, \overline{y})$

r_1

$C_1(-a, -b)$

$C_2(-a', -b')$

66.   (A)

Using elementary row operations, we transform $[M \mid I]$ into $[I \mid M^{-1}]$:

$$\begin{bmatrix} 2 & 1 & 3 & 1 & 0 & 0 \\ 0 & -1 & 2 & 0 & 1 & 0 \\ 4 & 3 & 1 & 0 & 0 & 1 \end{bmatrix}$$

$$\begin{bmatrix} 2 & 1 & 3 & 1 & 0 & 0 \\ 4 & 3 & 1 & 0 & 0 & 1 \\ 0 & -1 & 2 & 0 & 1 & 0 \end{bmatrix} \quad R_2 \Leftrightarrow R_3$$

$$\begin{bmatrix} 2 & 1 & 3 & 1 & 0 & 0 \\ 0 & 1 & -5 & -2 & 0 & 1 \\ 0 & -1 & 2 & 0 & 1 & 0 \end{bmatrix} \quad -2R_1 + R_2 \Rightarrow R_2$$

$$\begin{bmatrix} 2 & 1 & 3 & 1 & 0 & 0 \\ 0 & 1 & -5 & -2 & 0 & 1 \\ 0 & 0 & -3 & -2 & 1 & 1 \end{bmatrix} \quad R_2 + R_3 \Rightarrow R_3$$

$$\begin{bmatrix} 2 & 1 & 0 & -1 & 1 & 1 \\ 0 & 1 & -5 & -2 & 0 & 1 \\ 0 & 0 & -3 & -2 & 1 & 1 \end{bmatrix} \quad R_3 + R_1 \Rightarrow R_1$$

$$\begin{bmatrix} 2 & 1 & 0 & \Big| & -1 & 1 & 1 \\ 0 & 1 & 0 & \Big| & 4/3 & -5/3 & -2/3 \\ 0 & 0 & -3 & \Big| & -2 & 1 & 1 \end{bmatrix} \qquad -5/3R_3 + R_2 \Rightarrow R_2$$

$$\begin{bmatrix} 2 & 0 & 0 & \Big| & -7/3 & 8/3 & 5/3 \\ 0 & 1 & 0 & \Big| & 4/3 & -5/3 & -2/3 \\ 0 & 0 & -3 & \Big| & -2 & 1 & 1 \end{bmatrix} \qquad R_1 - R_2 \Rightarrow R_1$$

$$\begin{bmatrix} 1 & 0 & 0 & \Big| & -7/6 & 8/6 & 5/6 \\ 0 & 1 & 0 & \Big| & 4/3 & -5/3 & -2/3 \\ 0 & 0 & 1 & \Big| & 2/3 & -1/3 & -1/3 \end{bmatrix} \qquad \begin{array}{l} 1/2R_1 \Rightarrow R_1 \\ -1/3R_3 \Rightarrow R_3 \end{array}$$

GRE

MATH TEST

TEST II

THE GRADUATE RECORD EXAMINATION

MATH TEST

ANSWER SHEET

1. Ⓐ Ⓑ Ⓒ Ⓓ Ⓔ
2. Ⓐ Ⓑ Ⓒ Ⓓ Ⓔ
3. Ⓐ Ⓑ Ⓒ Ⓓ Ⓔ
4. Ⓐ Ⓑ Ⓒ Ⓓ Ⓔ
5. Ⓐ Ⓑ Ⓒ Ⓓ Ⓔ
6. Ⓐ Ⓑ Ⓒ Ⓓ Ⓔ
7. Ⓐ Ⓑ Ⓒ Ⓓ Ⓔ
8. Ⓐ Ⓑ Ⓒ Ⓓ Ⓔ
9. Ⓐ Ⓑ Ⓒ Ⓓ Ⓔ
10. Ⓐ Ⓑ Ⓒ Ⓓ Ⓔ
11. Ⓐ Ⓑ Ⓒ Ⓓ Ⓔ
12. Ⓐ Ⓑ Ⓒ Ⓓ Ⓔ
13. Ⓐ Ⓑ Ⓒ Ⓓ Ⓔ
14. Ⓐ Ⓑ Ⓒ Ⓓ Ⓔ
15. Ⓐ Ⓑ Ⓒ Ⓓ Ⓔ
16. Ⓐ Ⓑ Ⓒ Ⓓ Ⓔ
17. Ⓐ Ⓑ Ⓒ Ⓓ Ⓔ
18. Ⓐ Ⓑ Ⓒ Ⓓ Ⓔ
19. Ⓐ Ⓑ Ⓒ Ⓓ Ⓔ
20. Ⓐ Ⓑ Ⓒ Ⓓ Ⓔ
21. Ⓐ Ⓑ Ⓒ Ⓓ Ⓔ
22. Ⓐ Ⓑ Ⓒ Ⓓ Ⓔ

23. Ⓐ Ⓑ Ⓒ Ⓓ Ⓔ
24. Ⓐ Ⓑ Ⓒ Ⓓ Ⓔ
25. Ⓐ Ⓑ Ⓒ Ⓓ Ⓔ
26. Ⓐ Ⓑ Ⓒ Ⓓ Ⓔ
27. Ⓐ Ⓑ Ⓒ Ⓓ Ⓔ
28. Ⓐ Ⓑ Ⓒ Ⓓ Ⓔ
29. Ⓐ Ⓑ Ⓒ Ⓓ Ⓔ
30. Ⓐ Ⓑ Ⓒ Ⓓ Ⓔ
31. Ⓐ Ⓑ Ⓒ Ⓓ Ⓔ
32. Ⓐ Ⓑ Ⓒ Ⓓ Ⓔ
33. Ⓐ Ⓑ Ⓒ Ⓓ Ⓔ
34. Ⓐ Ⓑ Ⓒ Ⓓ Ⓔ
35. Ⓐ Ⓑ Ⓒ Ⓓ Ⓔ
36. Ⓐ Ⓑ Ⓒ Ⓓ Ⓔ
37. Ⓐ Ⓑ Ⓒ Ⓓ Ⓔ
38. Ⓐ Ⓑ Ⓒ Ⓓ Ⓔ
39. Ⓐ Ⓑ Ⓒ Ⓓ Ⓔ
40. Ⓐ Ⓑ Ⓒ Ⓓ Ⓔ
41. Ⓐ Ⓑ Ⓒ Ⓓ Ⓔ
42. Ⓐ Ⓑ Ⓒ Ⓓ Ⓔ
43. Ⓐ Ⓑ Ⓒ Ⓓ Ⓔ
44. Ⓐ Ⓑ Ⓒ Ⓓ Ⓔ

45. Ⓐ Ⓑ Ⓒ Ⓓ Ⓔ
46. Ⓐ Ⓑ Ⓒ Ⓓ Ⓔ
47. Ⓐ Ⓑ Ⓒ Ⓓ Ⓔ
48. Ⓐ Ⓑ Ⓒ Ⓓ Ⓔ
49. Ⓐ Ⓑ Ⓒ Ⓓ Ⓔ
50. Ⓐ Ⓑ Ⓒ Ⓓ Ⓔ
51. Ⓐ Ⓑ Ⓒ Ⓓ Ⓔ
52. Ⓐ Ⓑ Ⓒ Ⓓ Ⓔ
53. Ⓐ Ⓑ Ⓒ Ⓓ Ⓔ
54. Ⓐ Ⓑ Ⓒ Ⓓ Ⓔ
55. Ⓐ Ⓑ Ⓒ Ⓓ Ⓔ
56. Ⓐ Ⓑ Ⓒ Ⓓ Ⓔ
57. Ⓐ Ⓑ Ⓒ Ⓓ Ⓔ
58. Ⓐ Ⓑ Ⓒ Ⓓ Ⓔ
59. Ⓐ Ⓑ Ⓒ Ⓓ Ⓔ
60. Ⓐ Ⓑ Ⓒ Ⓓ Ⓔ
61. Ⓐ Ⓑ Ⓒ Ⓓ Ⓔ
62. Ⓐ Ⓑ Ⓒ Ⓓ Ⓔ
63. Ⓐ Ⓑ Ⓒ Ⓓ Ⓔ
64. Ⓐ Ⓑ Ⓒ Ⓓ Ⓔ
65. Ⓐ Ⓑ Ⓒ Ⓓ Ⓔ
66. Ⓐ Ⓑ Ⓒ Ⓓ Ⓔ

GRE MATHEMATICS
TEST II

TIME: 2 hours and 50 minutes
66 Questions

DIRECTIONS: Choose the best answer for each question and mark the letter of your selection on the corresponding answer sheet.

1. Find the sum of the series $\displaystyle\sum_{n=1}^{\infty} \frac{n}{4^{n+1}}$.

   (A) $\dfrac{1}{12}$ (D) $\dfrac{4}{3}$

   (B) $\dfrac{1}{9}$ (E) $\dfrac{1}{3}$

   (C) $\dfrac{1}{6}$

2. A rectangle has dimensions a units by b units with $a > b$. A diagonal divides the rectangle into two triangles. A square, with sides parallel to those of the rectangle, is inscribed in each triangle. Find the distance between the vertices (of the squares) that lie in the interior of the rectangle.

   (A) $\dfrac{(a - b)\sqrt{a^2 + b^2}}{a + b}$ (D) $\dfrac{a^2 - b^2}{\sqrt{a^2 + b^2}}$

   (B) $\sqrt{a^2 - b^2}$ (E) $\dfrac{(a - b)\sqrt{a^2 - b^2}}{a + b}$

   (C) $\dfrac{a^2 - b^2}{\sqrt{ab}}$

3. Find the index of the subgroup generated by the permutation

$$\begin{pmatrix} 1 & 2 & 3 & 4 & 5 \\ \downarrow & \downarrow & \downarrow & \downarrow & \downarrow \\ 3 & 1 & 2 & 4 & 5 \end{pmatrix}$$

in the alternating group A_5 .

(A) 20

(D) 3

(B) 40

(E) 5

(C) 24

4. In a pure radioactive decay model, the rate of change in the mass, M, satisfies the differential equation, $dM/dt = -M/10$. If the initial value of M is M_0, find M in terms of M_0 after 20 units of time, t, have elapsed.

(A) $\dfrac{1}{2} M_0$

(D) $\dfrac{M_0}{e}$

(B) $\dfrac{1}{4} M_0$

(E) $\dfrac{M_0}{e^2}$

(C) $\dfrac{M_0}{2e}$

5. Let $f(x) = x^{2n} - x^{2n-1} + \ldots + x^4 - x^3 + x^2 - ax + b$. Which value for the pair (a, b) will insure that the x-axis will be tangent to the graph of $f(x)$ at $x = 1$?

(A) $(1, 1)$

(B) $(n, n{-}1)$

(C) $(n-1, n)$

(D) $(n+1, n)$

(E) $(n, n+1)$

6. Let the set S be infinite and let the set T be countably infinite. Let $\bar{S}$ denote the complement of S. If S and T are both subsets of the real numbers, which of the following pairs of sets must be of the same cardinality?

(A) T and $S \cap T$

(D) Both (A) and (B)

(B) S and $S \cup T$

(E) Both (A) and (C)

(C) T and $\bar{S} \cup T$

7. Find the maximum value of $f(x) = 5 \sin 7x + 12 \cos 7x$.

(A) 12

(D) 17

(B) 5

(E) 13

(C) 7

8. In a computer program, separate loops with distinct indices produce M and N operations respectively. If these reside internally in a loop with an independent index producing P

operations, find the total number of operations represented by the three loops.

(A) P^{M+N}

(D) $P^M + P^N$

(B) $(M + N)^P$

(E) $M^P + N^P$

(C) $P(M + N)$

9. Give that the Taylor series for $g(x)$ is

$$\sum_{n=0}^{\infty} a_n x^n \text{ and} f(x) = [g(x)]^3, \text{ find } f''(0).$$

(A) $3a_0(2a_1^2 + a_0 a_2)$

(D) $6a_0(a_1 + a_0 a_1)$

(B) $6a_0(a_1^2 + a_0 a_2)$

(E) None of these

(C) $3a_0(2a_1 + a_0 a_2)$

10. If $f(x) = x/(1 - x)$, find $f(f(f(x)))$.

(A) $\dfrac{x^3}{1 - x^3}$

(D) $\dfrac{3x}{1 - 3x}$

(B) $\dfrac{3x}{3 - x}$

(E) $\dfrac{x}{1 - 3x}$

(C) $\dfrac{x}{3 - x}$

11. Define $S_k = \{\frac{k}{j} \mid j = k, k+1, \ldots\}$ for $k = 1, 2, \ldots$. Find the intersection $\bigcap_{k=1}^{\infty} S_k$.

(A) S_1

(D) the interval $(0, 1)$

(B) the empty set

(E) $\{\frac{k}{j} \mid 0 < \frac{k}{j} \leq 1\}$

(C) the interval $[0, 1]$

12. Evaluate $\lim_{n \to \infty} \sum_{k=1}^{n} \dfrac{1}{n(1 + \frac{k}{n})}$.

(A) 1

(D) $+\infty$

(B) $\ln 2$

(E) Does not exist

(C) 0

13. Evaluate the definite integral $\displaystyle\int_0^a \dfrac{x^2 + b^2}{x^2 + a^2}\, dx$.

(A) $\dfrac{((4 - \pi)a + \pi b^2)}{4a}$

(D) $a + (b^2 - a^2)\ln 2$

(B) $4a^2 + \pi(b^2 - a^2)$

(E) $(4 - \pi)\dfrac{a}{4} + \dfrac{\pi b^2}{4a}$

(C) $\dfrac{((2 - \pi)a + \pi b^2)}{2a}$

14. Let $f(x, y) = x^3 - axy + y^2 - x$. Find the greatest lower bound for a so that $f(x, y)$ has a relative minimum point.

(A) 0

(D) 6

(B) $\sqrt{48}$

(E) Does not exist

(C) 12

15. Given that S and T are subspaces of a vector space, which of the following is also a subspace?

(A) $S \cap T$

(D) Both (A) and (C)

(B) $S \cup T$

(E) Both (B) and (C)

(C) $2S$

16. Find the point $x + iy$ at which the complex function $f(x + iy) = x^2 + y^2 + 2xi$ is differentiable.

(A) 0

(D) $1 + i$

(B) i

(E) $-i$

(C) $1 - i$

17. Define a function, $f(x)$, to be <u>differentiably redundant</u> of order n if the n-th derivative $f^{(n)}(x) = f(x)$ but $f^{(k)}(x) \neq f(x)$ when $k < n$. For easy examples, in this context, e^x is of order 1, e^{-x} is of order 2, and $\cos x$ is of order 4. Which of the following functions is differentiably redundant of order 6?

(A) $e^{-x} + e^{\frac{-x}{2}} \cos\left(\dfrac{\sqrt{3x}}{2}\right)$

(B) $e^{-x} + \cos x$

(C) $e^{\frac{x}{2}} \sin\left(\dfrac{\sqrt{3x}}{2}\right)$

(D) Both (A) and (C)

(E) (A), (B) and (C)

18. In a homogeneous system of 5 linear equations in 7 unknowns, the rank of the coefficient matrix is 4. The maximum number of independent solution vectors is

(A) 5   (D) 1

(B) 2   (E) 3

(C) 4

19. The number, up to isomorphism, of abelian groups of order 40 is

(A) 40   (B) 20

(C) 8   (D) 7

(E) 5

20.   From the set of integers {1, 2, ..., 9}, how many nonempty
       subsets sum to an even integer?

       (A) 512   (D) $\dfrac{9!}{2!}$

       (B) 255   (E) None of these

       (C) $\dfrac{9!}{2!\,7!}$

21.   How many topologies are possible on a set of 2 points?

       (A) 5   (D) 2

       (B) 4   (E) 1

       (C) 3

22.   In the (ε, δ) definition of the limit, $\lim\limits_{x \to c} f(x) = L$, let $f(x) =$
       $x^3 + 3x^2 - x + 1$ and let $c = 2$. Find the least upper bound on δ
       so that $f(x)$ is bounded within ε of L for all sufficiently small
       $\varepsilon > 0$.

       (A) $\dfrac{\varepsilon}{8}$ (D) $\dfrac{(\varepsilon^2)}{16}$

       (B) $\dfrac{\varepsilon}{23}$ (E) $\dfrac{\varepsilon}{19}$

       (C) $\dfrac{(\varepsilon^3)}{4}$

23. Find the remainder on dividing 3^{20} by 7.

(A) 1   (D) 4

(B) 2   (E) 5

(C) 3

24. In the partial fractions expansion of $\dfrac{s^2 + 1}{(s^2 - 2)(s^2 + 3)}$, the numerator of the fraction with denominator $s^2 + 3$ is

(A) 3   (D) $2s + 1$

(B) $\dfrac{3}{5}$ (E) $1 - 2s$

(C) $\dfrac{2}{5}$

25. For how many distinct real coefficients, a, will the system of equations $y = ax^2 + 2$ and $x = ay^2 + 2$ admit a solution with $y = 1$?

(A) 0   (D) 3

(B) 1   (E) 4

(C) 2

26. A subgroup H in group G is invariant if $gH = Hg$ for every g in G. If H and K are both invariant subgroups of G, which of the following is also an invariant subgroup?

(A) $H \cap K$ (D) Both (A) and (B)

(B) HK (E) Both (B) and (C)

(C) $H \cup K$

27. Let R be a ring such that $x^2 = x$ for each $x \in R$. Which of the following must be true?

(A) $x = -x$ for all $x \in R$

(B) R is commutative

(C) $xy + yx = 0$ for all $x, y \in R$

(D) Both (A) and (C)

(E) (A), (B), and (C)

28. In the integral domain $D = \{r + s\sqrt{17} \mid r, s \text{ integers}\}$, which of the following is irreducible?

(A) $8 + 2\sqrt{17}$ (D) $7 + \sqrt{17}$

(B) $3 - \sqrt{17}$ (E) $13 + \sqrt{17}$

(C) $9 - 2\sqrt{17}$

29. For which value of k is x^k a solution for the differential equation
$x^2 y'' - 3xy' - 4y = 0$?

(A) 4

(D) 1

(B) 3

(E) None of these

(C) 2

30. Which of the following is a factor of $x^4 + 1$?

(A) $x + 1$

(D) $x^2 + \sqrt{2}\,x - 1$

(B) $x^2 + 1$

(E) None of these

(C) $x^2 - \sqrt{2}\,x + 1$

31. The surface given by $z = x^2 - y^2$ is cut by the plane given by
$y = 3x$, producing a curve in the plane. Find the slope of this
curve at the point $(1, 3, -8)$.

(A) 3

(D) 0

(B) -16

(E) $\dfrac{18}{\sqrt{10}}$

(C) $-8\sqrt{\dfrac{2}{5}}$

32. If A is an $n \times n$ matrix with diagonal entries, a, and other entries, b, then one eigenvalue of A is $a - b$. Find another eigenvalue of A .

(A) $b - a$

(D) 0

(B) $nb + a - b$

(E) None of these

(C) $nb - a + b$

33. In ancient Egypt, the formula $A = \left(\dfrac{8d}{9}\right)^2$ was used for the area of a circle of diameter d . Using the correct multiple, relating the volume of a sphere to the area of a circle, what should the Egyptian formula be for the volume of the sphere of diameter d ?

(A) $\dfrac{\pi d^3}{3}$

(D) $\dfrac{2^8 \pi d^3}{3^5}$

(B) $\left(\dfrac{8d}{9}\right)^3$

(E) $\dfrac{2^7 d^3}{3^5}$

(C) $4\left(\dfrac{8}{9}d\right)^3$

34. Find k so that the matrix

$$A = \begin{pmatrix} k & 1 & 2 \\ 1 & 2 & k \\ 1 & 2 & 3 \end{pmatrix}$$

has eigenvalue $\lambda = 1$.

(A) $\dfrac{1}{2}$

(B) $-\dfrac{1}{2}$

(C) 0   (D) 1

(E) − 1

35.   Express z^{14} in the form $a + bi$ if $z = \dfrac{(1 + i)}{\sqrt{2}}$.

(A) $-i$ (D) i

(B) -1 (E) $\dfrac{(1 + i)}{128}$

(C) 1

36.   Which number is nearest a solution of $e^{\frac{-x}{100}} - e^{-x} = e^{-1}$?

(A) $1 - \dfrac{1}{2}\ln 4$ (D) -1

(B) $1 - \dfrac{1}{2}\ln 3$ (E) 0

(C) $1 - \dfrac{1}{2}\ln 2$

37.   In the Laurent series for $f(z) = \dfrac{1}{(z - 4)}$ centered at $z = 1$, the coefficient of $(z - 1)^{-2}$ is

(A) 9   (D) 3

(B) -9 (E) -1

(C) -3

38. If $f(x) = \int_{1}^{x^2} \dfrac{dt}{1+t^3}$ then $f'(2)$ is

(A) $\dfrac{4}{65}$

(B) $\dfrac{1}{9}$

(C) $\ln\left(\dfrac{65}{2}\right)$

(D) $\ln\left(\dfrac{9}{2}\right)$

(E) 0.23

39. The series $\displaystyle\sum_{n=2}^{\infty} \dfrac{1}{n \cdot 3^n}$ must

(A) converge to a value greater than 1/4

(B) converge to a value greater than 1/9

(C) converge to a value less than 1/18

(D) converge to a value less than 1/12

(E) diverge

40. If A is a square matrix of order $n \geq 4$ and $a_{ij} = i + j$ represents the entry in row i and column j, then the rank of A is always

(A) 1

(B) 2

(C) $n-2$

(D) $n-1$

(E) None of these

41. In the finite field, Z_{17}, the multiplicative inverse of 10 is

(A) 13

(D) 9

(B) 12

(E) 7

(C) 11

42. The system of equations $x^2 - y = a$ and $y - x = b$ has exactly one value of x in its solution(s). This value of x must be

(A) 0

(D) $-\dfrac{1}{2}$

(B) 1

(E) $\dfrac{1}{2}$

(C) $\dfrac{3}{2}$

43. $\log_4 64$ is identical to

(A) $\log_7 343$

(D) Both (A) and (B)

(B) $\dfrac{\log_{10} 64}{\log_{10} 4}$

(E) Both (A) and (C)

(C) $\log_8 256$

44. Let $S = \{\tan (k) \mid k = 1, 2, \ldots\}$. Find the set of limit points of S on the real line.

(A) $(-\infty, \infty)$

(D) $(-\infty, 0]$

(B) $\left[-\dfrac{\pi}{2}, \dfrac{\pi}{2}\right]$

(E) The empty set

(C) $[0, \infty)$

45. Given the sequence $a_n = \sin n$, $n \geq 1$, find

$$\lim_{n \to \infty} \inf\{a_n\} - \lim_{n \to \infty} \sup\{a_n\}.$$

(A) 2

(D) -1

(B) 1

(E) -2

(C) 0

46. Find the length of a diagonal of a regular pentagon of side length 1.

(A) $2\cos\dfrac{\pi}{5}$

(D) $\sqrt{2}$

(B) $\sqrt{2}\left(1 + \cos\left(\dfrac{\pi}{5}\right)\right)$

(E) $\sqrt{2} + \sqrt{2\cos\left(\dfrac{2\pi}{5}\right)}$

(C) $\sqrt{2}\left(1 + \cos\left(\dfrac{2\pi}{5}\right)\right)$

47. Which of the following is a solution to the differential equation $y'' = 2y' + 8y$?

(A) $e^{2x} - e^{-4x}$

(D) $e^{4x} - e^{-2x}$

(B) xe^{4x}

(E) xe^{-2x}

(C) e^{2x}

48. Let $f(x)$ be defined and strictly increasing on $(a, b]$. Find the maximum value of $g(x) = -f(x)$ on $(a, b]$.

(A) $g(b)$

(D) $f(a)$

(B) $f(b)$

(E) Does not exist

(C) $g(a)$

49. Find the number of distinguishable permutations of six colored blocks if one is red, two are yellow, and three are blue.

(A) 360

(D) 120

(B) 60

(E) 240

(C) 720

50. Two vertices of an isosceles triangle are (1,2) and (4,6). The inradius of the triangle is 3/2. Find the maximum possible area for the triangle.

(A) $\dfrac{45}{4}$

(D) $\dfrac{9\sqrt{19}}{2}$

(B) $\dfrac{9\sqrt{19}}{4}$

(E) None of these

(C) $\dfrac{45}{2}$

51. The volume, V, of the region in space bounded above by the surface $x^2 + y^2 + z^2 = 4$ and below by $z = -\sqrt{x^2 + y^2}$ is represented by a triple integral in spherical coordinates as

$$\iiint\limits_{V} \rho^2 \sin\phi\, d\rho\, d\phi\, d\theta.$$

find the upper limit of integration for ϕ .

(A) π

(D) $\dfrac{\pi}{4}$

(B) $\dfrac{3\pi}{4}$

(E) $\dfrac{\pi}{6}$

(C) $\dfrac{\pi}{2}$

52. The reliability of component C is R. A system is designed as a series of n subcomponents each of which is doubly redundant using two components, C. Find the reliability of the system.

(A) $R^n(1-R)^n$

(B) $R^n(2-R)^n$

(C) R^{2n}

(D) $\dfrac{R^n}{2^n}$

(E) $1 - (1-R)^{2n}$

53. A family of curves is represented by the differential equation $ydx - xdy = 0$. Which of the following best describes the family of orthogonal trajectories to this given family?

(A) all parabolas with vertex at $(0, 0)$

(B) all hyperbolas with centers at $(0, 0)$

(C) all lines through $(0, 0)$

(D) all circles with centers at $(0, 0)$

(E) all lines parallel to the y-axis

54. Which of the following sequences is a solution for the difference equation $x_{n+2} + 36_n = x_{n+1} + 6x_n$?

(A) $3^n + 6n$

(D) $3^n + 6 + n$

(B) $2^n + 6n + 1$

(E) $(-1)^n 2^{n+1} + 6n + 1$

(C) $6^n + 6n$

55. Let f be a mapping from a topological space $\overline{X}$ onto itself. Which of the following is true for continuous f?

   (A) Every open set in $\overline{X}$ is the image of an open set in $\overline{X}$

   (B) $f^{-1}(B)$ is bounded for each bounded set B in $\overline{X}$

   (C) f is one-to-one

   (D) Both (A) and (B)

   (E) Both (A) and (C)

56. At the point $(2, -1, 2)$ on the surface $z = xy^2$, find a direction vector for the greatest rate of decrease of z.

   (A) $\hat{i} - 2\hat{j}$ (D) $-\hat{i} + 4\hat{j}$

   (B) $\hat{i} - 4\hat{j}$ (E) $\hat{i} + \hat{j}$

   (C) $\dfrac{(\hat{i} - 4\hat{j})}{\sqrt{17}}$

57. Let G be a polyhedron with 27 vertices and 40 edges. Find the number of faces on G.

   (A) 12   (D) 15

   (B) 13   (E) Cannot be decided based on the given information

   (C) 14

58. Find the coefficient of x^2y^3 in the binomial expansion of $(x - 2y)^5$.

(A) -160

(D) 8

(B) 80

(E) -8

(C) -80

59. In the evaluation of the integral $\int \dfrac{dx}{x(2 + 3x)^2}$, the coefficient of $\ln | (2 + 3x) |$ is

(A) $-\dfrac{3}{4}$

(D) $\dfrac{1}{4}$

(B) $-\dfrac{1}{4}$

(E) $-\dfrac{1}{36}$

(C) $\dfrac{3}{4}$

60. A biased coin is tossed repeatedly until the first "tail" occurs. The expected number of tosses required to produce the first tail is estimated as T. Assuming this is true, find the probability of at least two tails in $3T$ tosses.

(A) $\dfrac{T^{3T} - (T - 1)^{3T-1}(4T)}{T^{3T}}$

(B) $\dfrac{T^{3T} - (T - 1)^{3T-1}(3T)}{T^{3T}}$

(C) $\dfrac{T^{3T} - (T - 1)^{3T-1}(3T - 1)}{T^{3T}}$

(D) $\dfrac{T^{3T} - (T-1)^{3T-1}(4T-1)}{T^{3T}}$

(E) None of these

61. The vertices of a quadrilateral are $(0,0), (1,4), (3,2),$ and $(5,5)$. Find the first coordinate of the centroid of the region.

(A) $\dfrac{9}{4}$ (D) $\dfrac{17}{6}$

(B) $\dfrac{13}{6}$ (E) $\dfrac{8}{3}$

(C) $\dfrac{7}{3}$

62. Let R be a ring and let $x \neq 0$ be a fixed element in R. Which of the following is a subring of R ?

(A) $\{ r \mid xr = 0 \}$

(B) $\{ x \mid x^{-1} \text{ exists in } R\}$

(C) $\{ x^n \mid n = 1, 2, \dots \}$

(D) $\{ nx \mid n \text{ is an integer}\}$

(E) Both (A) and (D)

63. If $f(x) = \ln x$, find

$$\lim_{m \to 0} \left[\lim_{n \to 0} \frac{f(2+m+n) - f(2+m) - f(2+n) + f(2)}{mn} \right]$$

(A) $\frac{1}{4}$

(D) $\frac{1}{2}$

(B) 1

(E) $-\frac{1}{4}$

(C) -1

64. Let $S = \{ x_1, x_2, ..., x_n, ... \}$ be a topological space where the open sets are $U_n = \{ x_1, ..., x_n \}$, $n = 1, 2, ...$. Let $E = \{ x_2, x_4, ..., x_{2k}, ... \}$. Find the set of cluster points of E.

(A) $S - \{x_1, x_2\}$

(D) $E - \{x_2\}$

(B) $\{x_1\}$

(E) $S - E$

(C) $\{x_2\}$

65. A stiff beam on two supports that are 20ft. apart is loaded by two uniform blocks with dimensions and weights as shown below.

How much of the total weight is supported at the left support?

(A) 150

(D) 100

(B) 120

(E) None of these

(C) 110

66.   Given that $\sum\limits_{n=1}^{\infty} a_n$ converges to L, which conclusion is valid

for $\sum\limits_{n=1}^{\infty} a_n^2$?

(A) It may diverge

(B) It converges absolutely

(C) It converges to $M < L$

(D) It converges to $M > L$

(E) It converges to L^2

GRE MATHEMATICS
TEST II

ANSWER KEY

1.	B	23.	B	45.	E
2.	A	24.	C	46.	A
3.	A	25.	D	47.	D
4.	E	26.	D	48.	E
5.	D	27.	E	49.	B
6.	B	28.	B	50.	A
7.	E	29.	E	51.	B
8.	C	30.	C	52.	B
9	B	31.	C	53.	D
10.	E	32.	B	54.	E
11.	A	33.	E	55.	A
12.	B	34.	A	56.	D
13.	E	35.	A	57.	D
14.	E	36.	B	58.	C
15.	D	37.	D	59.	B
16.	E	38.	A	60.	D
17.	D	39.	D	61.	B
18.	E	40.	B	62.	A
19.	D	41.	B	63.	E
20.	B	42.	E	64.	A
21.	B	43.	D	65.	C
22.	B	44.	A	66.	A

GRE MATHEMATICS
TEST II

DETAILED EXPLANATIONS
OF ANSWERS

1. **(B)**

It is well-known that $(1 - x)^{-1} = \sum_{n=0}^{\infty} x^n$, so $(1 - x)^{-2} = \sum_{n=1}^{\infty} nx^{n-1}$ by differentiation. Of course $|x| < 1$ is required for convergence. The given series is $\frac{1}{16} \sum_{n=1}^{\infty} n\left(\frac{1}{4}\right)^{n-1} = \frac{1}{16}\left(1 - \frac{1}{4}\right)^{-2} = \frac{1}{9}$.

2. **(A)**

From the diagram shown, vertex E must lie on the lines $y = x$ and $y = -\frac{b}{a}x + b$, so it has coordinates $\left(\frac{ab}{a + b}, \frac{ab}{a + b}\right)$, found by solving these equations simultaneously. By symmetry we must have coorindates for vertex F as $\left(\frac{a^2}{a + b}, \frac{b^2}{a + b}\right)$.

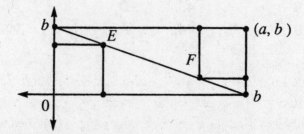

Applying the distance formula,

$$d = \frac{\sqrt{a^2(a-b)^2 + b^2(b-a)^2}}{(a+b)}$$

which reduces to (A).

3.   (A)

If $\lambda = (1\ 3\ 2)\ (4)\ (5)$, then $\lambda^2 = (1\ 2\ 3)\ (4)\ (5)$ and $\lambda^3 = (1)\ (2)\ (3)$ $(4)\ (5)$, the identity. Hence the <u>cyclic</u> subgroup generated by λ is of order 3. A_5 is of order $5!/2 = 60$ and so the required index is $60/3 = 20$.

4.   (E)

The equation can be solved by separation of variables $\dfrac{dM}{M} = -\dfrac{dt}{10}$ and integration, yielding $\ln M = -\dfrac{t}{10} + C$. The value $M = M_0$ when $t = 0$ implies that $C = \ln M_0$. Taking the exponential of both sides of the solution yields

$$M = M_0 e^{-\frac{t}{10}} \quad \text{so } M(20) = M_0 e^{-2} = \frac{M_0}{e^2}.$$

5.   (D)

First, we must have $f(1) = 1 - a + b = 0$. Then since $f'(1) = n - 1 + 2 - a = 0$ is also required, we must have $a = n + 1$ so $b = n$.

6.   (B)

If S is countable, then $S \cup T$ is the union of countable sets and hence countable. If S is uncountable, then $S \cup T$ is uncountable as its cardinality is at least that of S. Counterexamples for the other cases:

(A) $S \cap T$ is countable but it may be finite.
For example, $S = \{ 0, 1, 2, \ldots \}$, $T = \{ 0, -1, -2, \ldots \}$.

(C) $\bar{S}$ may be uncountable and then $\bar{S} \cup T$ is also.

7.　(E)

The amplitude of any wave in the form $a \sin kx + b \cos kx$ is $\sqrt{a^2 + b^2}$. This follows since factoring $\sqrt{a^2 + b^2}$ from the expression leaves coefficients $\dfrac{a}{\sqrt{a^2 + b^2}}$ and $\dfrac{b}{\sqrt{a^2 + b^2}}$ which have sum of squares equal to one. Hence we can rewrite the wave as

$$\sqrt{a^2 + b^2} \, \sin (kx \pm \theta) \quad \text{where } \theta = \sin^{-1} \left(\frac{b}{\sqrt{a^2 + b^2}} \right).$$

As $\sin (kx \pm \theta)$ can be at most 1, the maximum is at

$$\sqrt{a^2 + b^2} = \sqrt{5^2 + 12^2} = \sqrt{169} = 13.$$

A calculus approach is much more difficult..

8.　(C)

Each of the P passes through the external loop creates $M + N$ operations in the internal loops. Basic counting technique implies the product $P (M + N)$, gives the total number of operations.

9.　(B)

Directly, using the chain rule, $f'(x) = 3 [g (x)]^2 \cdot g'(x)$ and then $f''(x) = 6 g (x)[g'(x)]^2 + 3 [g (x)]^2 g''(x)$. Now the coefficients of the

series are related to $g(x)$ in general as $g^{(n)}(0) = n!a_n$. So $g(0) = a_0$, $g'(0)$
$= a_1$ and $g''(0) = 2a_2$. Hence $f''(0) = 6a_0a_1^2 + 3a_0^2 \cdot 2a_2 = 6a_0(a_1^2 + a_0a_2)$.

10. (E)

$$f(f(x)) = f\left(\frac{x}{1-x}\right) = \frac{\dfrac{x}{1-x}}{\left(1 - \dfrac{x}{1-x}\right)} = \frac{x}{1-x-x} = \frac{x}{1-2x}$$

Likewise,

$$f(f(f(x))) = f\left(\frac{x}{1-2x}\right) = \frac{\dfrac{x}{1-2x}}{\left(1 - \dfrac{x}{1-2x}\right)} = \frac{x}{1-3x}$$

11. (A)

S_1 contains 1 and all unit fractions $1/n$. In all other S_k, only the numerators of the fractions change. Since the unit fraction $\dfrac{1}{n} = \dfrac{k}{nk}$ and this is in S_k, we find that

$$S_k \subseteq S_1 \text{ for all } k, \text{ so } \bigcap_{k=1}^{\infty} S_k = S_1.$$

12. (B)

It is simplest to view the limit as a definite integral in the form

$$\lim_{n \to \infty} \sum_{k=1}^{n} f(a + k\Delta x) \Delta x.$$

In this case, $\Delta x = 1/n$ and $a = 1$ so $f(x) = 1/x$. As usual, we can use $\Delta x(b - a)/n$ for interval $[a, b]$ to conclude that $b = 2$. Thus, the limit is

$$\int_{1}^{2} \frac{dx}{x} = \ln x \Big|_{1}^{2} = \ln 2 = \ln 1 = \ln 2.$$

13. (E)

$$\int_0^a \frac{x^2 + b^2}{x^2 + a^2}\, dx = \int_0^a \left(\frac{x^2 + a^2}{x^2 + a^2} + \frac{b^2 - a^2}{x^2 + a^2} \right) dx$$

$$= \int_0^a \left(1 + \frac{b^2 - a^2}{x^2 + a^2} \right) dx$$

$$= \left(x + \frac{b^2 - a^2}{a} \tan^{-1}\left(\frac{x}{a}\right) \right)\Big|_0^a$$

$$= a + \frac{\left(b^2 - a^2\right)}{a} \frac{\pi}{4}$$

$$= \frac{4a^2}{4a} + \frac{\left(b^2 - a^2\right)\pi}{4a}$$

$$= \frac{4a^2 + b^2\pi - a^2\pi}{4a}$$

$$= \frac{(4 - \pi)\, a^2 + b^2\pi}{4a}$$

$$= (4 - \pi)\frac{a}{4} + \frac{\pi b^2}{4a}.$$

14. (E)

For a relative minimum, we must simultaneously have $f_x = 3x^2 - ay - 1 = 0$, $f_y = -ax + 2y = 0$, and $D = f_{xx} \cdot f_{yy} - f^2_{xy} = 12x - a^2 > 0$ since $f_{yy} = 2 > 0$ independent of x, y. The first two conditions imply $y = ax/2$ and $3x^2 - \frac{a^2}{2}x - 1 = 0$. Solving the quadratic always yields two roots,

$$x = \frac{\left(\frac{a^2}{2} \pm \sqrt{\frac{a^4}{4} + 12} \right)}{6}$$

where the + sign will yield the necessary positive root for $D > 0$. Then

91

$D = a^2 + \sqrt{a^4 + 48} - a^2 = \sqrt{a^4 + 48} > 0$ independent of the choice of a. No lower bound exists.

15.   (D)

The result (A) is a standard theorem in vector spaces. For (C), we need only note that subspaces are closed under scalar multiplication so $2S \subseteq S$. But, for every x in S, $1/2\,x$ is in S and $2(1/2\,x) = x$ so $S \subseteq 2S$, and we can conclude that $S = 2S$, so $2S$ is a subspace.

To show that (B) is not necessarily true, let the vector space be R^2, $S = \{ (a, 0) \mid a \,\varepsilon\, R \}$, $T = \{ (a, b) \mid a + b = 0,\ a, b \,\varepsilon\, R \}$. Then S and T are subspaces of R^2 (this is easily checked), and $S \cup T = \{ (a, b) \mid b = 0 \text{ or } a + b = 0, a, b \,\varepsilon\, R \}$. We see that $S \cup T$ is not a subspace of R^2 because it is not closed under addition. For example, if we take $s, t \,\varepsilon\, S \cup T$ where $s = (1, 0)$ and $t = (1, -1)$, then $s + t = (2, -1) \notin S \cup T$.

16.   (E)

The Cauchy-Riemann conditions to be satisfied are

$$\frac{\partial(x^2 + y^2)}{\partial x} = \frac{\partial(2x)}{\partial y} \quad \text{and} \quad \frac{\partial(x^2 + y^2)}{\partial y} = -\frac{\partial(2x)}{\partial x},$$

which imply $x = 0$ and $y = -1$.

17.   (D)

If $y = f(x)$ is differentiably redundant of order n then $y^{(n)} - y = 0$ and solutions are related to the nth roots of unity. Clearly, the sum of two functions, one of order m and the other of order n, yields a function of order $l\,cm(m, n)$. This eliminates (B) which must be of order 4. (A) is of order 6 since $-1/2 \pm i\sqrt{3}/2$ are 3rd roots of unity. (C) is of order

6 since $1/2 \pm i\sqrt{3}/2$ are 6th roots of unity. In each of these latter cases we have primitive roots and this is necessary. For instance -1 is also a 6th root of unity but e^{-x} is not of order 6.

18.   (E)
The dimension of the solution space of a matrix always is given by the number of columns (7) or unknowns less the rank of the matrix (4).

19.   (D)
Non-isomorphic abelian groups of the same order, n, are effectively the direct products $Z_{n1} \times Z_{n2} \times \ldots \times Z_{nk}$ where $n_1 \times n_2 \times \ldots n_k = n$ and each n_i is a divisor of n. In this case, the products yielding 40 are 40, 10×4, 8×5, 20×2, $10 \times 2 \times 2$, $5 \times 4 \times 2$, and $5 \times 2 \times 2 \times 2$.

20.   (B)
It may simply be well known that half the sums will be even (including sum zero for the empty set) and the number of subsets is $2^9 = 512$, so $1/2(512) - 1 = 255$ (for the empty set). A more direct anaylsis follows in that an even sum results in each of the $2^4 = 16$ subsets containing only the even integers, 2, 4, 6, 8. These may be combined with either 0, 2, or 4 odd numbers and the number of ways to choose these is

$$\binom{5}{0} = 1, \binom{5}{2} = 10, \text{ or } \binom{5}{4} = 5, \text{ respectively.}$$

Hence the total $16(1 + 10 + 5) = 16^2 = 256$ which includes the empty set.

21.   (B)

Given $\overline{X} = \{x, y\}$, every topology must contain the open sets $\overline{X}$ and ϕ, the empty set. When these are the only open sets, we have one (trivial) topology. The other three possible topologies are $\{\{x\}\}$, $\{\{y\}\}$, and $\{\{x\}, \{y\}\}$.

22.   (B)

This is very tedious by direct means, but generally the bound is ε / |$f'(c)$| when f is differentiable and $f'(c) \neq 0$, on an interval containing c. In this case $f'(2) = 23$.

23.   (B)

Since $3^3 = 27 \equiv (-1) \pmod 7$ we find $3^{18} \equiv (-1)^6 \equiv 1 \pmod 7$, so $3^{20} \equiv 3^2 \pmod 7 \equiv 2 \pmod 7$.

24.   (C)

The Heaviside method yields the coefficient

$$\frac{s^2 + 1}{s^2 - 2}\bigg|_{s^2 = -3} = \frac{-2}{-5} = \frac{2}{5}.$$

25.   (D)

By substitution $y = a(ay^2 + 2)^2 + 2$. Then $y = 1$ implies $a(a + 2)^2 + 1 = 0$ or $a^3 + 4a^2 + 4a + 1 = 0$ with obvious solution $a = -1$ yielding the factor $a^2 + 3a + 1$ with two real (irrational) roots.

26. (D)

$H \cap K$ is always a subgroup and invariance follows easily. HK is a subgroup since invariance guarantees that $HK = KH$. Finally, HK is invariant since $gHK = HgK = HKg$, for all $g \, \varepsilon \, G$.

27. (E)

Since $x = x^2$ we must have $x + y = (x + y)^2 = x^2 + y^2 + xy + yx = x + y + xy + yx$. So $xy + yx = 0$. When $x = y$ we get $2x^2 = 2x = 0$ so $x = -x$. Combining we find $xy = -yx = yx$ and R is commutative.

28. (B)

For $a = r + s\sqrt{17} \, \varepsilon \, D$ let $\bar{a} = r - s\sqrt{17} \, \varepsilon \, D$. The norm of a is $N(a) = a\bar{a} = r^2 - 17s^2$. It is well known that $N(a)N(b) = N(ab)$ and this implies that whenever $N(a)$ is prime then a is irreducible. The norms of the choices show only one prime, $N(9 - 2\sqrt{17}) = 81 - 68 = 13$.

29. (E)

Direct substitution yields

$$k \, (k - 1) \, x^k - 3kx^k - 4x^k = 0,$$

and since x is not always 0, we can claim that $k^2 - 4k - 4 = 0$ and solve for $k = 2 \pm 2\sqrt{2}$.

30. (C)

Since $(x^2 + 1)^2 = x^4 + 2x^2 + 1$ we can find that

$$x^4 + 1 = (x^2 + 1 + \sqrt{2}\,x)(x^2 + 1 - \sqrt{2}\,x).$$

31. (C)

This slope is the directional derivative of z at $(1, 3)$ in the direction given by $\hat{i} + 3\hat{j} = \overline{v}$ (a vector of slope 3). To compute this, we need the gradient vector $\nabla z = z_x \hat{i} + z_y \hat{j}$ or $2x\hat{i} - 2y\hat{j} = 2\hat{i} - 6\hat{j}$. Then the directional derivative is

$$\nabla z \cdot \frac{\overline{v}}{|\overline{v}|} = \frac{(2 - 18)}{\sqrt{10}} = -8\sqrt{\frac{2}{5}} \,.$$

32. (B)

Since the row sums are all equal to $a + (n - 1)b$ this must be an eigenvalue corresponding to the eigenvector, $\overline{x} = (1, 1, \ldots, 1)$.

33. (E)

The correct relationship is

$$\frac{\text{VOLUME}}{\text{AREA}} = \frac{\dfrac{(4\pi r^3)}{3}}{\pi r^2} = \frac{4}{3} r \,.$$

The formula should be

$$\frac{4}{3} \frac{d}{2} \left(\frac{8}{9} d \right)^2 = \frac{2^7 d^3}{3^5} \,.$$

34. (A)

To have eigenvalue $\lambda = 1$ we must have $|A - I| = 0$.

$$\Rightarrow \begin{vmatrix} k - 1 & 1 & 2 \\ 1 & 1 & k \\ 1 & 2 & 2 \end{vmatrix} = 2k^2 - 5k + 2 = (2k - 1)(k - 2) = 0 \,,$$

so $k = 1/2$ or $k = 2$ will suffice.

35.   (A)

In polar form, $z = e^{i\pi/4}$ and $z^{14} = e^{i\,14\pi/4}$. The periodic quality of e^z means $z^{14} = e^{-i\pi/2} = -i$.

36.   (B)

For a solution of relatively small magnitude, as proposed, we may approximate $e^{-x/100}$ by $e^0 = 1$. Then solving $1 - e^{-x} = e^{-1}$ implies $e^{-x} = 1 - e^{-1}$ or $-x = \ln(1 - e^{-1})$ or

$$x = \ln\left(\frac{e}{(e-1)}\right) = 1 - \ln(e-1) = 1 - \ln(1.718 +).$$

Since $\sqrt{3} = 1.732 +$ the best choice is $1 - \ln\sqrt{3} = 1 - \frac{1}{2}\ln 3$.

37.   (D)

The necessary algebra is

$$\frac{1}{z-4} = \frac{1}{z-1-3} = \frac{\dfrac{1}{(z-1)}}{1-\left[\dfrac{3}{(z-1)}\right]} = \frac{1}{z-1}\sum_{n=0}^{\infty}\left(\frac{3}{z-1}\right)^n,$$

by the formula for the sum of a geometric series. Then the coefficient corresponds to $n = 1$ in the form

$$\sum_{n=0}^{\infty} 3^n (z-1)^{-n-1}.$$

38.   (A)

The Fundamental Theorem of Calculus states that

$$\frac{d}{dx}\left[\int_a^x f(t)\,dt\right] = f(x).$$

Then by the chain rule we must have

$$\frac{d}{dx}\left[\int_a^{x^2} f(t)\, dt\right] = 2x\, f(x^2) = \frac{2x}{(1+x^6)}$$

in this case. Evaluation at $x = 2$ yields $\dfrac{4}{(1+64)} = \dfrac{4}{65}$.

39.   (D)
   By comparison methods the series has partial sums

$$\frac{1}{2\cdot 3^2} + \frac{1}{3\cdot 3^3} + \frac{1}{4\cdot 3^4} + \dots + \frac{1}{n\cdot 3^n} < \frac{1}{2\cdot 3^2} + \frac{1}{2\cdot 3^3}$$

$$+ \frac{1}{2\cdot 3^4} + \dots + \frac{1}{2\cdot 3^n}.$$

The latter sum is geometric and its corresponding series sums to

$$\frac{1}{18}\left(\frac{1}{1-\dfrac{1}{3}}\right) = \frac{1}{12}.$$

40.   (B)
   Since the entries in each row are one unit apart, the given matix is row equivalent to the matrix shown where the rank of 2 is easily visible. Actually $n \geq 2$ could be used without changing the result.

$$\begin{pmatrix} 2 & 3 & 4 & \dots & (n+1) \\ 1 & 1 & 1 & \dots & 1 \\ 0 & 0 & 0 & \dots & 0 \\ \vdots & \vdots & \vdots & \vdots\vdots & \vdots \\ 0 & 0 & 0 & \dots & 0 \end{pmatrix}$$

41.   (B)

The inverse x, must satisfy the equation $10x \equiv 1$ (17) in modular arithmetic or $10x = 17y + 1$. Apparently $17y$ ends in the digit 9, and so $y = 7$ must be the case. Then $10x = 119 + 1$ implies $x = 12$.

42.   (E)

By substitution of $y = x + b$ from the latter equation we get $x^2 - x - b = a$ or $x^2 - x - (a + b) = 0$ in the former. The quadratic formula implies two distinct solutions for x unless $(a + b) = -1/4$, and then $x = 1/2$ follows from $(x - 1/2)^2 = 0$.

43.   (D)

By basic properties, $\log_4 64 = \log_4 4^3 = 3$. Clearly, $\log_7 343 = \log_7 7^3 = 3$. Also a standard identity for change of base is $\log_b x = \dfrac{\log_a x}{\log_a b}$, so (B) is also correct.

44.   (A)

The points on the unit circle corresponding to arcs of integral measurement (whole radians) are dense in the circle. We know that y is a limit point of S if every neighborhood of y contains $x \neq y$ such that $x \varepsilon S$. Since the whole radians are dense in the circle, the values of $\tan k$, $K = 1, 2, 3, \ldots$ are dense in the real numbers. Hence if y is any real number, then any neighborhood of y will also contain a value of $\tan (k)$ $\neq y$, $k = 1, 2, 3, \ldots$, so the limit points of S consist of all the points on the real line. This means that the entire range $(-\infty, \infty)$ of the real function $f(x) = \tan x$ is the set of limit points.

45.   (E)

As in problem 44, the points on the unit circle corresponding to whole radians are dense in the circle. Hence the values of $\sin(n)$, $n = 1, 2, 3, \ldots$ are dense in the range of $\sin n$, namely $[-1, 1]$. Therefore,

$$\lim_{n \to \infty} \inf\{\sin n\} = \inf\{-1, 1\} = -1 \text{ and } \lim_{n \to \infty} \sup \{\sin n\} \sup\{-1, 1\}$$

$= 1$ so the difference is $-1 - 1 = -2$.

46.   (A)

In the diagram, the diagonal is the base of an isosceles triangle with external angle $2\pi/5$. The base angles must be $\pi/5$. Therefore, the base is $2 \cos \pi/5$.

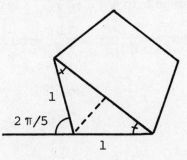

47.   (D)

The characteristic polynomial of the equation is $m^2 - 2m - 8 = (m - 4)(m + 2)$, implying that the general form of all solutions is $y = c_1 e^{4x} + c_2 e^{-2x}$. Only (D) is in this form.

48.   (E)

If $f(x)$ is strictly increasing then $g(x) = -f(x)$ must be strictly decreasing and hence has no maximum since $g(a)$ is undefined.

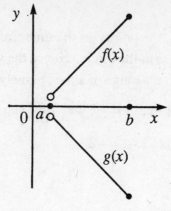

49.　(B)

Permutations of $n = n_1 + n_2 + n_3$ objects, when groups of $n_1, n_2,$ and n_3 are not distinguishable, total $\dfrac{n!}{n_1! n_2! n_3!}$. In this case $n = 6, n_1 = 1,$ $n_2 = 2, n_3 = 3.$ So we get $\dfrac{6!}{1! 2! 3!} = \dfrac{720}{12} = 60.$

50.　(A)

There are two possible structures. In the first, the side of length 5 is the base, and then the median from the opposite vertex is 3 times the inradius in length so the area is $3(3/2)(5/2) = 45/4$. In the second, the side of length 5 is one of two equal sides, and then the base must be $2\sqrt{25 - 9(3/2)^2} = \sqrt{19} < 5$ so the maximum is $45/4$.

51.　(B)

In spherical coordinates, ϕ represents the angle from the positive z-axis to the line generating a cone with z-axis of symmetry and center at the origin. In spherical coordinates $\rho^2 = x^2 + y^2 + z^2 = 4$, so $\rho = 2$.

Also $2\cos\Phi = z = -\sqrt{x^2 + y^2}$

$$= -\sqrt{\rho^2\sin^2\Phi\cos^2\Phi + \rho^2\sin^2\Phi\sin^2\theta}$$

$$\Rightarrow 2\cos\Phi = -\sqrt{\rho^2\sin^2\Phi} = -\rho\,\sin\Phi = -2\sin\theta$$

$$\Rightarrow \frac{\sin\theta}{\cos\theta} = -1$$

$$\Rightarrow \theta = \frac{3\pi}{4}.$$

So in this case, the surfaces, in spherical coordinates, have equations $\rho = 2$, (a sphere) and $\Phi = 3\pi/4$ (a lower half-cone).

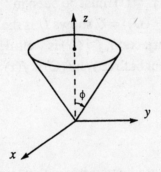

52. (B)

Each subcomponent has reliability $1 - (1-R)^2 = R(2-R)$. Then the series $0 \mid n$ subcomponents must have reliability $R^n(2-R)^n$.

53. (D)

For the given family, $y' = y/x$; thus, the orthogonal family satisfies the differential equation $y' = -x/y$. In separated form, we have $x\,dx + y\,dy = 0$, which can be integrated directly to yield $\frac{x^2}{2} + \frac{y^2}{2} = C$, where C is arbitrary, so $x^2 + y^2 = 2C = r^2$, giving circles centered at $(0, 0)$.

54.   (E)

In standard form the linear difference equation is $x_{n+2} - x_{n+1} - 6x_n = -36n$, which implies characteristic roots 3 and -2 and a particular solution in the form $An + B$. Substitution leads to matching of coefficients via $-6An + A - 6B = -36n$, so $-6A = -36$ and $A = 6$. Then $6 - 6B = 0$ and $B = 1$. All solutions must be in the form $x_n = c_1 3^n + c_2 (-2)^n + 6n + 1$ where c_1, c_2 are arbitrary constants. (E) is in this form with $c_1 = 0$ and $c_2 = 2$.

55.   (A)

Continuity implies $f^{-1}(U)$ must be open in $\overline{X}$ for every open set U in $\overline{X}$. But then $f(f^{-1}(U)) = U$ shows U is the image under f of an open set. Since f is a surjection, $f^{-1}(U)$ is well-defined for every open set. A counterexample for both (B) and (C) is $f(x) = e^x \sin x$ on the reals.

56.   (D)

The negative of the gradient vector always supplies this direction. Here

$$-\nabla z = -\left. y^2 \hat{i} + 2xy\hat{j}\right)\Big|_{(2,-1)}$$
$$= -\hat{i} + 4\hat{j}.$$

57.   (D)

Euler's formula states that $V - E + F = 2$. Here $V = 27$ and $E = 40$ so $F = 15$.

58. (C)

The term in the expansion is given combinatorially by

$$\binom{5}{3} x^2(-2y)^3 = -80 \, x^2 y^3 \, .$$

59. (B)

The partial fractions expansion multiplied by x gives

$$x\left[\frac{A}{x} + \frac{B}{2+3x} + \frac{C}{(2+3x)^2}\right] = \frac{x}{x(2+3x)^2}$$

Taking limits as $x \to +\infty$ yields $A + B/3 = 0$. $A = 1/4$ by the following calculations:

$$\frac{A}{x} + \frac{B}{2+3x} + \frac{Cx+D}{(2+3x)^2} = \frac{1}{x(2+3x)^2}$$

$$\Rightarrow A(2+3x)^2 + Bx(2+3x) + (Cx+D)x = 1$$

$$\Rightarrow 4A = 1 \, , \text{ since all other terms will contain a factor of } x \, ,$$

$$\Rightarrow A = \frac{1}{4} \, .$$

So $B = -3/4$ and the integral of this term is $\left(-\frac{3}{4}\right)\left(\frac{1}{3}\right) \ln |2 + 3x|.$

60. (D)

It is well known that in the waiting time model the probability of a tail will be $1/T$. Then the probability of at least two tails is the complement of zero or one tail. As usual, this is

$$1 - \left(1 - \frac{1}{T}\right)^{3T} - 3T\left(1 - \frac{1}{T}\right)^{3T-1}\left(\frac{1}{T}\right).$$

Using T^{3T} as a common denominator yields the numerator

$$T^{3T} - (T-1)^{3T} - 3T(T-1)^{3T-1}$$

$$= T^{3T} - (T-1)^{3T-1}(T-1+3T).$$

61. (B)

The quadrilateral can be split into two triangles by the diagonal joining $(1,4)$ and $(3,2)$ as shown. The triangles have simple centroidal first coordinates 4/3 and 9/3 as the average of those for their vertices. The sides of the triangles are identical, so the average of these is the centroid coordinate $4/6 + 9/6 = 13/6$.

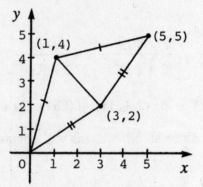

62. (A)

All that is needed is to show closure under the operations. For (A), if $xr = 0$ and $xs = 0$ then $xr + xs = 0 + 0 = 0$ and $(xr)(xs) = 0 \cdot 0 = 0$.

(B) will not contain 0 and this is a must for a subring.

(C) may not contain 0 if x is not nilpotent.

(D) fails to guarantee that $(mx)(nx) = mnx^2$ is a multiple of x. For example, let R be the ring of 2×2 matrices.

63. (E)

The limit can be simplified as

$$\lim_{m \to 0} \frac{1}{m} \left[\lim_{n \to 0} \frac{f(2+m+n)-f(2+m)}{n} - \lim_{n \to 0} \frac{f(2+n)-f(2)}{n} \right]$$

$$= \lim_{m \to 0} \left[\frac{f'(2+m)-f'(2)}{m} \right] = f''(2) = \frac{-1}{2^2} = -\frac{1}{4}$$

by the definition of derivative since f is twice differentiable at $x = 2$.

64. (A)

Every open set containing a cluster point of E must contain some other point in E. Since $\{x_1\}$ is open, x_1 can never be a cluster point. Likewise $\{x_1, x_2\}$ is open and contains only x_2 in E so x_2 is not a cluster point. For $x_n, n \geq 3$, every open set containing x_n also contains x_2 in E, so these are all cluster points.

65. (C)

The weights can be thought to act as their centers. Further, the proportion of the weight supported at the left is the ratio of the distance to the right support and the total distance between supports. In this case, we get $100 (16/20) + 200(3/20) = 80 + 30 = 110$.

66. (A)

The series may diverge if a_n is not a series of terms all of the same sign. For example, let $a_n = \frac{(-1)^n}{\sqrt{n}}$. Then $\sum_{n=1}^{\infty} a_n$ converges by the alternating series test. However, $\sum_{n=1}^{\infty} a_n^2$ is the well-known divergent harmonic series.

GRE

MATH TEST

TEST III

THE GRADUATE RECORD EXAMINATION

MATH TEST

ANSWER SHEET

1. Ⓐ Ⓑ Ⓒ Ⓓ Ⓔ
2. Ⓐ Ⓑ Ⓒ Ⓓ Ⓔ
3. Ⓐ Ⓑ Ⓒ Ⓓ Ⓔ
4. Ⓐ Ⓑ Ⓒ Ⓓ Ⓔ
5. Ⓐ Ⓑ Ⓒ Ⓓ Ⓔ
6. Ⓐ Ⓑ Ⓒ Ⓓ Ⓔ
7. Ⓐ Ⓑ Ⓒ Ⓓ Ⓔ
8. Ⓐ Ⓑ Ⓒ Ⓓ Ⓔ
9. Ⓐ Ⓑ Ⓒ Ⓓ Ⓔ
10. Ⓐ Ⓑ Ⓒ Ⓓ Ⓔ
11. Ⓐ Ⓑ Ⓒ Ⓓ Ⓔ
12. Ⓐ Ⓑ Ⓒ Ⓓ Ⓔ
13. Ⓐ Ⓑ Ⓒ Ⓓ Ⓔ
14. Ⓐ Ⓑ Ⓒ Ⓓ Ⓔ
15. Ⓐ Ⓑ Ⓒ Ⓓ Ⓔ
16. Ⓐ Ⓑ Ⓒ Ⓓ Ⓔ
17. Ⓐ Ⓑ Ⓒ Ⓓ Ⓔ
18. Ⓐ Ⓑ Ⓒ Ⓓ Ⓔ
19. Ⓐ Ⓑ Ⓒ Ⓓ Ⓔ
20. Ⓐ Ⓑ Ⓒ Ⓓ Ⓔ
21. Ⓐ Ⓑ Ⓒ Ⓓ Ⓔ
22. Ⓐ Ⓑ Ⓒ Ⓓ Ⓔ

23. Ⓐ Ⓑ Ⓒ Ⓓ Ⓔ
24. Ⓐ Ⓑ Ⓒ Ⓓ Ⓔ
25. Ⓐ Ⓑ Ⓒ Ⓓ Ⓔ
26. Ⓐ Ⓑ Ⓒ Ⓓ Ⓔ
27. Ⓐ Ⓑ Ⓒ Ⓓ Ⓔ
28. Ⓐ Ⓑ Ⓒ Ⓓ Ⓔ
29. Ⓐ Ⓑ Ⓒ Ⓓ Ⓔ
30. Ⓐ Ⓑ Ⓒ Ⓓ Ⓔ
31. Ⓐ Ⓑ Ⓒ Ⓓ Ⓔ
32. Ⓐ Ⓑ Ⓒ Ⓓ Ⓔ
33. Ⓐ Ⓑ Ⓒ Ⓓ Ⓔ
34. Ⓐ Ⓑ Ⓒ Ⓓ Ⓔ
35. Ⓐ Ⓑ Ⓒ Ⓓ Ⓔ
36. Ⓐ Ⓑ Ⓒ Ⓓ Ⓔ
37. Ⓐ Ⓑ Ⓒ Ⓓ Ⓔ
38. Ⓐ Ⓑ Ⓒ Ⓓ Ⓔ
39. Ⓐ Ⓑ Ⓒ Ⓓ Ⓔ
40. Ⓐ Ⓑ Ⓒ Ⓓ Ⓔ
41. Ⓐ Ⓑ Ⓒ Ⓓ Ⓔ
42. Ⓐ Ⓑ Ⓒ Ⓓ Ⓔ
43. Ⓐ Ⓑ Ⓒ Ⓓ Ⓔ
44. Ⓐ Ⓑ Ⓒ Ⓓ Ⓔ

45. Ⓐ Ⓑ Ⓒ Ⓓ Ⓔ
46. Ⓐ Ⓑ Ⓒ Ⓓ Ⓔ
47. Ⓐ Ⓑ Ⓒ Ⓓ Ⓔ
48. Ⓐ Ⓑ Ⓒ Ⓓ Ⓔ
49. Ⓐ Ⓑ Ⓒ Ⓓ Ⓔ
50. Ⓐ Ⓑ Ⓒ Ⓓ Ⓔ
51. Ⓐ Ⓑ Ⓒ Ⓓ Ⓔ
52. Ⓐ Ⓑ Ⓒ Ⓓ Ⓔ
53. Ⓐ Ⓑ Ⓒ Ⓓ Ⓔ
54. Ⓐ Ⓑ Ⓒ Ⓓ Ⓔ
55. Ⓐ Ⓑ Ⓒ Ⓓ Ⓔ
56. Ⓐ Ⓑ Ⓒ Ⓓ Ⓔ
57. Ⓐ Ⓑ Ⓒ Ⓓ Ⓔ
58. Ⓐ Ⓑ Ⓒ Ⓓ Ⓔ
59. Ⓐ Ⓑ Ⓒ Ⓓ Ⓔ
60. Ⓐ Ⓑ Ⓒ Ⓓ Ⓔ
61. Ⓐ Ⓑ Ⓒ Ⓓ Ⓔ
62. Ⓐ Ⓑ Ⓒ Ⓓ Ⓔ
63. Ⓐ Ⓑ Ⓒ Ⓓ Ⓔ
64. Ⓐ Ⓑ Ⓒ Ⓓ Ⓔ
65. Ⓐ Ⓑ Ⓒ Ⓓ Ⓔ
66. Ⓐ Ⓑ Ⓒ Ⓓ Ⓔ

GRE MATHEMATICS
TEST III

TIME: 2 hours and 50 minutes
66 Questions

DIRECTIONS: Choose the best answer for each question and mark the letter of your selection on the corresponding answer sheet.

1. The generating function $f(x)$ for the Fibonacci numbers $1, 1, 2, 3, 5, 8, 13, 21, \ldots$ is given by

    (A) $(1 - x + x^2 - x^3)^{1/2}$

    (B) $(1 - x - x^2)^{-1}$

    (C) $(1 - x - x^2 - x^3)^{-1}$

    (D) $(1 + x + x^2)^{-1/2}$

    (E) $(1 - x^2 + x^3)^{-1}$

2. The number of solutions of $p(x) = x^2 + 3x + 2$ in Z_6 is

    (A) 0

    (B) 1

    (C) 2

    (D) 3

    (E) 4

3. Which of the following matrices is normal? $(i = \sqrt{-1})$

(A) $\begin{bmatrix} 1 & -1 \\ 0 & 1 \end{bmatrix}$ (D) $\begin{bmatrix} i & 1 \\ -1 & 0 \end{bmatrix}$

(B) $\begin{bmatrix} 0 & i \\ -1 & 1 \end{bmatrix}$ (E) $\begin{bmatrix} -1 & 1 \\ 0 & 1 \end{bmatrix}$

(C) $\begin{bmatrix} 1 & -1 \\ 0 & -1 \end{bmatrix}$

4. Find the locus of all points (x, y), such that the sum of those distances from $(0, 1)$ and $(1, 0)$ is 2.

(A) $x^2 + xy + y^2 - 2x - 2y + 2 = 0$

(B) $3x^2 - 2xy + 3y^2 - 4x + 4y - 2 = 0$

(C) $4x^2 - 2xy + 4y^2 - 2x - 2y = 0$

(D) $3x^2 + 2xy + 3y^2 - 4x - 4y = 0$

(E) $x^2 - 2xy + y^2 + 2x - 2y + 4 = 0$

5. Find $\prod\limits_{k=2}^{+\infty} \left(1 - \dfrac{1}{k^2}\right)$

(A) $\dfrac{1}{2}$ (D) $\dfrac{3}{4}$

(B) $\dfrac{1}{4}$ (E) $\dfrac{1}{8}$

(C) 0

6.   The cross ratio of the following set of lines is

(A) $\dfrac{4}{3}$ (D) $-\dfrac{5}{6}$

(B) $\dfrac{3}{2}$ (E) 1

(C) $\dfrac{1}{5}$

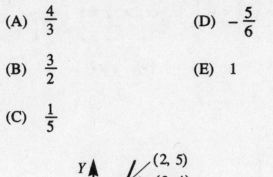

7.   Find the characteristic of the ring $Z_2 + Z_3$.

(A) 0   (D) 4

(B) 6   (E) 2

(C) 3

8.   Find $\lim\limits_{n \to +\infty} \left(\sqrt{n^4 + i\, n^2} - n^2 \right)$

(A) $\dfrac{i}{2}$ (D) $-\dfrac{1}{2}$

(B) 0   (E) $\sqrt{i}$

(C) $+\infty$

9. Which of the following is a solution of

$$u(x) = x + \int_0^x (t - x)\, u(t)\, dt \,?$$

(A) $\sin x$

(D) $x\, e^{-x}$

(B) $x \cos x$

(E) $x\, e^x$

(C) $\ln (x + 1)$

10. Find $\displaystyle \int_0^1 \left(\ln \frac{1}{x} \right)^5 dx$

(A) 120

(D) 720

(B) $+ \infty$

(E) 24

(C) 1

11. Find the Laplace transform of

$$f(x) = \begin{cases} 0 & \text{if } x \in (-\infty, 1) \\ 1 & \text{if } x \in (1, +\infty) \end{cases}$$

(A) e^{-p}

(D) $p\, e^p$

(B) $\dfrac{1}{p}$

(E) $\dfrac{1}{p\, e^p}$

(C) $\dfrac{1}{e^{p-1}}$

12. Let $T: R^2 \to R^2$ be defined by

$$T(x,y) = \begin{bmatrix} 2x - y \\ x + 3y \end{bmatrix}.$$

Find the adjoint T^* of T.

(A) $\begin{bmatrix} 2x + y \\ -x + 3y \end{bmatrix}$

(D) $\begin{bmatrix} \frac{x}{2} - y \\ -x + \frac{y}{3} \end{bmatrix}$

(B) $\begin{bmatrix} x + 2y \\ x - 3y \end{bmatrix}$

(C) $\begin{bmatrix} 2x + y \\ x - 3y \end{bmatrix}$

(E) $\begin{bmatrix} 3x - y \\ x + 2y \end{bmatrix}$

13. The value of $I = \int_0^{\frac{\pi}{2}} \frac{\cos x}{\cos x + \sin x}\, dx$ is

(A) 1

(D) $\frac{\pi}{4}$

(B) $\frac{\pi}{2}$

(E) π

(C) 0

14. Find the discriminant of the ternary quadratic form $x^2 - y^2 + z^2 - 2xy + 4yz - 6xz$

(A) 25

(D) 15

(B) 13

(E) 19

(C) 0

112

15. The radius of curvature of $f(x) = x + \frac{1}{x}$ at $P(1,2)$ is

(A) 1

(D) 2

(B) $\sqrt{2}$

(E) $\frac{1}{2}$

(C) 4

16. If $\Gamma(p)$ represents the gamma function, then $\int_0^{+\infty} e^{-x^2} \, dx$ is equal to $\frac{1}{2} \Gamma(p)$ when p is equal to

(A) -1

(D) $\frac{1}{4}$

(B) $\frac{1}{2}$

(E) 2

(C) 1

17. The factor group $\dfrac{(Z_2 \times Z_3)}{<(1,0)>}$ has order

(A) 2

(D) 1

(B) 3

(E) 6

(C) 4

18. Let R [0, 1] denote the set of Riemann integrable functions defined on [0, 1]. Which of the following is <u>not</u> satisfied by the function d defined on R [0, 1] by

$$d(f,g) = \int_0^1 |f(x) - g(x)|\, dx\ ?$$

(A) $d(f, f) = 0$

(B) $d(f, g) \geq 0$

(C) $d(f, g) > 0$ if $f \neq g$

(D) $d(f, g) = d(g, f)$

(E) $d(f, g) \leq d(f, h) + d(h, g)$

19. Find the simple continued fraction for $\dfrac{13}{42}$.

(A) $\cfrac{1}{2 + \cfrac{1}{3 + \cfrac{1}{3}}}$

(D) $\cfrac{1}{4 + \cfrac{1}{4 + \cfrac{1}{3}}}$

(B) $\cfrac{1}{3 + \cfrac{1}{3 + \cfrac{1}{4}}}$

(E) $\cfrac{1}{3 + \cfrac{1}{4 + \cfrac{1}{3}}}$

(C) $\cfrac{1}{3 + \cfrac{1}{2 + \cfrac{1}{4}}}$

20. Which of the following polynomials satisfies an Eisenstein criterion for irreducibility over the rationals?

(A) $x^5 + 3x^4 + 18x^2 + 15x + 9$

(B) $2x^5 + 9x^4 + 15x^2 + 3x + 18$

(C) $3x^5 + 18x^4 + 15x^2 + 9x + 3$

(D) $4x^5 + 15x^4 + 9x^2 + 3x + 18$

(E) $5x^5 + 9x^4 + 18x^2 + 3x + 15$

21. The number of degrees that the conic, defined by
$$x^2 - y^2 + 2\sqrt{3}\ xy = 2$$
must be rotated in order to eliminate the xy term is

(A) 15   (D) 60

(B) 30   (E) 75

(C) 45

22. For the initial value problem $y'' + 6y' + 9y = 0$; $y(0) = 3$; $y'(0) = -11$ find $\pounds(y)$, the Laplace transform of y.

(A) $\dfrac{1}{p + 3} + \dfrac{2}{(p + 3)^2}$

(B) $\dfrac{-2}{p + 3} - \dfrac{3}{(p + 3)^2}$

115

(C) $\dfrac{3}{(p+3)^2}$

(D) $\dfrac{3}{p+3} - \dfrac{2}{(p+3)^2}$

(E) $\dfrac{1}{p+3} - \dfrac{2}{(p+3)^2}$

23.   Find the join of the subgroups <4> and <6> of Z_{12}.

(A) <0>   (D) <4>

(B) <2>   (E) <5>

(C) <3>

24.   For which n is the regular n-gon <u>not</u> constructible with a straightedge and compass?

(A) 6   (D) 17

(B) 9   (E) 20

(C) 15

25.   Given $T = \begin{bmatrix} 1 & 0 \\ 1 & 1 \end{bmatrix}$, the sum of the elements in T^n is

(A) $3n$ (B) $n+3$

(C) n

(D) $2n$

(E) $n + 2$

26. Let $b: R \times R \to$ be the bilinear form defined by

$$b(X;Y) = x_1 y_1 - 2x_1 y_2 + x_2 y_1 + 3x_2 y_2$$

where $X = (x_1, x_2)$ and $Y = (y_1, y_2)$. Find the 2×2 matrix B of b relative to the basis $U = \{u_1, u_2\}$ where $u_1 = (0, 1)$ and $u_2 = (1,1)$.

(A) $\begin{bmatrix} 5 & -3 \\ 0 & 2 \end{bmatrix}$

(D) $\begin{bmatrix} 0 & 4 \\ -1 & 3 \end{bmatrix}$

(B) $\begin{bmatrix} 2 & 2 \\ -1 & 1 \end{bmatrix}$

(E) $\begin{bmatrix} 3 & -1 \\ 1 & 2 \end{bmatrix}$

(C) $\begin{bmatrix} -1 & 4 \\ 2 & 3 \end{bmatrix}$

27. Let $X = \{a, b, c\}$. Which of the following classes of subsets of X does <u>not</u> form a topology on X ?

(A) $\{X, \emptyset\}$

(B) $\{X, \emptyset, \{a\}\}$

(C) $\{X, \emptyset, \{a\}, \{b\}, \{a, b\}\}$

(D) $\{X, \emptyset, \{a, b\}, \{a, c\}, \{b, c\}, \{a, b, c\}\}$

(E) $P(X)$, the power set of X

117

28. The eigenvalues for the initial value–eigenvalue problem

$$y'' + \lambda y = 0$$

$$y(0) = 0; \quad y(\pi) = 0$$

are given by

(A) $1, 2, 3, 4, \ldots$ (D) $0, \pm 1, \pm 4, \pm 9, \pm 16, \ldots$

(B) $1, 4, 9, 16, \ldots$ (E) $\ldots, -3, -2, -1$

(C) $0, \pm 1, \pm 2, \pm 3, \pm 4, \ldots$

29. For switching functions f, g, and h, the expression $(f \vee g)$ $(\bar{f} \vee h)$ is equivalent to

(A) $g\bar{f} \wedge gh$ (D) $g\bar{f} \vee fh \vee gh$

(B) $g \vee h$ (E) $g\bar{f} \wedge fh \vee gh$

(C) $g \wedge f h$

30. For the inner product $<A, B> = \text{trace}(B'A)$ defined on the vector space of 2 by 2 matrices on R, find the square of the norm of

$$T = \begin{bmatrix} 1 & 3 \\ 2 & -1 \end{bmatrix}.$$

(A) 5   (B) 10

(C) 15　　　　　　　　　　　　(D) 20

(E) 25

31.　Find the limit of the series

$$x^4 + \frac{x^4}{1 + x^2} + \frac{x^4}{(1 + x^2)^2} + \frac{x^4}{(1 + x^2)^3} + \dots$$

(A) $x^6 + x^4$　　　　　　　　(D) $x^4 + \dfrac{x^6}{1 + x^2}$

(B) $\dfrac{x^6}{1 + x^2}$　　　　　　　(E) $x^4 + x^2$

(C) x^6

32.　The domain of $f(x) = \displaystyle\int (x + 2x^2 + 3x^3 + \dots) \, dx$ is

(A) $(-1, 1)$　　　　　　　　(D) $\left[\dfrac{1}{2}, \dfrac{1}{2}\right)$

(B) $[-1, 1)$　　　　　　　　(E) $(-1, 1]$

(C) $\left[-\dfrac{1}{2}, \dfrac{1}{2}\right]$

33.　Determine the number of homomorphisms from the group Z_8 onto the group Z_4.

(A) 0　　　　　　　　　　　　(B) 1

(C) 2 (D) 3

(E) 4

34. The solution of $x^2 y'' + 6xy' + 6y = 0$, for $x > 0$, is given by

(A) $c_1 x^3 - c_2 x^2$ (D) $c_1 e^{-2x} + c_2 e^{-3x}$

(B) $c_1 x + c_2 \ln x$ (E) $c_1 x \ln x + c_2 \ln x$

(C) $\dfrac{c_1}{x^3} + \dfrac{c_2}{x^2}$

35. The remainder of 5^{34} when divided by 17 is

(A) 0 (D) 6

(B) 2 (E) 8

(C) 4

36. Find the curl of $\vec{u} = xyz\,\vec{i} + xy^2\vec{j} + yz\,\vec{k}$

(A) $xz\,\vec{i} + (x - yz)\,\vec{j} + 2y\,\vec{k}$

(B) $(x - z)\,\vec{i} - yz\,\vec{j} + xyz\,\vec{k}$

(C) $z\,\vec{i} + xy\,\vec{j} + (y^2 - xz)\,\vec{k}$

(D) $xy \vec{i} - (z - y) \vec{j} + (xy - yz) \vec{k}$

(E) $(xy - yz) \vec{i} - yz \vec{j} + x \vec{k}$

37.   The inverse of the function $f(x) = \dfrac{x}{x - 1}$ is

(A) $\dfrac{x}{x + 1}$

(D) $1 - \dfrac{1}{x}$

(B) $\dfrac{x}{x - 1}$

(E) $\dfrac{x - 1}{x + 1}$

(C) $1 + \dfrac{1}{x}$

38.   Find the slope of the tangent line to the ellipse

$$2x^2 + y^2 + 30 = 8y - 12x$$

at (x_0, y_0), where $x_0 = -2$ and $y_0 > 4$.

(A) $\dfrac{1}{\sqrt{2}}$

(D) $\dfrac{1}{2}$

(B) $-\sqrt{2}$

(E) -2

(C) 2

39.   For matrices

$$A = \begin{bmatrix} 1 & 1 \\ 0 & -1 \end{bmatrix}, \ B = \begin{bmatrix} 0 & 1 \\ 1 & 1 \end{bmatrix}, \ C = \begin{bmatrix} -1 & 0 \\ 1 & 1 \end{bmatrix},$$

$$\text{and} \quad D = \begin{bmatrix} 3 & 3 \\ 0 & -2 \end{bmatrix},$$

the matrix D is a linear combination $(aA + bB + cC)$ of A,B,C for a,b,c, given by

(A) $1, 1, -1$ (D) $1, -2, 1$

(B) $2, 1, -1$ (E) $-1, 1, -2$

(C) $2, 2, -2$

40. Given $p(x) = \sum_{k=1}^{+\infty} \dfrac{(x-2)^k}{k^2}$, find the interval in which $p'(x)$ converges.

(A) $\{2\}$ (D) $(1, 3]$

(B) $[1, 3)$ (E) $R \to R$

(C) $[1, 3]$

41. Find the Laplace transform of $\displaystyle\int_0^x \sin 2t \, dt$.

(A) $\dfrac{1}{p^2 + 4}$ (D) $\dfrac{4}{p^4 + 16}$

(B) $\dfrac{2p}{p^2 + 4}$ (E) $\dfrac{1}{p^2 + 2p}$

(C) $\dfrac{2}{p^3 + 4p}$

42. If $f'(x_0) = \sqrt{3}$, then the tangent line to the graph of f at x_0 makes an angle of β degrees with the positive x-axis. Find β .

(A) 0

(D) 60

(B) 30

(E) 90

(C) 45

43. Let $T : R^3 \rightarrow R^3$ be defined by $T(x, y, z) = (x + y, x - y + z, y + 2z)$. Find the trace of T.

(A) 5

(D) 7

(B) -1

(E) 2

(C) 0

44. Find the sum of $\dfrac{1}{2!} + \dfrac{2}{3!} + \dfrac{3}{4!} + \cdots$.

(A) $\dfrac{3}{4}$

(D) $\dfrac{3}{2}$

(B) 1

(E) $\dfrac{7}{4}$

(C) $\dfrac{5}{4}$

45. Which of the following is <u>not</u> a proper ideal of the ring Z_{12} ?

(A) $<5>$ (D) $<3>$

(B) $<8>$ (E) $<4>$

(C) $<2>$

46. Assuming that a person selects an answer to each of the first ten questions on this examination at random and that the selections are independent, what is the probability that he/she will guess exactly five answers correct?

(A) $\dfrac{(63)\,4^6}{5^{10}}$ (D) $\dfrac{(61)\,4^6}{5^{10}}$

(B) $\dfrac{(65)\,4^6}{5^{10}}$ (E) $\dfrac{(67)\,4^6}{5^{10}}$

(C) $\dfrac{4^9}{5^{10}}$

47. Find the Jacobian of the transformation from the xy-plane to the uv-plane defined by
$$u = f(x,y) = xe^{xy}$$
$$v = g(x,y) = ye^{xy}$$

(A) $2xye^{xy}$ (D) $(2xy + 1)\,e^{2xy}$

(B) $(1 - x^2y^2)\,e^{2xy}$ (E) 0

(C) $2e^{2xy}$

48. On average, a baseball player gets a hit in one out of three attempts. Assuming that the attempts are independent, what is the probability that he gets exactly three hits in six attempts?

(A) $\dfrac{50}{3^5}$

(D) $\dfrac{80}{3^6}$

(B) $\dfrac{160}{3^5}$

(E) $\dfrac{40}{3^6}$

(C) $\dfrac{1}{2}$

49. Find the number of units in the ring Z_5 .

(A) 0

(D) 3

(B) 1

(E) 4

(C) 2

50. Define $f(x) = x$ for $x \varepsilon (0, 1)$. Find the coefficient of the third term in the half range Fourier sine series.

(A) $\dfrac{2}{3\pi}$

(D) $\dfrac{1}{3\pi}$

(B) $\dfrac{4}{9\pi^2}$

(E) $\dfrac{1}{9\pi^2}$

(C) $\dfrac{2}{9\pi^2}$

51. Let V be the vector space of functions $f: R \rightarrow R$. Let S be the subspace generated by $\{e^x, e^{2x}, e^{-2x}\}$. Define D_x to be the derivative operator on S. Find the determinant of D_x.

(A) 2   (D) 1

(B) 0   (E) -1

(C) -4

52. Find Green's function for $y'' + 5y' + 6y = \sin x$

(A) $2e^{2(t-x)} + 3e^{3(t-x)}$ (D) $2e^{(t-x)} - 3e^{(t-x)}$

(B) $e^{2(t-x)} - e^{3(t-x)}$ (E) $e^{3(x-t)} - e^{2(x-t)}$

(C) $e^{(t+x)} - e^{(t-x)}$

53. The Maclaurin series for xe^{-x^2} is given by

(A) $x - x^3 + \dfrac{x^5}{2!} - \dfrac{x^7}{3!} + \ldots$

(B) $x^3 - \dfrac{x^5}{2!} + \dfrac{x^7}{3!} - \dfrac{x^9}{4!}$

(C) $x - \dfrac{x^3}{2!} + \dfrac{x^5}{3!} - \dfrac{x^7}{5!} + \ldots$

(D) $x + x^3 + \dfrac{x^5}{2!} + \dfrac{x^7}{3!} + \ldots$

(E) $x + x^3 - \dfrac{x^5}{2!} + \dfrac{x^7}{3!} - \ldots$

54. The symmetric difference of the sets $S = \{1, 2, 3, 4, 5\}$ and $T = \{4, 5, 6, 7, 8\}$ is

(A) $\{4, 5\}$

(D) $\{3, 4, 5, 6\}$

(B) $\varnothing$

(E) $\{1, 2, 3, 6, 7, 8\}$

(C) $\{1, 2, 3, 4, 5, 6, 7, 8\}$

55. Given
$$x_{n+2} + 6x_{n+1} + 9x_n = 0 \quad (n = 0, 1, 2, \ldots)$$
$$x_0 = 1; \quad x_1 = 0,$$
then $x_5 =$

(A) 576

(D) -972

(B) -834

(E) 774

(C) 1068

56. Let V be the vector space of real polynomials with inner product
$$(f, g) = \int_0^1 f(x)\, g(x)\, dx$$
where $f, g \in V$. Find the cosine of the angle between $f(x) = 2$ and $g(x) = x$.

(A) $\dfrac{1}{2}$

(B) $\dfrac{\sqrt{3}}{2}$

(C) 0   (D) 1

(E) $\dfrac{\sqrt{2}}{2}$

57. The integral $\displaystyle\int_{-24}^{4} \dfrac{dx}{\sqrt[3]{(x-3)^2}}$

(A) converges to 6   (D) converges to 12

(B) diverges to $+\infty$ (E) diverges to $-\infty$

(C) converges to 9

58. Let n be a positive integer greater than 3. Then $n^3 + (n+1)^3 + (n+2)^3$ is divisible by

(A) 9   (D) 6

(B) 4   (E) 15

(C) 12

59. If F is a finite field, then which of the following numbers can be the cardinality of F ?

(A) 21   (B) 45

(C) 27   (D) 14

(E) 33

60.   Consider the set $S = \{2, 3, 4, 6, 8, 9\}$ ordered by "s is a multiple
      of t". How many minimal elements does S have?

(A) 0   (D) 3

(B) 1   (E) 4

(C) 2

61.   Which of the following is a neighborhood of 0 relative to the
      usual topology τ for the real numbers?

(A) $(0, 1)$ (D) $[0, 1]$

(B) $[-1, 1]$ (E) $(-1, 0)$

(C) $[-1, 0]$

62.   Find the Cauchy number for the permutation

$$\sigma = \begin{bmatrix} 1 & 2 & 3 & 4 & 5 & 6 & 7 \\ 3 & 6 & 5 & 1 & 4 & 7 & 2 \end{bmatrix} \varepsilon\, S_7.$$

(A) 1   (B) 2

(C) 3   (D) 4

(E) 5

63.   Which of the following ordinary differential equations is
      exact?

      (A) $(x + e^y)\, dx + (xe^y - 2xye^y - x^2y)\, dy = 0$

      (B) $(ye^{xy} + \cos x)\, dx + (xe^{xy} + 1)\, dy = 0$

      (C) $(\sin x \sin y + y^2)\, dx + (\cos x \cos y - 2xy)\, dy = 0$

      (D) $(x^2y - y^2)\, dx + (2 - xy)\, dy = 0$

      (E) $(2x + 3y - 4)\, dx + (6x + 9y + 2)\, dy = 0$

64.   Let G be a graph with vertices x_1, x_2, x_3, x_4, x_5. If $\mathrm{val}(x_1) = 2$,
      $\mathrm{val}(x_2) = 2$, $\mathrm{val}(x_3) = 3$, $\mathrm{val}(x_4) = 3$ and $\mathrm{val}(x_5) = 4$, where the
      valence of vertex x is denoted $\mathrm{val}(x)$, how many edges does G
      have?

      (A) 4   (D) 8

      (B) 9   (E) 5

      (C) 7

65. If τ is the discrete topology on the real numbers R, find the closure of (a, b).

(A) (a, b) (D) $[a, b]$

(B) $(a, b]$ (E) R

(C) $[a, b)$

66. Define $f: \mathbb{C}^3 \to \mathbb{C}$ by $f(c) = x - iy + (2 + i) z$ where $c = (x, y, z)$. Find a $\hat{c} \in \mathbb{C}^3$ such that $f(c) = (c, \hat{c})$ for every $\hat{c} \in \mathbb{C}^3$ where $(c, \hat{c})$ is the usual inner product on c^3.

(A) $(1, i, 2 - i)$ (D) $(-1, i, -2 - i)$

(B) $(-1, -i, 2 - i)$ (E) $(-1, i, -2 - i)$

(C) $(1, -i, 2 + i)$

GRE MATHEMATICS
TEST III

ANSWER KEY

1.	B	23.	B	45.	A
2.	E	24.	B	46.	A
3.	D	25.	E	47.	D
4.	D	26.	D	48.	A
5.	A	27.	D	49.	E
6.	A	28.	B	50.	A
7.	B	29.	D	51.	C
8.	A	30.	C	52.	B
9	A	31.	E	53.	A
10.	A	32.	A	54.	E
11.	E	33.	C	55.	D
12.	A	34.	C	56.	B
13.	D	35.	E	57.	D
14.	D	36.	C	58.	A
15.	E	37.	B	59.	C
16.	B	38.	B	60.	D
17.	B	39.	B	61.	B
18.	C	40.	B	62.	E
19.	E	41.	C	63.	B
20.	E	42.	D	64.	C
21.	B	43.	E	65.	D
22.	D	44.	B	66.	A

GRE MATHEMATICS
TEST III

DETAILED EXPLANATIONS
OF ANSWERS

1.   (B)

Let $a_0, a_1, a_2, \ldots, a_n, \ldots$ be a sequence. The generating function for this sequence is given by

$$f(x) = a_0 + a_1 x + a_2 x^2 + a_3 x^3 + \ldots + a_n x^n + \ldots.$$

Since the Fibonacci sequence satisfies $a_n = a_{n-1} + a_{n-2}$ for $n = 2, 3, 4,$ $\ldots$, we have

$$f(x) = a_0 + a_1 x + (a_0 + a_1)x^2 + (a_1 + a_2)x^3 + \ldots$$

$$+ (a_{n-1} + a_{n-2})x^n + \ldots$$

$$= a_0 + x(a_1 + a_1 x + a_2 x^2 + \ldots) + x^2(a_0 + a_1 x + \ldots)$$

$$= 1 + x f(x) + x^2 f(x)$$

where use was made of the fact that $a_0 = a_1 = 1$. Hence

$$(1 - x - x^2) f(x) = 1$$

so that

$$f(x) = (1 - x - x^2)^{-1}$$

2.   (E)

We have

$$p(0) = 0 + 0 + 2 = 2 \equiv 2 \pmod 6$$
$$p(1) = 1 + 3 + 2 = 6 \equiv 0 \pmod 6$$
$$p(2) = 4 + 6 + 2 = 12 \equiv 0 \pmod 6$$
$$p(3) = 9 + 9 + 2 = 20 \equiv 2 \pmod 6$$
$$p(4) = 16 + 12 + 2 = 30 \equiv 0 \pmod 6$$
$$p(5) = 25 + 15 + 2 = 42 \equiv 0 \pmod 6$$

so that there are four elements of Z_6 satisfying $p(x) = 0$.

3.   (D)

A complex matrix M is said to be normal if $M M^* = M^* M$, where M^* is the conjugate transpose of M. If M is real then $M^* = M^T$, where M^T is the transpose of M. We have for

$$M = \begin{bmatrix} i & 1 \\ -1 & 0 \end{bmatrix}, \quad M^* = \begin{bmatrix} -i & -1 \\ 1 & 0 \end{bmatrix}$$

so that

$$M M^* = \begin{bmatrix} i & 1 \\ -1 & 0 \end{bmatrix} \begin{bmatrix} -i & -1 \\ 1 & 0 \end{bmatrix} = \begin{bmatrix} 2 & -i \\ i & 1 \end{bmatrix}$$

and

$$M^* M = \begin{bmatrix} -i & -1 \\ 1 & 0 \end{bmatrix} \begin{bmatrix} i & 1 \\ -1 & 0 \end{bmatrix} = \begin{bmatrix} 2 & -i \\ i & 1 \end{bmatrix},$$

so M is normal.

4.   (D)

We have

$$\sqrt{x^2 + (y-1)^2} + \sqrt{(x-1)^2 + y^2} = 2$$

$$\sqrt{x^2 + (y-1)^2} = 2 - \sqrt{(x-1)^2 + y^2}$$

$$4\sqrt{(x-1)^2 + y^2} = 4 - 2x + 2y$$

$$3x^2 + 2xy + 3y^2 - 4x - 4y = 0$$

5. (A)

Let $\{u_k\}_k^{+\infty} = 1$ be a sequence of non-zero numbers and form the sequence $\{p_n\}_n^{+\infty} = 1$ of partial products $p_n = u_1 \cdot u_2 \ldots u_n = \prod_{k=1}^{n} uk$ for $n = 1, 2, \ldots$. (actually, this sequence does not have to start at $n = 1$). If p_n converges to p, we say that the infinite product $\prod_{k=1}^{+\infty} u_k$ converges to p. For $u_k = 1 - \dfrac{1}{k^2}$ we have

$$p_2 = \frac{3}{4} \qquad\qquad \left(= \frac{2+1}{2 \cdot 2}\right)$$

$$p_3 = \frac{3}{4}\frac{8}{9} = \frac{2}{3} \qquad\qquad \left(= \frac{3+1}{2 \cdot 3}\right)$$

$$p_4 = \frac{2}{3}\frac{15}{16} = \frac{5}{8} \qquad\qquad \left(= \frac{4+1}{2 \cdot 4}\right)$$

$$p_5 = \frac{5}{8}\frac{24}{25} = \frac{3}{5} \qquad\qquad \left(= \frac{5+1}{2 \cdot 5}\right)$$

We claim that $p_n = \dfrac{n+1}{2n}$. This is true for $p_2 = \dfrac{2+1}{4} = \dfrac{3}{4}$.

We assume that it is true for $m = n$ and let $m = n + 1$. Then

$$p_n + 1 = p_n u_{n+1}$$

$$= \left[\frac{n+1}{2n}\right]\left[\frac{(n+1)^2 - 1}{(n+1)^2}\right]$$

$$= \frac{n^2 + 2n}{2n(n+1)}$$

$$= \frac{(n+1) + 1}{2(n+1)}$$

135

Therefore $p_n = \dfrac{n+1}{2n}$ for $n = 2, 3, \ldots$ so that

$$\prod_{k=2}^{+\infty} \left(1 - \frac{1}{k^2}\right) = \lim_{n \to +\infty} p_n$$

$$= \lim_{n \to +\infty} \frac{n+1}{2n}$$

$$= \frac{1}{2}$$

6.   (A)

The cross ratio R_c of a set of four distinct concurrent lines $l_1, l_2, l_3, l_4,$ is given by

$$R_c = \frac{(m_3 - m_1)(m_4 - m_2)}{(m_3 - m_2)(m_4 - m_1)}$$

where $m_1, m_2, m_3,$ and m_4 represent the slopes of l_1, l_2, l_3 and $l_4,$ respectively. We have $m_1 = 1/2, m_2 = 2/2, m_3 = 3/2,$ and $m_4 = 4/2$ so that

$$R_c = \frac{(3-1)(4-2)}{(3-2)(4-1)} = \frac{4}{3}$$

7.   (B)

Let R be a ring and n a positive integer such that $n \cdot r = 0$ for all r εR. Then the least positive integer satisfying the equation is called the characteristic of R. If there does not exist a positive integer satisfying the equation, then R is said to have characteristic 0. The ring

$$Z_2 + Z_3 = \{(0, 0), (0, 1), (0, 2), (1, 0), (1, 1), (1, 2)\}$$

We have

$$1(0,1) \neq (0, 0)$$
$$2(0,1) = (0, 2) \neq (0, 0)$$

$$3(1,1) = (1, 0) \neq (0, 0)$$
$$4(1,1) = (0, 1) \neq (0, 0)$$
$$5(0,1) = (0, 2) \neq (0, 0)$$

However, $6(r,\bar{r}) = (0,0)$ for all $(r,\bar{r}) \; \varepsilon \; Z_2 + Z_3$, so the characteristic of $Z_2 + Z_3$ is 6.

8.　　(A)

We have

$$\lim_{n \to +\infty} \left(\sqrt{n^4 + in^2} - n^2 \right)$$

$$= \lim_{n \to +\infty} \left(\sqrt{n^4 + in^2} - n^2 \right) \frac{\sqrt{n^4 + in^2} + n^2}{\sqrt{n^4 + in^2} + n^2}$$

$$= \lim_{n \to +\infty} \frac{in^2}{\sqrt{n^4 + in^2} + n^2}$$

$$= \lim_{n \to +\infty} \frac{i}{\sqrt{1 + \dfrac{i}{n^2}} + 1}$$

$$= \frac{i}{2}$$

9.　　(A)

Successive substitutions of the right hand side of

$$u(x) = x + \int_0^x (t - x) \, u(t) \, dt$$

into the $u(t)$ in the integral yields

$$u(x) = x + \int_0^x (t - x) \left[t + \int_0^t (t_1 - t) \, u(t_1) \, dt_1 \right] dt$$

$$= x + \int_0^x (t^2 - xt) \, dt + \int_0^x (t - x) \int_0^t (t_1 - t) \, u(t_1) \, dt_1 \, dt$$

137

$$= x - \frac{x^3}{3!} + \int_0^x (t-x) \int_0^t (t_1 - t)\, u(t_1)\, dt_1\, dt$$

$$= x - \frac{x^3}{3!} + \int_0^x (t-x) \int_0^t (t_1 - t) \left[t_1 + \int_0^{t_1} (t_2 - t_1)\, u(t_2) dt_2 \right] dt_1 dt$$

$$= x - \frac{x^3}{3!} + \int_0^x (t-x) \int_0^t (t_1 - t)\, u(t_1)\, dt_1\, dt$$

$$\qquad + \int_0^x (t-x) \int_0^t (t_1 - t) \int_0^{t_1} (t_2 - t_1)\, u(t_2)\, dt_2\, dt_1\, dt$$

$$= x - \frac{x^3}{3!} + \int_0^x (t-x) \left[-\frac{t^3}{3!} \right] dt$$

$$\qquad + \int_0^x (t-x) \int_0^t (t_1 - t) \int_0^{t_1} (t_2 - t_1)\, u(t_2)\, dt_2\, dt_1\, dt$$

$$= x - \frac{x^3}{3!} + \frac{x^5}{5!} + \int_0^x (t-x) \int_0^t (t_1 - t) \int_0^{t_1} (t_2 - t_1)\, u(t_2)\, dt_2\, dt_1\, dt$$

$$= \ldots = \sin x$$

10. (A)

Setting $u = \ln x^{-1}$, we obtain $x = e^{-u}$ and $dx = -e^{-u}\, du$. Also, $x \to 0^+$ implies $u \to +\infty$ and $x \to 1^-$ implies $u \to 0^+$. Thus

$$\int_0^1 \left(\ln \frac{1}{x} \right)^5 dx = \int_{+\infty}^0 u^5 (-e^{-u})\, du$$

$$= \int_0^{+\infty} u^{6-1} e^{-u}\, du$$

$$= \Gamma(6) = 5! = 120$$

11.   (E)

Let $f(x)$ be defined on $[0, +\infty)$. The Laplace transform of $f(x)$, denoted $£[f(x)](p)$, is the function of p defined by

$$£[f(x)](p) = \int_0^{+\infty} e^{-px} f(x) \, dx$$

The domain of $£[f(x)](p)$ is the set of all real numbers p for which the integral converges. We have

$$£[f(x)](p) = \int_1^{+\infty} e^{-px} \, dx$$

$$= \lim_{b \to +\infty} \int_1^b e^{-px} \, dx$$

$$= \lim_{b \to +\infty} \left[-\frac{e^{-px}}{p} \right]_1^b$$

$$= \lim_{b \to +\infty} \left[\frac{e^{-p}}{p} - \frac{e^{-pb}}{p} \right]$$

$$= \frac{e^{-p}}{p}$$

for $p \, \varepsilon \, (0, +\infty)$.

12.   (A)

The matrix M_T of T relative to $\{(1, 0), (0, 1)\}$ is given by

$$M_T = \begin{bmatrix} 2 & -1 \\ 1 & 3 \end{bmatrix}$$

The matrix $M_T{}^*$ for the adjoint T^* of T is

$$M_T{}^* = M_T^* = \begin{bmatrix} 2 & 1 \\ -1 & 3 \end{bmatrix}$$

Thus

$$T^*(x,y) = \begin{bmatrix} 2 & 1 \\ -1 & 3 \end{bmatrix} \begin{bmatrix} x \\ y \end{bmatrix} = \begin{bmatrix} 2x + y \\ -x + 3y \end{bmatrix}$$

13.   (D)

Set $x = \pi/2 - u$. Then $dx = -du$, $x = 0$ implies that $u = \pi/2$, and $x = \pi/2$ implies that $u = 0$. Using the identities $\sin(\pi/2 - u) = \cos u$ and $\cos(\pi/2 - u) = \sin u$, we obtain

$$I = \int_0^{\frac{\pi}{2}} \frac{\cos x}{\cos x + \sin x}\, dx = \int_{\frac{\pi}{2}}^0 \frac{\sin u}{\sin u + \cos u}\, (-du)$$

$$= \int_0^{\frac{\pi}{2}} \frac{\sin u}{\sin u + \cos u}\, du$$

Hence

$$2I = \int_0^{\frac{\pi}{2}} \frac{\cos x}{\cos x + \sin x}\, dx + \int_0^{\frac{\pi}{2}} \frac{\sin x}{\sin x + \cos x}\, dx$$

$$= \int_0^{\frac{\pi}{2}} 1\, dx$$

$$= \frac{\pi}{2}$$

so that $I = \pi/4$.

14.   (D)

The discriminant D of the ternary quadratic form

$$a_{11}\, x^2 + a_{22}\, y^2 + a_{33}\, z^2 + 2\, a_{12}\, xy + 2\, a_{23}\, yz + 2\, a_{13}\, xz$$

140

is the determinant

$$A = \begin{bmatrix} a_{11} & a_{12} & a_{13} \\ a_{12} & a_{22} & a_{23} \\ a_{13} & a_{23} & a_{33} \end{bmatrix}$$

Thus

$$D = \det \begin{bmatrix} 1 & -1 & -3 \\ -1 & -1 & 2 \\ -3 & 2 & 1 \end{bmatrix}$$

$$= (-1 + 6 + 6) - (-9 + 4 + 1)$$

$$= 15$$

15. (E)

The curvature $\kappa(x)$ of $f(x)$ at $P(x_0, f(x_0))$ is given by

$$\kappa(x_0) = \frac{f''(x_0)}{\{1 + [f'(x_0)]^2\}^{3/2}}$$

and the radius of curvature $R(x)$ of $f(x)$ at $P(x_0, f(x_0))$ is given by

$$R(x_0) = \frac{1}{|\kappa(x_0)|}.$$

We have

$$f'(x) = 1 - \frac{1}{x^2} \; ; f'(1) = 0$$

$$f''(x) = -\frac{2}{x^3} \; ; \quad f''(1) = -2$$

so that $\kappa(1) = -2$ and $R(1) = 1/2$.

16.   (B)

The gamma function $\Gamma(p)$ is defined by

$$\Gamma(p) = \int_0^{+\infty} x^{p-1} e^{-x} dx$$

Setting $x = u^{1/2}$, we obtain $dx = u^{1/2} du$ so that

$$\int_0^{+\infty} e^{-x^2} dx = \int_0^{+\infty} \frac{1}{2} u^{-1/2} e^{-u} du$$

$$= \frac{1}{2} \int_0^{+\infty} u^{1/2-1} e^{-u} du$$

$$= \frac{1}{2} \Gamma\left(\frac{1}{2}\right)$$

17.   (B)

We have

$$<(1, 0)> = \{(0, 0), (1, 0)\}$$

so that all cosets of $<(1, 0)>$ must have two elements. Since $Z_2 \times Z_3$ has six elements, $(Z_2 \times Z_3)/<(1, 0)>$ contains three elements:

$$(0, 1) + <(1, 0)> = \{(0, 1), (1, 1)\}$$
$$(0, 0) + <(1, 0)> = \{(0, 0), (1, 0)\}$$
$$(1, 2) + <(1, 0)> = \{(1, 2), (0, 2)\}$$

18.   (C)

The function d would be called a metric for $R[0, 1]$ if it satisfied all of the conditions (A) – (E). Since condition (C) is not satisfied, the function d is called a pseudometric for $R[0, 1]$. To see this, define

$$f(x) = 1 \text{ if } x \in [0, 1]$$

142

and

$$g(x) = \begin{cases} 1 \text{ if } x \, \varepsilon \, [0,1) \\ 2 \text{ if } x = 1 \end{cases}.$$

Then $f, g \, \varepsilon \, R[0, 1]$ with $f \neq g$, but $d(f, g) = 0$, as

$$\int_0^1 \left| f(x) - g(x) \right| dx = \int_0^1 \left| 1 - 1 \right| dx = 0 \, .$$

19.   (E)

Let m (> 0) and n be integers. The Division Algorithm states that there exist unique integers q and r such that

$$\frac{n}{m} = q + \frac{r}{m} \text{ where } 0 \leq \frac{r}{m} < 1.$$

Repeated applications of this algorithm yield

$$\frac{13}{42} = 0 + \cfrac{1}{\cfrac{42}{13}}$$

$$= \cfrac{1}{3 + \cfrac{1}{\cfrac{13}{3}}}$$

$$= \cfrac{1}{3 + \cfrac{1}{4 + \cfrac{1}{3}}} \, .$$

20.   (E)

Let $p(x) = a_N x^N + a_{N-1} x^{N-1} + \ldots + a_1 x + a_0$ be an element of $Z[x]$. The Eisenstein criterion states that for a prime p, if $a_N \not\equiv 0 \pmod{p}$, $a_j \equiv 0 \pmod{p}$ for $j = 0, 1, 2, \ldots, N - 1$ and $a_0 \not\equiv 0 \pmod{p^2}$, then $p(x)$ is irreducible over the rationals. We have, for $p = 3$,

$5 \not\equiv 0 \pmod 3$

$9 \equiv 0 \pmod 3$

$$0 \equiv 0 \pmod{3}$$

$$18 \equiv 0 \pmod 3$$

$$3 \equiv 0 \pmod{3}$$

$$15 \equiv 0 \pmod 3$$

$$15 \not\equiv 0 \pmod 9$$

Therefore $5x^5 + 9x^4 + 18x^2 + 3x + 15$ satisfies an Eisenstein criterion $(p = 3)$.

21.   (B)

The angle θ that a conic $Ax^2 + Bxy + Cy^2 + Dx + Ey + F = 0$ must be rotated in order to eliminate the xy term must satisfy

$$\cot 2\theta = \frac{A - C}{B}.$$

For the given conic, we must have

$$\cot 2\theta = \frac{1 + 1}{2\sqrt{3}} \text{ or } \tan 2\theta = \sqrt{3}.$$

Therefore $\theta = 30^\circ$.

22.   (D)

We have

$$0 = \pounds[y'' + 6y' + 9y]$$

$$= p^2 \pounds(y) - [p\, y(0) + y'(0)] + 6\{p\, \pounds(y) - y(0)\} + 9\, \pounds(y)$$

$$= [p^2 + 6p + 9]\, \pounds(y) = 3p + 7$$

Thus

$$\pounds(y) = \frac{3p+7}{(p+3)^2}$$

$$= \frac{A}{p+3} + \frac{B}{(p+3)^2}$$

Setting $p = -3$ in $3p + 7 = A(p+3) + B$ yields $B = -2$. For $p = 0$, we obtain $A = 3$.

23.   (B)

The join of subgroups S_1 and S_2 of G is the smallest subgroup of G containing S_1 and S_2. Thus the join must contain $\{0, 4, 6, 8\}$. Since $4 + 6 \equiv 10 \pmod{12}$ and $6 + 8 \equiv 2 \pmod{12}$, the join equals $<2>$.

24.   (B)

Since a 60° angle cannot be trisected, a 20° angle cannot be constructed. A regular 9–gon is constructible if and only if the angle $\frac{360}{9} = 40°$ is constructible. Thus, a 9–gon is not constructible because one of the 40° angles formed could then be bisected to construct a 20° angle.

25.   (E)

We have

$$T^2 = \begin{bmatrix} 1 & 0 \\ 1 & 1 \end{bmatrix}^2 = \begin{bmatrix} 1 & 0 \\ 2 & 1 \end{bmatrix}$$

$$T^3 = \begin{bmatrix} 1 & 0 \\ 1 & 1 \end{bmatrix}^3 = \begin{bmatrix} 1 & 0 \\ 3 & 1 \end{bmatrix}$$

and, in general,

$$T^n = \begin{bmatrix} 1 & 0 \\ 1 & 1 \end{bmatrix}^n = \begin{bmatrix} 1 & 0 \\ n & 1 \end{bmatrix}.$$

Hence, the sum of the elements in T^n is $n + 2$.

26.   (D)

Let V be a finite dimensional vector space over a field F. A bilinear form $b(v; \overline{v})$ is a function $b: V \times V \to F$ which satisfies

1) $b(\alpha v_1 + \beta v_2; \overline{v}) = \propto b(v_1; \overline{v}) + \beta\, b(v_2; \overline{v})$

2) $b(v; \delta \overline{v}_1 \upsilon \overline{w}_2) = \delta(v; \overline{v}_1) + \upsilon b(v; \overline{v}_2)$

where $v_1, v_2, \overline{v}_1, \overline{v}_2 \varepsilon V$ and $\alpha, \beta, \delta, \upsilon, \varepsilon\, F$. The matrix $B = (b_{ij})$ is given by $b_{ij} = b(u_i, u_j)$ for $1 \le i \le 2$; $1 \le j \le 2$. We have

$b_{11}\,(u_1, u_1) = b\,((0, 1); (0, 1)) = 0 + 0 + 0 + 0 = 0$

$b_{12}\,(u_1, u_2) = b\,((0, 1); (1, 1)) = 0 + 0 + 1 + 3 = 4$

$b_{21}\,(u_2, u_1) = b\,((1, 1); (0, 1)) = 1 - 2 + 0 + 0 = -1$

$b_{22}\,(u_2, u_2) = b\,((1, 1); (1, 1)) = 1 - 2 + 1 + 3 = 3$

Thus

$$B = \begin{bmatrix} 0 & 4 \\ -1 & 3 \end{bmatrix}$$

27.   (D)

A class of subsets τ of $\mathcal{X}$ is called a topology on $\mathcal{X}$ if τ satisfies the following axioms:

146

(1) $\cancel{X} \varepsilon \tau$; $\emptyset \varepsilon \tau$

(2) $S_{\propto} \varepsilon \tau$ for $\propto \varepsilon A$ implies $\underset{\alpha \varepsilon A}{\bigcup} S_\alpha \varepsilon \tau$

(3) $S_1, S_2 \varepsilon \tau$ implies $S_1 \cap S_2 \varepsilon \tau$

Consider $\tau = \{\cancel{X}, \emptyset, \{a,b\}, \{a,c\}, \{b,c\}, \{a,b,c\}\}$. We have $\{a, b\}$ $\varepsilon \tau$ and $\{b, c\} \varepsilon \tau$ but $\{b\} = \{a, b\} \cap \{b, c\}$ is not an element of τ. Thus τ does not form a topology on $\cancel{X}$.

28.   (B)

An eigenvalue λ for a differential equation of the form $y'' + \lambda y = 0$ with initial conditions $y(x_1) = y_1$; $y(x_2) = y_2$ is a number for which the initial value problem has a non-trivial solution. The auxiliary equation of the given equation is $m^2 + \lambda = 0$ so that $m = \pm \sqrt{-\lambda}$. We consider three cases: $\lambda = 0$; $\lambda < 0$; $\lambda > 0$. For $\lambda = 0$, the general solution is $y(x) = c_1 + c_2 x$. Since $y(0) = 0$ and $y(\pi) = 0$, we have

$$0 = y(0) = c_1$$

$$0 = y(\pi) = c_2 \pi$$

so that $y(x) \equiv 0$. For $\lambda < 0$, the general solution is

$$y(x) = c_1 e \sqrt{-\lambda} x + c_2 e - \sqrt{-\lambda} x.$$

Substitution of the initial conditions into $y(x)$ yields

$$0 = y(0) = c_1 + c_2$$

$$0 = c_1 e \sqrt{-\lambda} \pi + c_2 e - \sqrt{-\lambda} \pi.$$

Since

$$\begin{vmatrix} 1 & 1 \\ e\sqrt{-\lambda}\pi & e-\sqrt{-\lambda}\pi \end{vmatrix} \neq 0$$

$c_1 = c_2 = 0$, so that $y(x) \equiv 0$. For $\lambda > 0$, the general solution is

$$y(x) = c_1 \sin \sqrt{\lambda} x + c_2 \cos \sqrt{\lambda} x.$$

147

Substitution of the initial conditions into $y(x)$ yields

$$0 = y(0) = c_2$$

$$0 = y(\pi) = c_1 \sin \sqrt{\lambda}\, x.$$

To obtain a non-trivial solution, $\sin\sqrt{\lambda}\, x = 0$, that is $\sqrt{\lambda}\, \pi = k\pi$ for $k = 1, 2, 3, \ldots$. Therefore, the eigenvalues are $\lambda = k^2$ for $k = 1, 2, 3, \ldots$.

29.   (D)

Switching algebra is similar to set algebra with union ($\cup$) replaced with disjunction ($\vee$), intersection replaced with conjunction (or juxtaposition) and complementation denoted by ($\bar{\ }$). We have

$$(f \vee g)\, (\bar{f} \vee h) = (f \vee g)\bar{f} \vee (f \vee g)h$$

$$= f\bar{f} \vee g\bar{f} \vee fh \vee gh$$

$$= 0 \vee g\bar{f} \vee fh \vee gh$$

$$= g\bar{f} \vee fh \vee gh$$

30.   (C)

Using the identity $\|T\|^2 = \langle T, T \rangle$, we obtain

$$\|T\| = \text{trace}\,(T^t T)$$

$$= \text{trace}\left[\begin{bmatrix} 1 & 2 \\ 3 & -1 \end{bmatrix}\begin{bmatrix} 1 & 3 \\ 2 & -1 \end{bmatrix}\right]$$

$$= \text{trace}\begin{bmatrix} 5 & 1 \\ 1 & 10 \end{bmatrix}$$

$$= 15$$

31.   (E)

A geometric series is a series of the form $a + ar + ar^2 + \ldots + ar^{n-1} + \ldots$. If $|r| < 1$, the series converges to $\dfrac{a}{1-r}$. For the given series, $r = \dfrac{1}{1+x^2} < 1$ so that its sum is

$$\frac{x^4}{1 - \dfrac{1}{1+x^2}} = \frac{x^4}{\dfrac{1+x^2-1}{1+x^2}} = x^4 + x^2 \, .$$

32.   (A)

To within an additive constant,

$$f(x) = \frac{x^2}{2} + \frac{2x^3}{3} + \ldots + \frac{n \, x^{n+1}}{n+1} + \ldots$$

Using the ratio test with $u_n = \dfrac{n \, x^{n+1}}{n+1}$, we have

$$L = \lim_{n \to +\infty} \left| \frac{u_{n+1}}{u_n} \right|$$

$$= \lim_{n \to +\infty} \left| \frac{(n+1)(n+1) \, x \, x^{n+1}}{n(n+2) \, x^{n+1}} \right|$$

$$= |x|$$

so that the series is absolutely convergent for $|x| < 1$ and divergent for $|x| > 1$. For

$$x = -1, \; u_n = \frac{(-1)^{n+1} n}{n+1}$$

which does not go to 0 which implies that -1 is not in Dom(f). For

$$x = 1, \; u_n = \frac{n}{n+1} \, ,$$

which does not approach 0 which imples that 1 is not in Dom(f). Thus Dom(f) = $(-1, 1)$.

33. **(C)**

Let $(G, *)$ and $(G', *')$ be groups. A homomorphism from G into G' is a function $\emptyset$ such that $\emptyset(gh) = \emptyset(g)\,\emptyset(h)$. A homomorphism $\emptyset$ must take the identity $e \,\varepsilon\, G$ onto the identity $\emptyset(e) \,\varepsilon\, G'$. When G is cyclic, the homomorphism $\emptyset$ is completely determined by $\emptyset(g)$ where g is a generator of G. Since 1 is a generator of Z_8, the value $\emptyset(1)$ $\varepsilon\ \{0, 1, 2, 3\}$ is critical. Because we desire only the "onto" homomorphisms, $\emptyset(1)$ must be a generator of Z_4. The generators of Z_4 are the elements of $\{0, 1, 2, 3\}$ relatively prime to 4, namely 1 and 3. The functions "defined by" $\emptyset_1(1) = 1$ and $\emptyset_2(1) = 3$ are both homomorphisms from Z_8 onto Z_4. In particular, note that they both take the identity element in Z_8 onto the identity element in Z_4.

34. **(C)**

Setting $x = e^t$, we have

$$\frac{dy}{dt} = \frac{dy}{dx}\frac{dx}{dt} = y'\,x, \quad \text{since } \frac{dx}{dt} = \frac{d(e^t)}{dt} = e^t = x$$

and

$$\frac{d^2y}{dt^2} = \frac{d}{dt}\left(x\frac{dy}{dx}\right) = x\,\frac{d}{dt}\left(\frac{dy}{dx}\right) + xy'$$

$$= x\,\frac{d}{dx}\left(\frac{dy}{dx}\right)\frac{dx}{dt} + xy' = x^2 y'' + xy'$$

Thus

$$xy' = \frac{dy}{dt} \quad \text{and} \quad x^2 y'' = \frac{d^2y}{dt^2} - \frac{dy}{dt}.$$

We have

$$\frac{d^2y}{dt^2} - \frac{dy}{dt} + 6\frac{dy}{dt} + 6y = 0$$

$$\frac{d^2y}{dt^2} + 5\frac{dy}{dt} + 6y = 0.$$

The auxiliary equation is given by $m^2 + 5m + 6 = 0$, so that the general solution is $c_1\,e^{-3t} + c_2\,e^{-2t}$ which equals $\dfrac{c_1}{x^3} + \dfrac{c_2}{x^2}$.

35.   (E)

Fermat's "little" theorem states that if t is an integer and p a prime not dividing t, then $t^{p-1} \equiv 1 \pmod{p}$. Thus

$$5^{34} \equiv (5^{16})^2 \, 5^2 \equiv (5^{17-1})^2 \, 5^2 \equiv 1^2 \, 5^2 \equiv 25 \equiv 8 \pmod{17}$$

36.   (C)

Let $\vec{u} = u_1 \vec{i} + u_2 \vec{j} + u_3 \vec{k}$. The curl of $\vec{u}$, denoted curl $(\vec{u})$, is the cross product of the vector operator $\nabla \equiv \vec{i} \frac{\partial}{\partial x} + \vec{j} \frac{\partial}{\partial y} + \vec{k} \frac{\partial}{\partial z}$ and the vector $\vec{u}$:

$$\text{curl}(\vec{u}) = \nabla \times \vec{u} = \begin{vmatrix} \vec{i} & \vec{j} & \vec{k} \\ \frac{\partial}{\partial x} & \frac{\partial}{\partial y} & \frac{\partial}{\partial z} \\ u_1 & u_2 & u_3 \end{vmatrix}$$

For $\vec{u} = xyz \, \vec{i} + xy^2 \, \vec{j} + yz \, \vec{k}$, we have

$$\text{curl}(\vec{u}) = (z - 0) \, \vec{i} + (xy - 0) \, \vec{j} + (y^2 - xz) \, \vec{k}$$

37.   (B)

The inverse f^{-1} of f is found from $y = \frac{x}{x-1}$ by first solving for x in terms of y and then replacing y with x and x with y. Thus

$$y = \frac{x}{x-1}$$

$$xy - y = x$$

$$x(y-1) = y \Rightarrow x = \frac{y}{y-1}$$

$$f^{-1}(x) = \frac{x}{x-1}$$

Thus $f^{-1}(x) = f(x)$.

38.   (B)

For $x_0 = -2$, we have $8 + y_0^2 + 30 = 8y_0 + 24$ so that

$$y_0 = \frac{8 \pm \sqrt{64 - 4(14)}}{2} = 4 \pm \sqrt{2}$$

Since $y_0 > 4$, $y_0 = 4 \pm \sqrt{2}$. Taking the derivative of both sides of $2x^2 + y^2 + 30 = 8y - 12x$ with respect to x yields

$$4x + 2yy' \; 8y' - 12$$

$$4x + 12 = y'(8 - 2y)$$

$$y' = \frac{2x + 6}{4 - y}$$

Therefore, the slope of the tangent line at $(-2, 4 \pm \sqrt{2})$ is

$$y' = \frac{-4 + 6}{4 - (4 + \sqrt{2})} = -\sqrt{2}$$

39.   (B)

The equation $D = aA + bB + cC$ implies that

$$\begin{bmatrix} 3 & 3 \\ 0 & -2 \end{bmatrix} = \begin{bmatrix} a - c & a + b \\ b + c & -a + b + c \end{bmatrix}$$

Thus,

$$a - c = 3$$

$$a + b = 3$$

$$b + c = 0$$

$$-a + b + c = -2$$

Since $b + c = 0$, $a = 2$ which implies that $b = 1$, $c = -1$.

40.   (B)

The derivative of $p(x)$ is given by

$$p'(x) = \sum_{n=1}^{+\infty} \frac{(x - 2)^{n-1}}{n}$$

The nth term of $p'(x)$ is $a_n = \dfrac{(x-2)^{n-1}}{n}$.

$$\rho = \lim_{n \to \infty} \left| \frac{a_n + 1}{a_n} \right|$$

$$= \lim_{n \to \infty} \left| \frac{(x-2)^n n}{(x-2)^{n-1}(n+1)} \right|$$

$$= \lim_{n \to \infty} \left| \frac{(x-2)n}{n+1} \right|$$

$$= |x-2|$$

By the Ratio Test, the series converges absolutely if $|x-2| < 1$, i.e., $1 < x < 3$. Now we consider endpoints. When $x = 1$, the series converges by the Alternating Series Test. When $x = 3$, the series is the divergent harmonic series. Therefore, the series converges in $[1, 3]$.

41.   (C)

Let $f(x)$ be defined on $[0, +\infty)$. The Laplace transformation of f, denoted $\pounds[f(x)](p)$, is defined by

$$\pounds[f(x)](p) = \int_0^{+\infty} e^{-px} f(x)\, dx$$

for all p for which the integral converges. If, in addition, f is of exponential order and is piecewise continuous on $[0, b]$ for every $b > 0$, then

$$\pounds\left[\int_0^x f(t)\, dt \right](p) = \frac{1}{p}\, \pounds[f(x)]\,(p)$$

Since $\pounds[\sin ax]\,(p) = \dfrac{a}{p^2 + a^2}$, we have

$$\pounds\left[\int_0^x \sin 2t\, dt \right](p) = \frac{2}{p^3 + 4p}.$$

42.   (D)

The slope of the tangent line to the graph of f at x_0 is equal to $f'(x_0)$. It is also equal to the $\tan A$ where A is the angle formed by the tangent line and the positive x-axis. Thus $\tan A = f'(x_0) = \sqrt{3}$ so that $a = 60°$.

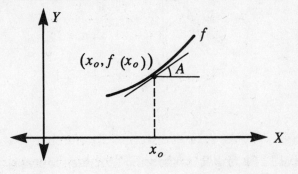

43.   (E)

The trace of T is the trace of M_T where M_T is a matrix representing T in some fixed basis. For the basis $\{(1, 0, 0), (0, 1, 0), (0, 0, 1)\}$,

$$M_T = \begin{bmatrix} 1 & 1 & 0 \\ 1 & -1 & 1 \\ 0 & 1 & 2 \end{bmatrix}$$

so that the trace of T is 2.

44.   (B)

The n'th partial sum s_n can be written as

$$s_n = \frac{1}{2!} + \frac{2}{3!} + \frac{3}{4!} + \ldots + \frac{n}{(n+1)!}$$

$$= \frac{2-1}{2!} + \frac{3-1}{3!} + \frac{4-1}{4!} + \ldots + \frac{(n+1)-1}{(n+1)!}$$

$$= 1 - \frac{1}{2!} + \frac{1}{2!} - \frac{1}{3!} + \frac{1}{3!} - \frac{1}{4!} + \ldots + \frac{1}{n!} - \frac{1}{(n+1)!}$$

$$= 1 - \frac{1}{(n+1)!} \to 1 \quad \text{as} \quad n \to +\infty .$$

Therefore, the sum is 1.

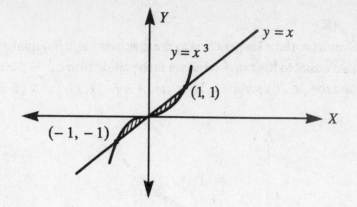

45. **(A)**

An ideal I of a ring R is a subring of R such that $rI \subseteq I$ and $Ir \subseteq I$, for all $r \varepsilon R$. An ideal I is called proper if $I \neq R$ and $I \neq \{0\}$. Since 5 and 12 are relatively prime, 5 is a generator of Z_{12}, that is, $<5> = Z_{12}$. Thus, $<5>$ is not a proper ideal of Z_{12}.

46. **(A)**

A set of answers to the ten questions is a 10-tuple of the form $(a_1, \ldots, a_{10})$ where a_j represents an answer to question Q_j, $1 \leq j \leq 10$. An answer is an element of the set $\{r_j, w_{j1}, \ldots, w_{j4}\}$ where r_j represents the right answer and $w_{j1}, \ldots, w_{j4}$ represent wrong answers. There are 5^{10} possible sets of answers. The number of ways to obtain a 10-tuple with exactly five correct answers is

$$\begin{bmatrix} 10 \\ 5 \end{bmatrix} = \frac{10!}{5! \, 5!} = 252,$$

each with probability

$$\left(\frac{1}{5}\right)^5 \left(\frac{4}{5}\right)^5 = \frac{4^5}{5^{10}} .$$

Hence the probability desired is

$$\frac{252 \; 4^5}{5^{10}} = \frac{(63) \, 4^6}{5^{10}} .$$

47. (D)

The Jacobian J of a transformation from the xy-plane into the uv-plane defined by

$$u = f(x, y)$$

$$v = g(x, y)$$

is given by

$$J = \begin{vmatrix} \dfrac{\partial f}{\partial x} & \dfrac{\partial f}{\partial y} \\[2ex] \dfrac{\partial g}{\partial x} & \dfrac{\partial g}{\partial y} \end{vmatrix}$$

We have

$$J = \begin{vmatrix} xye^{xy} + e^{xy} & x^2 e^{xy} \\[1ex] y^2 e^{xy} & xye^{xy} + e^{xy} \end{vmatrix}$$

$$= e^{2xy}\left[(xy + 1)^2 - x^2 y^2\right]$$

$$= [2xy + 1]\, e^{2xy}.$$

48. (A)

The outcome of six attempts is a 6-tuple of the form $(O_1, \ldots, O_6)$, where O_j is either a hit (H) or an out (O). There are $2^6 = 64$ possible outcomes. The number of ways to select a 6-tuple with exactly 3 H's and 3 O's is

$$\begin{bmatrix} 6 \\ 3 \end{bmatrix} = \frac{6!}{3!\,3!} = 20,$$

each with probability

$$\left(\frac{1}{3}\right)^3 \left(\frac{2}{3}\right)^3 = \frac{8}{3^6}.$$

Hence the desired probability is $\dfrac{160}{3^6}$.

49. (E)

Let R be a ring with a multiplicative identity e ($re = er = r$, for all $r \varepsilon R$). A unit of R is an element u of R that possesses a multiplicative inverse in R. In $Z_5 = \{0, 1, 2, 3, 4\}$, we have that 1 is the multiplicative identity and

$$1 \cdot 1 \equiv 1 \pmod 5$$

$$2 \cdot 3 \equiv 1 \pmod 5$$

$$3 \cdot 3 \equiv 1 \pmod 5$$

$$4 \cdot 4 \equiv 1 \pmod 5$$

which means that Z_5 contains four units.

50. (A)

Let f be defined on an interval $(0, L)$. Define f in $(-L, L)$ to be odd. The half range Fourier sine series is given by

$$\sum_{k=1}^{+\infty} b_k \sin \frac{k \pi x}{L}$$

where

$$b_k = \frac{2}{L} \int_0^L f(x) \sin \frac{k \pi x}{L} \, dx$$

for $k = 1, 2, 3, \ldots$. We have

$$b_k = 2 \int_0^1 x \sin k \pi x \, dx$$

$$= 2 \left\{ \left[-\frac{x}{k \pi} \cos k \pi x \right]_0^1 + \int_0^1 \frac{1}{k \pi} \cos k \pi x \, dx \right\}$$

$$= 2 \left\{ -\frac{1}{k \pi} \cos k \pi + \frac{1}{k \pi} \left[\frac{1}{k \pi} \sin k \pi x \right]_0^1 \right\}$$

$$= -\frac{2}{k \pi} \cos k \pi .$$

For $k = 3$, $b_3 = -\dfrac{2}{3\pi} \cos 3\pi = \dfrac{2}{3\pi}$.

51.   (C)

Since $\{e^x, e^{2x}, e^{-2x}\}$ is a linearly independent set, it forms a basis for S. In this basis, we have

$$D_x(e^x) = 1e^x + 0e^{2x} + 0e^{-2x}$$

$$D_x(e^{2x}) = 0e^x + 2e^{2x} + 0e^{-2x}$$

$$D_x(e^{-2x}) = 0e^x + 0e^{2x} - 2e^{-2x}$$

so that the corresponding matrix M_{D_x} of D_x is given by

$$M_{D_x} \begin{bmatrix} 1 & 0 & 0 \\ 0 & 2 & 0 \\ 0 & 0 & -2 \end{bmatrix}.$$

The determinant of D_x is -4.

52.   (B)

Let $a_2(x), a_1(x), a_0(x)$, and $f(x)$ be continuous on an interval I with $a_2(x) \neq 0$ for each $x \, \varepsilon \, I$. The Green's function for the ordinary differential equation $a_2(x)y'' + a_1(x)y' + a_0(x)y = f(x)$ is given by

$$G(x,t) = -\frac{1}{a_2(t)} \frac{\begin{vmatrix} y_1(x) & y_2(x) \\ y_1(t) & y_2(t) \end{vmatrix}}{\begin{vmatrix} y_1(t) & y_2(t) \\ y_1'(t) & y_2'(t) \end{vmatrix}}$$

where y_1 and y_2 are linearly independent solutions of the corresponding homogeneous equation. Note that

$$\int_{x_0}^{x} G(x,t)f(t)\,dt$$

is a particular solution of the non-homogeneous equation. We have $m^2 + 5m + 6 = 0$ so that $y_1(x) = e^{-3x}$ and $y_2(x) = e^{-2x}$. Since

$$\begin{vmatrix} e^{-3x} & e^{-2x} \\ e^{-3t} & e^{-2t} \end{vmatrix} = e^{-(3x+2t)} - e^{-(3t+2x)}$$

and

$$\begin{vmatrix} e^{-3t} & e^{-2t} \\ -3e^{-3t} & -2e^{-2t} \end{vmatrix} = e^{-5t}.$$

Therefore,

$$G(x,t) = -e^{5t}(e^{-(3x+2t)} - e^{-(3t+2x)}) = e^{2(t-x)} - e^{3(t-x)}.$$

53. (A)

The Maclaurin series for e^u is given by

$$e^u = 1 + u + \frac{u^2}{2!} + \dots + \frac{u^n}{n!} + \dots$$

Setting $u = -x^2$ and multiplying the result by x yields the Maclaurin series for xe^{-x^2}:

$$xe^{-x^2} = x\left(1 - x^2 + \frac{x^4}{2!} - \frac{x^6}{3!} + \dots\right)$$

$$= x - x^3 + \frac{x^5}{2!} - \frac{x^7}{3!} + \dots.$$

54. (E)

The symmetric difference is defined by

$$S\Delta T = (S\backslash T) \cup (T\backslash S).$$

159

We have
$$S \backslash T = \{1, 2, 3\}$$
and
$$T \backslash S = \{6, 7, 8\}$$
so that
$$S \Delta T = \{1, 2, 3, 6, 7, 8\} .$$

55. (D)

Set $x_n = \alpha^n$ for $n = 0, 1, 2, 3, \ldots$. Then

$$\alpha^{n+2} + 6 \alpha^{n+1} + 9 \alpha^n = 0$$

$$\alpha^2 + 6 \alpha + 9 = 0$$

$$\alpha = 3, 3 .$$

Thus, the general solution is given by $x_n = a \, 3^n + b \, n \, 3^n$ where $a, b \in R$. Since $x_0 = 1$ and $x_1 = 0$, we have

$$1 = x_0 = a$$

$$0 = x_1 = 3a + 3b$$

so that $a = 1$ and $b = -1$. Therefore, $x_5 = 3^5 - 5(3^5) = -4(3^5) = -972$.

56. (B)

If A represents the angle between f and g, then

$$\cos A = \frac{(f, g)}{\|f\| \, \|g\|} .$$

We have

$$\|f\|^2 = (f, f) = \int_0^1 2^2 \, dx = 4 \qquad (\|f\| = 2)$$

$$\|g\|^2 = (g, g) = \int_0^1 x^2 \, dx = \frac{1}{3} \qquad (\|g\| = 1/\sqrt{3})$$

$$(f,g) = \int_0^1 2x \; dx = 1 .$$

Therefore $\cos A = \sqrt{3}/2$.

57. (D)

The integral is improper since the integrand has a vertical asymptote at $x = 3$. Hence

$$\int_{-24}^4 \frac{dx}{\sqrt[3]{(x-3)^2}} = \int_{-24}^3 \frac{dx}{\sqrt[3]{(x-3)^2}} + \int_3^4 \frac{dx}{\sqrt[3]{(x-3)^2}}$$

$$= \lim_{\delta \to 0^+} \int_{-24}^{3-\delta} \frac{dx}{\sqrt[3]{(x-3)^2}} + \lim_{\varepsilon \to 0^+} \int_{3+\varepsilon}^4 \frac{dx}{\sqrt[3]{(x-3)^2}}$$

$$= \lim_{\delta \to 0^+} \left[3\sqrt[3]{x-3} \right]_{-24}^{3-\delta} + \lim_{\varepsilon \to 0^+} \left[3\sqrt[3]{x-3} \right]_{3+\varepsilon}^4$$

$$= 3 \lim_{\delta \to 0^+} \left[\sqrt[3]{-\delta} - \sqrt[3]{-27} \right] + 3 \lim_{\varepsilon \to 0^+} \left[\sqrt[3]{1} - \sqrt[3]{\varepsilon} \right]$$

$$= 12.$$

58. (A)

The statement is actually true for all positive integers. For $n = 1$, we have $1^2 + 2^2 + 3^2 = 36$ which is divisible by 9. Assume that $n^3 + (n+1)^3 + (n+2)^3$ is divisible by 9 for some positive integer n. We have

$$(n + 1)^3 + (n + 2)^3 + (n + 3)^3$$

$$= (n + 1)^3 + (n + 2)^3 + n^3 + 9n^2 + 27n + 27$$

$$= \{n^3 + (n + 1)^3 + (n + 2)^3\} + 9\{n^2 + 3n + 3\}$$

which is divisible by 9. Thus the statement is true for all positive integers.

59.   (C)

If F is a finite field, then it must have p^n elements for p a prime and n a non-negative integer. Since $27 = 3^3$, there exists a field with 27 elements.

60.   (D)

The following diagram represents S with the given ordering:

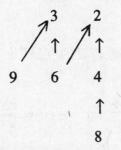

Therefore, the minimal elements of S are 6, 8, 9.

61.   (B)

A subset of a topological space is a neighborhood of a point if it contains an open set containing the point. Since $0 \varepsilon (-1, 1) \subseteq [-1, 1]$ and $(-1, 1)$ is open with respect to the usual topology on R, $[-1, 1]$ is a neighborhood of 0.

62.   (E)

Let $\sigma \varepsilon S_n$, the symmetric group of degree n. If

$$\sigma = \sigma_m \, \sigma_{m-1} \cdots \sigma_i \cdots \sigma_2 \sigma_1$$

is the decomposition of σ into disjoint cycles where σ_i is a K_i-cycle, the Cauchy number of σ is given by

$$C(\sigma) = \sum_{i=1}^{m} (k_i - 1).$$

We have $\sigma = (1\ 3\ 5\ 4)(2\ 6\ 7)$. Thus $C(\sigma) = (4-1) + (3-1) = 5$.

63.   (B)

Consider the ordinary differential equation $M(x, y)\, dx + N(x,y)\, dy = 0$. If $M(x, y)$, $N(x, y)$, $\dfrac{\partial M(x,y)}{\partial y}$, and $\dfrac{\partial N(x,y)}{\partial x}$ are continuous in a region R, then the differential equation is exact if and only if $\dfrac{\partial M}{\partial y} = \dfrac{\partial N}{\partial x}$. For

$$(ye^{xy} + \cos x)\, dx + (xe^{xy} + 1)\, dy = 0$$

we have

$$\frac{\partial M}{\partial y}\ yxe^{xy} + e^{xy} = \frac{\partial N}{\partial x}\ .$$

64.   (C)

Let x be a vertex of a graph G. The valence of x, denoted val(x), is the number of edges of G with x as one end point. The valences of the vertices and the number of vertices are related by val$(x_1) + \ldots + $ val(x_s) $= 2e$ where e represents the number of edges. Thus $2 + 2 + 3 + 3 + 4$ $= 2e$ so that $e = 7$.

65.   (D)

Since the discrete topology contains all subsets of R, every subset of R is both open and closed. Therefore, the closure of (a, b) is $[a, b]$.

66.   (A)

For $c, \hat{c}\ \varepsilon\ \mathit{C}^3$ the usual inner product is given by

$$(c,\hat{c}) = x\,\overline{\hat{x}} + y\,\overline{\hat{y}} + z\,\overline{\hat{z}}$$

where $c = (x, y, z)$ and $\hat{c} = (\hat{x}, \hat{y}, \hat{z})$. Therefore $\hat{c}$ can be chosen so that $\overline{\hat{x}} = 1$, $\overline{\hat{y}} = -i$, and $\overline{\hat{z}} = 2 + i$, that is $\hat{c} = (1, i, 2 - i)$.

GRE

MATH TEST

TEST IV

THE GRADUATE RECORD EXAMINATION

MATH TEST

ANSWER SHEET

1. Ⓐ Ⓑ Ⓒ Ⓓ Ⓔ
2. Ⓐ Ⓑ Ⓒ Ⓓ Ⓔ
3. Ⓐ Ⓑ Ⓒ Ⓓ Ⓔ
4. Ⓐ Ⓑ Ⓒ Ⓓ Ⓔ
5. Ⓐ Ⓑ Ⓒ Ⓓ Ⓔ
6. Ⓐ Ⓑ Ⓒ Ⓓ Ⓔ
7. Ⓐ Ⓑ Ⓒ Ⓓ Ⓔ
8. Ⓐ Ⓑ Ⓒ Ⓓ Ⓔ
9. Ⓐ Ⓑ Ⓒ Ⓓ Ⓔ
10. Ⓐ Ⓑ Ⓒ Ⓓ Ⓔ
11. Ⓐ Ⓑ Ⓒ Ⓓ Ⓔ
12. Ⓐ Ⓑ Ⓒ Ⓓ Ⓔ
13. Ⓐ Ⓑ Ⓒ Ⓓ Ⓔ
14. Ⓐ Ⓑ Ⓒ Ⓓ Ⓔ
15. Ⓐ Ⓑ Ⓒ Ⓓ Ⓔ
16. Ⓐ Ⓑ Ⓒ Ⓓ Ⓔ
17. Ⓐ Ⓑ Ⓒ Ⓓ Ⓔ
18. Ⓐ Ⓑ Ⓒ Ⓓ Ⓔ
19. Ⓐ Ⓑ Ⓒ Ⓓ Ⓔ
20. Ⓐ Ⓑ Ⓒ Ⓓ Ⓔ
21. Ⓐ Ⓑ Ⓒ Ⓓ Ⓔ
22. Ⓐ Ⓑ Ⓒ Ⓓ Ⓔ

23. Ⓐ Ⓑ Ⓒ Ⓓ Ⓔ
24. Ⓐ Ⓑ Ⓒ Ⓓ Ⓔ
25. Ⓐ Ⓑ Ⓒ Ⓓ Ⓔ
26. Ⓐ Ⓑ Ⓒ Ⓓ Ⓔ
27. Ⓐ Ⓑ Ⓒ Ⓓ Ⓔ
28. Ⓐ Ⓑ Ⓒ Ⓓ Ⓔ
29. Ⓐ Ⓑ Ⓒ Ⓓ Ⓔ
30. Ⓐ Ⓑ Ⓒ Ⓓ Ⓔ
31. Ⓐ Ⓑ Ⓒ Ⓓ Ⓔ
32. Ⓐ Ⓑ Ⓒ Ⓓ Ⓔ
33. Ⓐ Ⓑ Ⓒ Ⓓ Ⓔ
34. Ⓐ Ⓑ Ⓒ Ⓓ Ⓔ
35. Ⓐ Ⓑ Ⓒ Ⓓ Ⓔ
36. Ⓐ Ⓑ Ⓒ Ⓓ Ⓔ
37. Ⓐ Ⓑ Ⓒ Ⓓ Ⓔ
38. Ⓐ Ⓑ Ⓒ Ⓓ Ⓔ
39. Ⓐ Ⓑ Ⓒ Ⓓ Ⓔ
40. Ⓐ Ⓑ Ⓒ Ⓓ Ⓔ
41. Ⓐ Ⓑ Ⓒ Ⓓ Ⓔ
42. Ⓐ Ⓑ Ⓒ Ⓓ Ⓔ
43. Ⓐ Ⓑ Ⓒ Ⓓ Ⓔ
44. Ⓐ Ⓑ Ⓒ Ⓓ Ⓔ

45. Ⓐ Ⓑ Ⓒ Ⓓ Ⓔ
46. Ⓐ Ⓑ Ⓒ Ⓓ Ⓔ
47. Ⓐ Ⓑ Ⓒ Ⓓ Ⓔ
48. Ⓐ Ⓑ Ⓒ Ⓓ Ⓔ
49. Ⓐ Ⓑ Ⓒ Ⓓ Ⓔ
50. Ⓐ Ⓑ Ⓒ Ⓓ Ⓔ
51. Ⓐ Ⓑ Ⓒ Ⓓ Ⓔ
52. Ⓐ Ⓑ Ⓒ Ⓓ Ⓔ
53. Ⓐ Ⓑ Ⓒ Ⓓ Ⓔ
54. Ⓐ Ⓑ Ⓒ Ⓓ Ⓔ
55. Ⓐ Ⓑ Ⓒ Ⓓ Ⓔ
56. Ⓐ Ⓑ Ⓒ Ⓓ Ⓔ
57. Ⓐ Ⓑ Ⓒ Ⓓ Ⓔ
58. Ⓐ Ⓑ Ⓒ Ⓓ Ⓔ
59. Ⓐ Ⓑ Ⓒ Ⓓ Ⓔ
60. Ⓐ Ⓑ Ⓒ Ⓓ Ⓔ
61. Ⓐ Ⓑ Ⓒ Ⓓ Ⓔ
62. Ⓐ Ⓑ Ⓒ Ⓓ Ⓔ
63. Ⓐ Ⓑ Ⓒ Ⓓ Ⓔ
64. Ⓐ Ⓑ Ⓒ Ⓓ Ⓔ
65. Ⓐ Ⓑ Ⓒ Ⓓ Ⓔ
66. Ⓐ Ⓑ Ⓒ Ⓓ Ⓔ

GRE MATHEMATICS
TEST IV

TIME: 2 hours and 50 minutes
66 Questions

DIRECTIONS: Choose the best answer for each question and mark the letter of your selection on the corresponding answer sheet.

1. Given that $(1,2,3)$ is an eigenvector for the matrix

$$\begin{pmatrix} 2 & 3 & -1 \\ 3 & 2 & 1 \\ 2 & 2 & 3 \end{pmatrix}$$, find the corresponding eigenvalue.

   (A) 5

   (B) 4

   (C) 3

   (D) 2

   (E) None of these

2. A rectangular box resides in 3-space with one vertex at the origin, $(0, 0, 0)$ and three faces in the coordinate planes. If another vertex is $(x, 2, 3)$, $x > 0$, and the angle in radians between the diagonals from $(0, 0, 0)$ to $(x, 2, 3)$ and the other vertex in the xz plane is $\frac{\pi}{6}$, find x.

   (A) 1

   (B) $\sqrt{2}$

   (C) 2

   (D) 3

   (E) $\sqrt{3}$

166

3. The random variable, X, is discrete and uniformly distributed with values 1, 2, 3, 4, 5. The variance of X is

(A) 1   (D) 4

(B) 2   (E) None of these

(C) 3

4. Which collection of inequalities represents the shaded region as shown in the plane? The curves represent $y^2 = x - 1$ and $2xy = 1$.

(A) $y^2 + 1 < x$ and $2x > \dfrac{1}{y}$

(B) $x < y^2 + 1$ or $2x > \dfrac{1}{y}$

(C) $2x < \dfrac{1}{y}$ and $x - 1 > y^2$

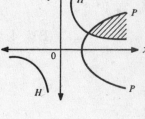

(D) $2x < \dfrac{1}{y}$ or $x - 1 < y^2$

(E) $2xy > 1$ and $y^2 + 1 > x$

5. A whispering gallery is constructed as part of the surface formed on rotation of the ellipse $\dfrac{x^2}{100} + \dfrac{y^2}{k} = 1$ with x and y in yards. Each whisperer stands at a focus on the x-axis that is three feet from the nearest vertex. Find k.

(A) 6   (B) 7

(C)   18   (E)   36

(D)   19

6.   Which of the following is a divisor of $3^{10} - 1$?

   (A)   3   (D)   17

   (B)   7   (E)   19

   (C)   11

7.   In the permutation group, S_5, find the product of the elements
       $(21453) \cdot (35214)$, where $(a\,b\,c\,d\,e)$ means $1 \to a$, $2 \to b$, etc.

   (A)   (41352)   (D)   (43125)

   (B)   (43215)   (E)   (34251)

   (C)   (43152)

8.   In the algebra of sets, which of the following is identical to
       $(\overline{S} \cap T)$, where $\overline{S}$ denotes the complement of S?

   (A) $S \cap \overline{T}$ (D) $S \cup \overline{T}$

   (B) $\overline{(\overline{S} \cup T)}$ (E)   None of these

   (C) ϕ

9. Find the interval on which the power series

$$\sum_{n=1}^{\infty} \frac{(-1)^n (x-3)^{2n+1}}{n \cdot 4^n}$$ converges.

(A) $(-1, 7)$ (D) $(1, 5)$

(B) $(-1, 7]$ (E) $[1, 5]$

(C) $(1, 5]$

10. Let f be a function such that the graph of f lies on a parabola through $(0, 0)$ and $(4, 2)$. If function g is the composition of f with itself, which of the following points could lie on the graph g?

(A) $(1, 1)$ (D) either (A) or (B)

(B) $(16, 2)$ (E) either (B) or (C)

(C) $(8, 8)$

11. When 4% interest is compounded quarterly, what is the effective annual rate to the nearest hundredth of a percent?

(A) 4.04   (D) 4.12

(B) 4.03   (E) 4.08

(C) 4.06

12. Given that f is a differentiable function with normal line
$4x + y = 9$ at $x = 2$ then

$$\lim_{x \to 0} \frac{f(2-x) - f(2+x)}{x} \text{ is}$$

(A) $\dfrac{1}{4}$

(D) $-\dfrac{1}{2}$

(B) $-\dfrac{1}{4}$

(E) Undefined

(C) $\dfrac{1}{2}$

13. Given that a 3×3 matrix A has only one eigenvalue, what is the dimension of the corresponding eigenspace?

(A) 1

(D) 1 or 2

(B) 2

(E) 1, 2 or 3

(C) 3

14. If $f(e^x) = \sqrt{x}$ for $x \geq 1$, then $f^{-1}(x)$ is

(A) $(\log x)^2$

(D) $e^{\sqrt{x}}$

(B) e^{x^2}

(E) $\sqrt{\log x}$

(C) $2 \log x$

170

15. Let * be a binary operation defined on the rational numbers by $a * b = a + b - ab$. Then the number of integers with integer *-inverse is

(A) 0

(D) 3

(B) 1

(E) 4

(C) 2

16. Evaluate the limit, $\lim\limits_{n \to \infty} \sum\limits_{k=1}^{n} \left[1 + \dfrac{2k}{n}\right]^2 \left[\dfrac{2}{n}\right].$

(A) $\dfrac{26}{3}$

(D) $\dfrac{7}{3}$

(B) 6

(E) 2

(C) $\dfrac{13}{3}$

17. Define a linear transformation from R^2 to R^3 by $(x, y) T = (x + y, x - y, x)$. Define S, a linear transformation from R^3 to R^2, to be an inverse of T if $((x, y) T) S = (x, y)$. Which of the following represent an inverse of T?

(A) $(x, y, z) S = \left(z, \dfrac{x}{2} - \dfrac{y}{2}\right)$

(B) $(x, y, z) S = \left(\dfrac{x}{2} + \dfrac{y}{2}, \dfrac{x}{2} - \dfrac{y}{2} - z\right)$

(C) $(x, y, z) S = \left(\dfrac{x}{3} + \dfrac{y}{3} + \dfrac{z}{3}, x - y\right)$

(D) both (A) and (B)

(E) all three, (A), (B), and (C)

18. The mapping $\phi : G \rightarrow G$ given by $g\phi = a^2 g a^2$ for fixed $a \in G$ and for each element g in G, is a homomorphism if

(A)
$$a^4 = e$$

(B)
$$a^3 = e$$

(C) $aG = Ga$

(D) G is abelian

(E) G is finite

19. Given the matrix $A = \begin{pmatrix} 1 & 2 & 3 \\ 2 & 3 & 4 \\ 1 & 1 & 5 \end{pmatrix}$ and $B = A^{-1}$, find the entry in row 3 and column 2 of B.

(A) $\dfrac{1}{4}$

(B) $\dfrac{1}{2}$

(C) 1

(D) $-\dfrac{1}{2}$

(E) $-\dfrac{1}{4}$

20. Given the function $f:(A \cup B) \rightarrow C$, which of the following is always true? ($\bar{A}$ denotes the complement of A).

(A) $f(A \cap B) = f(A) \cap f(B)$

(B) $f(\bar{A}) = \overline{f(A)}$

(C) $f(A - B) = f(A) - f(B)$

(D) $f(A \cup B) = f(A) \cup f(B)$

(E) All of these

21. Evaluate $\displaystyle\int_0^\pi \cos^2 nx \; dx$, where n is a positive integer.

(A) $\dfrac{\pi}{2}$

(D) $\dfrac{\pi}{2n}$

(B) π

(E) $n\pi$

(C) $\dfrac{n\pi}{2}$

22. Let R be the ring of integers modulo four. Which of the polynomials shown is irreducible over R?

(A) $x^2 + x + 2$

(D) $x^3 - 3$

(B) $x^2 + x + 3$

(E) $x^4 + 3$

(C) $x^2 + 3x - 2$

23. In a circle of radius $\dfrac{4}{\pi}$ find the area between an arc of length 2 and its chord.

(A) $\dfrac{4}{\pi}\left[1 - \dfrac{2}{\pi}\right]$

(D) $\dfrac{4}{\pi}$

(B) $\dfrac{2}{\pi} - \dfrac{4}{\pi^2}$

(E) $\dfrac{8}{\pi}$

(C) $\dfrac{2}{\pi}$

24. Let $f_n (x) = x^n$ on $[0, 1]$ and $f(x) = \lim\limits_{n \to \infty} f_n (x)$. Which of the following is true?

(A) f is constant.

(B) f is monotone.

(C) $\{f_n\}$ converges uniformly to f.

(D) Both (A) and (B)

(E) Both (B) and (C)

25. Find $\lim\limits_{x \to \infty} \dfrac{(e^x + e^{-x})}{2 - 3e^x}$.

(A) 0   (D) -2

(B) $\dfrac{1}{2}$ (E) $-\dfrac{1}{3}$

(C) Undefined

26. The column space of a 5 x 6 matrix is spanned by the vectors $(1,0,0,0,0), (0,0,1,0,0)$, and $(2,0,3,0,0)$. Find the dimension of the solution space of the matrix.

(A) 3   (D) 2

(B) 4   (E) 5

(C) 6

27. For $f(x,y) = x^2 + y^2$, find the rate of change of f at (1,2,5) in the direction $\overline{v} = 3\hat{i} - 4\hat{j}$.

(A) -2

(D) -13

(B) -10

(E) None of these

(C) -5

28. Which pair of the following elements of the symmetric group, S_4, has a product in the alternating group A_4?

(i) $\begin{pmatrix} 1 & 2 & 3 & 4 \\ 3 & 1 & 2 & 4 \end{pmatrix}$ (ii) $\begin{pmatrix} 1 & 2 & 3 & 4 \\ 3 & 2 & 1 & 4 \end{pmatrix}$ (iii) $\begin{pmatrix} 1 & 2 & 3 & 4 \\ 4 & 3 & 2 & 1 \end{pmatrix}$

(A) (i), (ii)

(D) both (i), (ii) and (i), (iii)

(B) (i), (iii)

(E) both (i), (ii) and (ii), (iii)

(C) (ii), (iii)

29. All functions, f, defined on the xy-plane such that
$$\frac{\partial f}{\partial x} = y^2(3x^2 + y^2) \quad \text{and} \quad \frac{\partial f}{\partial y} = 2xy(x^2 + 2y^2)$$
are given by

(A) $x^2y^3 + xy^4 + C$

(B) $xy^2(x^2 + y^2) + C$

175

(C) $x^2y(x^2 + y^2) + C$

(D) $x^4y + x^2y^3 + C$

(E) $xy(x^3 + y^3) + C$

30.   The moment with respect to the yz plane of the volume in the first octant bounded by the paraboloid $z = x^2 + y^2$ and the plane $z = 4$ is written as an integral in cylindrical coordinates as $\iiint\limits_V F(z, r, \theta)\, dz\, dr\, d\theta$. Find $F(z, r, \theta)$.

(A) $r \cos \theta$ (D) $r^2 \sin \theta$

(B) $r \sin \theta$ (E) $r^2 \cos \theta$

(C) $rz \cos \theta$

31.   In the solution of the differential equation $xy^2 dx = dy - x\, dx$ satisfying the initial condition $y(0) = -1$, find y when $x = \sqrt{\pi}$

(A) 0   (D) $\dfrac{\pi}{4}$

(B) –1   (E) $-\dfrac{\pi}{4}$

(C) 1

32. The set of all points in the plane satisfying $y = x \sin\left(\frac{1}{x}\right)$ together with the origin

    (A)   is compact but not connected

    (B)   is connected but not compact

    (C)   is compact and connected

    (D)   contains an open set

    (E)   does not contain all of its limit points.

33. A regular deck of 52 cards contains 4 suits of 13 denominations; $2, 3, \ldots, 10, J, Q, K, A$. In how many ways may we select a subset of 5 cards containing exactly 3 of the same denomination? In the answers below, $\cdot$ represents multiplication as usual.

    (A) $24 \cdot 47 \cdot 52$ (D) $39 \cdot 47 \cdot 48$

    (B) $47 \cdot 48 \cdot 52$ (E) $6 \cdot 47 \cdot 48 \cdot 52$

    (C) $24 \cdot 39 \cdot 47$

34. Find the integrating factor for the linear equation
$$xy' - 2y = x^2 .$$

    (A) x^{-2} (D) x

(B) e^{-2x} (E) x^2

(C) e^{2x}

35.   If T is a linear transformation mapping vectors (1,0,0), (0,1,0),
      and (0,0,1) to the vectors (1,2,3), (2,3,1), and (1,1,–2) respec-
      tively, which vector is the image of the vector (3,–2,1) under T?

(A) (1,1,7)   (D) (0,1,9)

(B) (1,0,5)   (E) (1,7,0)

(C) (0,1,5)

36.   If the ninth partial sum of the series $\displaystyle\sum_{n=1}^{\infty} \frac{(-1)^n}{n^2}$ is used to
      approximate its sum, which statement about E, the sum minus
      the approximation, is true?

(A) $E > .01$ (D) $-.01 < E < 0$

(B) $0 < E < .01$ (E) $E < -1/81$

(C) $E < -.01$

37.   The base ten number, 73, is given in binary as

(A) 10001001   (D) 101001

(B) 1001001   (E) 101011

(C) 10010001

38. For $f(x) = x^3 - 3x^2 + k$ on [1,3], the maximum and minimum
     values have the same absolute value. Find k.

(A) 4   (D) 1

(B) 3   (E) None of these

(C) 2

39. A regular polygon has ten times as many diagonals as it has
     vertices. How many sides does it have?

(A) 17   (D) 23

(B) 19   (E) None of these

(C) 21

40. An altitude is drawn to the hypotenuse of the triangle as shown.
     Find the ratio of the areas of the two smaller triangles.

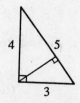

(A) $\dfrac{9}{16}$

(D) $\dfrac{4}{5}$

(B) $\dfrac{3}{4}$

(E) 1

(C) $\dfrac{3}{5}$

41. The number of different ways, not counting rotations, to seat 6 different people around a circular table is

(A) 720

(D) 180

(B) 60

(E) 120

(C) 360

42. Find the average value of the function $f(x) = \sqrt{4 - x^2}$ on $[0,2]$.

(A) 1

(D) $\dfrac{\pi}{2}$

(B) $\dfrac{3}{2}$

(E) None of these

(C) $\dfrac{\pi}{4}$

43. Let $F(x)$ represent the Fourier series of the periodic extension of the function $f(x) = x^2$ on the interval, $(0,2)$. Find $F(4)$.

(A) 16

(D) 8

(B) 2   (E) Undefined

(C) 4

44. Let f be a function on $[0,\infty)$ such that for each point in its graph, $(x,y) = (y^2, y)$. At how many points must each such f have a limit?

(A) 1   (D) 4

(B) 2   (E) Infinitely many

(C) 3

45. Given that $\{x_n\}$ is a bounded, divergent, infinite sequence of real numbers, which of the following must be true?

(A) $\{x_n\}$ contains infinitely many convergent subsequences

(B) $\{x_n\}$ contains convergent subsequences with different limits.

(C) $\left\{y_n = \min_{k \le n} x_k\right\}$ is convergent.

(D) All of the above

(E) (A) and (C) only

46. Let p, q, r, and s be statements with negations $\bar{p}$, $\bar{q}$, $\bar{r}$, and $\bar{s}$. If p implies q, r implies s, and $\bar{p}$ implies $\bar{q}$ and $\bar{r}$, which statements below must be true?

   I. $\bar{p}$ and $\bar{q}$ are equivalent

   II. $\bar{r}$ implies $\bar{s}$

   III. r implies q

   (A) I   (D) I and II

   (B) II   (E) I and III

   (C) III

47. Given $|x|$, $|y| \leq 2$ where x, y are real and $|x| \neq |y|$, we state

   I. $|x^2 - y^2| \geq 1$ if and only if $|x+y||x-y| \geq 1$,

   II. $|x+y||x-y| \geq 1$ if and only if $|x-y| \geq \dfrac{1}{|x+y|}$

   III. $|x-y| \geq \dfrac{1}{|x+y|}$ if and only if $|x-y| \geq \dfrac{1}{|x|+|y|}$

   IV. $|x-y| \geq \dfrac{1}{|x|+|y|}$ if and only if $|x-y| \geq \dfrac{1}{4}$

   Find all the general true statements above.

   (A) (I)   (D) (I), (II), and (III)

   (B) (II)   (E) (I), (II), and (IV)

   (C) (I) and (II)

48. In a sequence of consecutive throws of a die, find the probability that six will show before a one or a two.

(A) $\dfrac{1}{6}$ (D) $\dfrac{5}{6}$

(B) $\dfrac{1}{2}$ (E) $\dfrac{1}{3}$

(C) $\dfrac{2}{3}$

49. Given $x^2z - 2yz^2 + xy = 0$, find $\dfrac{\partial x}{\partial z}$ at $(1, 1, 1)$.

(A) 0 (D) 1

(B) $\dfrac{4}{3}$ (E) None of these

(C) -1

50. All commutators in a group, G, are of the form $aba^{-1}b^{-1}$. The inverse of this commutator is

(A) the identity element (D) $aba^{-1}b^{-1}$

(B) $a^{-1}b^{-1}ab$ (E) $b^{-1}a^{-1}ba$

(C) $bab^{-1}a^{-1}$

51. If H is a left ideal continuing the identity element of a ring R, then

(A) $RH = H$ 　　　　　　　(D) Both (B) and (C)

(B) $HR = H$ 　　　　　　　(E) Both (A) and (C)

(C) $HH = H$

52. Let C_n be a sequence of closed, bounded, nonempty intervals in the real line with the usual topology. The intervals are also nested in the sense that $C_{n+1} \subseteq C_n$. Which of the following is true of the intersection

$$S = \bigcap_{k=1}^{\infty} C_k$$

(A) S may be open or closed.

(B) S may be empty.

(C) S must be nonempty and closed.

(D) S must contain an interval.

(E) S must not contain an interval.

53. Find the best statement describing the output that the following subroutine, S, (flow chart) returns to the main program which provides the array $X(I)$.

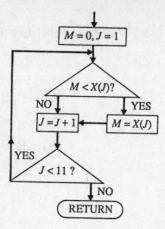

(A) S returns the minimum of the first 10 values of any $X(I)$

(B) S returns the maximum of the first 11 values of any $X(I)$

(C) S returns the maximum of the first 10 values of any positive $X(J)$

(D) S returns the minimum of the first 11 values of any $X(I)$

(E) S returns the maximum of the first 10 values of any $X(I)$ if one of these values is nonnegative.

54. In drawing two balls, from an urn containing 10 balls of each of the colors, red, white, and blue, find the probability of getting two different colors.

(A) $\dfrac{2}{3}$

(D) $\dfrac{20}{29}$

(B) $\dfrac{1}{3}$

(E) None of these

(C) $\dfrac{10}{29}$

55. A root of the polynomial $x^3 - 3x^2 + 5x - 3$ is

(A) -1

(D) $1 - \sqrt{2i}$

(B) $2 + \sqrt{2i}$

(E) 3

(C) $1 - \sqrt{8i}$

56. Find the fifth derivative, $f^{(5)}(2)$, of the given

$$f(x) = \sum_{n=0}^{\infty} \frac{(x-2)^n}{2^n(n+1)}$$

(A) 0

(D) $\dfrac{3}{4}$

(B) $\dfrac{1}{32}$

(E) $\dfrac{5}{8}$

(C) $\dfrac{1}{192}$

57. Let a and b be constants. If $f(x) = ae^{-x^2} + bx\tan x - |x|$ and if $f(7) = 5$, then $f(-7)$ is

(A) 5

(C) -2

(B) -5

(D) Undefined

(E) Not uniquely determined by the information given.

58. If the determinants $|A| = 3$ and $|B| = 2$, find $|2(AB)^{-1}|$ for 4 x 4 matrices A and B.

(A) $\frac{1}{3}$

(D) $\frac{8}{3}$

(B) $\frac{2}{3}$

(E) 12

(C) $\frac{4}{3}$

59. Let x and y be integers such that $7x + 3y$ is divisible by 13. For which value of k must $8x + ky$ by divisible by 13?

(A) 11

(D) 5

(B) 9

(E) 3

(C) 7

60. In Euler's method of tangents for approximating points on the solution curve of $x\,dy - (x + y)\,dx = 0$, $y(1) = 1$, find the approximation of $y(1.2)$ using two steps of length 0.1.

(A) $\frac{31}{22}$

(D) 2

(B) $\frac{7}{5}$

(E) $\frac{3}{2}$

(C) $\frac{29}{20}$

61. Find the number of distinct divisors of 1440.

   (A) 48   (D) 24

   (B) 36   (E) 10

   (C) 30

62. S is a set containing exactly 10 points. C is a collection of subsets of S. Find the maximum number of subsets that C may contain and satisfy the requirement that the intersection of all the subsets in C is nonempty.

   (A) 255   (D) 512

   (B) 256   (E) 1023

   (C) 511

63. Given that $f(x)$ and $g(x)$ are independent solutions of a linear homogeneous differential equation on (a, b), which of the following must also be solutions?

   (A) 0   (D) Both (A) and (B)

   (B) $2 f(x) - 3 g(x)$ (E) Both (B) and (C)

   (C) $f(x) g(x)$

64. Let $A = \begin{pmatrix} 1 & 2 \\ 3 & 4 \end{pmatrix}$ and let I be an identity matrix. Which matrix polynomial is zero?

(A) $A^2 - 10A + I$ (D) $A^2 + 5A - 2I$

(B) $A^2 - 10A$ (E) $A^2 + 5A + 2I$

(C) $A^2 - 5A - 2I$

65. Which of the following subsets of the plane may be translated or rotated into a proper subset of itself?

I. $Z = \{(x, y) \mid x \text{ and } y \text{ are positive integers}\}$

II. $I = \{(x, y) \mid y \geq x\}$

III. $C = \{(\cos n, \sin n) \mid n = 0, 1, 2, \ldots\}$

(A) I and II   (D) I, II, and III

(B) I and III   (E) None of these

(C) II and III

66. Which of the following is an eigenvalue of the matrix

$$A = \begin{pmatrix} 1 & 3 & 3 & 3 \\ 3 & 1 & 3 & 3 \\ 3 & 3 & 1 & 3 \\ 3 & 3 & 3 & 1 \end{pmatrix}$$

(A) -1

(B) -2

(C) 1

(D) 2

(E) 0

GRE MATHEMATICS
TEST IV

ANSWER KEY

1.	A	23.	A	45.	D
2.	E	24.	B	46.	E
3.	B	25.	E	47.	C
4.	A	26.	B	48.	D
5.	D	27.	A	49.	D
6.	C	28.	C	50.	C
7.	D	29.	B	51.	E
8.	D	30.	E	52.	C
9	E	31.	C	53.	E
10.	E	32.	B	54.	D
11.	C	33.	A	55.	D
12.	D	34.	A	56.	E
13.	E	35.	C	57.	A
14.	B	36.	B	58.	D
15.	C	37.	B	59.	B
16.	A	38.	C	60.	A
17.	A	39.	D	61.	B
18.	A	40.	A	62.	D
19.	E	41.	E	63.	D
20.	D	42.	D	64.	C
21.	A	43.	D	65.	A
22.	B	44.	A	66.	B

GRE MATHEMATICS
TEST IV

DETAILED EXPLANATIONS
OF ANSWERS

1.   (A)

When $\bar{x}$ is an eigenvector for matrix, A, then $A\bar{x} = \lambda\bar{x}$ defines the eigenvalue, λ. In this case,

$$A \begin{pmatrix} 1 \\ 2 \\ 3 \end{pmatrix} = \begin{pmatrix} 5 \\ 10 \\ 15 \end{pmatrix} = 5 \begin{pmatrix} 1 \\ 2 \\ 3 \end{pmatrix} \text{ so } \lambda = 5.$$

2.   (E)

The other vertex is $(x, 0, 3)$ and so, using dot products,

$$\cos\left(\frac{\pi}{6}\right) = \sqrt{\frac{3}{4}}$$

$$= \frac{x^2 + 9}{\sqrt{x^2 + 13}\sqrt{x^2 + 9}}$$

$$= \sqrt{\frac{x^2 + 9}{x^2 + 13}}$$

Then $4(x^2 + 9) = 3(x^2 + 13)$ implies $x^2 = 3$ and $x = \sqrt{3}$.

3.   (B)

"Uniform" means that each value has equal probabilty, $\frac{1}{5}$. Then variance of x is

$$E\left(x^2\right) - \left(E(x)\right)^2 = \sum_{x=1}^{5} \frac{x^2}{5} - \left(\sum_{x=1}^{5} \frac{x}{5}\right)^2$$

$$= 11 - 3^2$$

$$= 2.$$

4.   (A)

The parabola is $y^2 = x - 1$ (P) and the hyperbola is $2xy = 1 (H)$. Since the shaded region is above (H) we must have $y > 1/2x$ or $2x > 1/y$. And, since the shaded region is to the right of (P) we must have $x > y^2 + 1$ or $y^2 + 1 < x$. As usual "and" represents intersection.

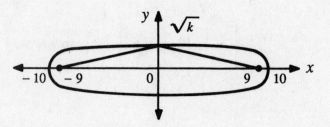

5.   (D)

The vertices from standard form are as shown. The statement implies that the foci must be at $(\pm 9, 0)$. The locus definition of an ellipse implies that $20 = 2\sqrt{k + 9^2}$ so that $100 = k + 9^2$ and $k = 19$.

6.   (C)

Fermat's Little Theorem states that $a^{p-1} \equiv 1 \pmod{p}$ for any prime p and any a which is not divisible by p. Here, the form indicates $p = 11$.

7.   (D)

Since permutations are functions, the "product" is actually a composition and proceeds from right to left. So, $1 \to 3 \to 4$, $2 \to 5 \to 3$, $3 \to 2 \to 1$, $4 \to 1 \to 2$, and $5 \to 4 \to 5$. We get (4 3 1 2 5).

8.   (D)

One can apply DeMorgan's Law which states $\overline{A \cap B} = \overline{A} \cup \overline{B}$. In this case $A = \overline{S}$ so $\overline{A} = \overline{\overline{S}} = S$.

9.   (E)

The ratio test, $\rho = \lim\limits_{n \to \infty} \dfrac{|x - 3|^2 \, n}{4 \cdot (n + 1)} = \left|\dfrac{x - 3}{2}\right|^2 < 1$, implies

$|x - 3| < 2$ or $-2 < x - 3 < 2$ and so $1 < x < 5$. Finally, checking endpoints directly we find for $x = 1$ that

$$2 \sum_{n=1}^{\infty} \frac{(-1)^{3n+1}}{n}$$

converges by the alternating series (Leibniz) test and for $x = 5$ that

$$2 \sum_{n=1}^{\infty} \frac{(-1)^{n}}{n}$$

likewise converges.

10.   (E)

There are two possible parabolic arcs that will contain $(4, 2)$. Either $f(x) = \sqrt{x}$ or $g(x) = \dfrac{x^2}{8}$ will do. $(16, 2)$ lies on the graph of $f(f(x)) = x^{1/4}$ and $(8, 8)$ lies on $g(g(x)) = \dfrac{x^4}{2^9}$.

11.   (C)

The effective rate is $(1 + .01)^4 - 1 = .04060401 \doteq 4.06\%$.

12.   (D)

The symmetric limit for the derivative at $x = 2$ has the form

$$\lim_{x \to 0} \frac{f(2 + x) - f(2 - x)}{2x} = f'(2) = \frac{1}{4}$$

since the tangent line slope is the negative reciprocal of the normal line slope. Since our limit has a reversed numerator and only $\dfrac{1}{2}$ the denominator, it has value $-\dfrac{1}{2}$.

13.   (E)

A single eigenvalue must then be of multiplicity 3 for a 3 x 3 matrix. In general the dimension of the eigenspace may be any number greater than zero and less than or equal to the multiplicity.

14.   (B)

Since $f(e^x) = \sqrt{x}$ we must have $f(x) = f(e^{\log x}) = \sqrt{\log x}$ and here is where $x \geq 1$ is needed for definition of the radical. Since $y = \sqrt{\log x}$ may be solved for $x = e^{y^2} = f^{-1}(y)$ we find that $f^{-1}(x) = e^{x^2}$.

195

15. (C)

The *–identity is 0 since $a*0 = 0*a = a$ for each rational, a. Then the *–inverse of a is found by solving $a*x = a + x - ax = 0$ for $x = \dfrac{a}{(a-1)}$, $a \neq 1$. Now x is an integer when $a = 0$ and $a = 2$ and in no other case.

16. (A)

In general

$$\int_a^b f(x)\ dx = \lim_{n \to \infty} \sum_{k=1}^{n} f(a + k\Delta x)\Delta x \quad \text{where} \quad \Delta x = \frac{(b-a)}{n}.$$

This may be called the limit of the right end point Riemann sum. In this case we let $f(x) = x^2$, $a = 1$, and $b = 3$ so $\Delta x = \dfrac{2}{n}$.

It follows by the fundamental theorem of calculus that the limit is

$$\int_1^3 x^2 dx = \frac{x^3}{3}\bigg|_1^3 = 9 - \frac{1}{3} = \frac{26}{3}.$$

17. (A)

T is representable as a 2 x 3 matrix $\begin{bmatrix} 1 & 1 & 1 \\ 1 & -1 & 0 \end{bmatrix}$.

Then S is an inverse if $TS = I_2 = \begin{bmatrix} 1 & 0 \\ 0 & 1 \end{bmatrix}$.

The given transformation for S are representable as 3 x 2 matrices

$$\begin{bmatrix} 0 & \frac{1}{2} \\ 0 & -\frac{1}{2} \\ 1 & 0 \end{bmatrix} \begin{bmatrix} \frac{1}{2} & \frac{1}{2} \\ \frac{1}{2} & -\frac{1}{2} \\ 0 & -1 \end{bmatrix}, \text{ and } \begin{bmatrix} \frac{1}{3} & 1 \\ \frac{1}{3} & -1 \\ \frac{1}{3} & 0 \end{bmatrix} \text{ respectively.}$$

Direct multiplications show that only (A) is inverse.

18.　(A)

The test for a homomorphism is to show that

$$\left(gh^{-1}\right)\phi = (g\phi)(h\phi)^{-1} \quad \text{for arbitrary } g, h \in G.$$

In this case

$$(g\phi)(h\phi)^{-1} = a^2 g a^2 \left(a^2 h a^2\right)^{-1} = a^2 g a^2 a^{-2} h^{-1} a^{-2} = a^2\left(gh^{-1}\right) a^{-2}$$

which will be $\left(gh^{-1}\right)\phi$ as desired if $a^2 = a^{-2}$ or $a^4 = e$.

19.　(E)

The entry is the cofactor of the entry in row 2 and column 3 divided by the determinant of A . The cofactor is

$$(-1)^5 \begin{vmatrix} 1 & 2 \\ 1 & 1 \end{vmatrix} = 1 \text{ and } |A| = -4.$$

20.　(D)

It is well-known that $f(A \cup B) = f(A) \cup f(B)$. (A) is contradicted by a constant function with disjoint A and B . Well-chosen constant functions and sets will also contradict (B) and (C).

21.　(A)

$$\cos^2 nx = \frac{1 + \cos^2 nx}{2} \quad \text{with integral } \left(\frac{x}{2} + \frac{\sin^2 nx}{4n}\right)\Big|_0^\pi = \frac{\pi}{2}$$

since $\sin^2 n\pi = \sin 0 = 0$ for all n.

22.　(B)

If we represent the polynomial by $p(x)$ then in (A) we find $p(1) = 4 = 0 \pmod 4$ so $p(x)$ is reducible. In (B) we find $p(0) = 3$, $p(1) = 1$, $p(2) = 1$, and $p(3) = 3$ modulo four and so $p(x)$ is irreducible.

23. (A)

The circumference is $2\pi\left(\frac{4}{\pi}\right) = 8$ and so the chord of an arc of length 2 is the hypotenuse of a right triangle of side lengths $\frac{4}{\pi}$ and area $\frac{1}{2}\left(\frac{4}{\pi}\right)^2 = \frac{8}{\pi^2}$. The area of the quarter-circle is $\frac{\pi}{4}\left(\frac{4}{\pi}\right)^2 = \frac{4}{\pi}$ and the desired area is the difference

$$\frac{4}{\pi} - \frac{8}{\pi^2} = \frac{4}{\pi}\left[1 - \frac{2}{\pi}\right].$$

24. (B)

The limit function $f(x) = 0$ for all x in $[0, 1)$ and $f(1) = 1$. Since the uniform limit of continuous functions is always continuous, (C) is impossible.

25. (E)

Dividing both numerator and denominator by e^x results in a determinate form.

26. (B)

Since the third vector is a linear combination of the two elementary basis vectors, the column rank is two. The dimension of the solution space must be $6 - 2 = 4$.

27. (A)

The rate of change is the directional derivative,

$$(f_x\hat{i} + f_y\hat{j}) \cdot \frac{(3\hat{i} - 4\hat{j})}{5} = \frac{(6x - 8y)}{5} = -\frac{10}{5} = -2$$

at $(1, 2, 5)$.

28.   (C)

A_4 is the subgroup of even permutations in S_4. It is easy to inspect that

$$\begin{pmatrix} 1 & 2 & 3 & 4 \\ 3 & 1 & 2 & 4 \end{pmatrix}^3 = \begin{pmatrix} 1 & 2 & 3 & 4 \\ 1 & 2 & 3 & 4 \end{pmatrix} = e, \text{ so (i) is odd.}$$

Likewise $\begin{pmatrix} 1 & 2 & 3 & 4 \\ 3 & 2 & 1 & 4 \end{pmatrix}^2 = e$, so (ii) is even

and $\begin{pmatrix} 1 & 2 & 3 & 4 \\ 3 & 2 & 4 & 1 \end{pmatrix}^3 = e$, so (iii) is odd. The product of odd and

even is odd and the product of odd and odd is even so on (i), (iii) will product an even product.

29.   (B)

By partially integrating the given derivatives we find at first that

$$f(x,y) = \int (3x^2y^2 + y^4)dx = x^3y^2 + xy^4 + g(y)$$

where $g(y)$ can be any function of y. Finding

$$\frac{\partial f}{\partial y} = 2x^3y + 4xy^3 + g'(y)$$

from this representation implies that

$$g'(y) = 0 \text{ so } g(y) = C.$$

So $f(x,y) = x^3y^2 + xy^4 + C = xy^2(x^2 + y^2) + C.$

30.   (E)

The distance (directed) from the yz plane to any point (x,y,z) is the coordinate $x = r\cos\theta$ in cylindrical coordinates. The representation of dV is $rdzdrd\theta$. The integrand must be $r^2\cos\theta$.

31.   (C)

The equation is separable as $x\,dx = \dfrac{dy}{(y^2 + 1)}$ and solved as

$\dfrac{x^2}{2} = \tan^{-1} y + C$ where $y(0) = -1$ implies $C = \dfrac{\pi}{4}$. Then $x =$

$\sqrt{\pi}$ implies $\tan^{-1} y = \dfrac{\pi}{2} - \dfrac{\pi}{4} = \dfrac{\pi}{4}$ and $y = 1$.

32.   (B)

The point $(0, 0)$ connects the well known graph of $x \sin \left(\dfrac{1}{x}\right)$ as shown. Since the domain is $(-\infty, \infty)$, the graph cannot be compact. It is a closed subset since the only missing limit point on the graph of $x \sin \left(\dfrac{1}{x}\right)$ is $(0, 0)$.

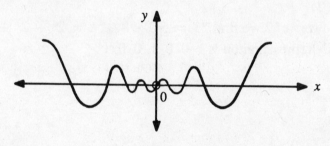

33.   (A)

As subtasks we may first choose any one of 13 denominations and then find 4 different subsets of three of the same denomination. Finally the number of ways to choose the remaining two cards from the 48 not in the selected denomination is $48 \cdot 47/2$. Division by two is required as subsets are desired and so orders of selection should not be counted. The counting principle for products implies the solution $13 \cdot 4 \cdot 14 \cdot 47 = 24 \cdot 47 \cdot 52$.

34.   (A)

In standard form, $y' - \dfrac{2}{x} y = x$ and so the integrating factor is

$$e^{\int -\frac{2}{x}\,dx} = e^{-2\ln x} = e^{\ln x^{-2}} = x^{-2}$$

200

35.   (C)

Since $(3, -2, 1) = 3(1, 0, 0) - 2(0, 1, 0) + 1(0, 0, 1)$ its image must be $3(1, 2, 3) - 2(2, 3, 1) + (1, 1, -2) = (0, 1, 5)$.

36.   (B)

The 9th partial sum of a convergent alternating series with decreasing absolute terms has absolute error less than the 10th term which is $1/100$. Since the approximation ends with a negative term it is less than the sum of the series and so $0 < E < .01$.

37.   (B)

In powers of 2 we find $73 = 64 + 8 + 1 = 2^6 + 2^3 + 2^0$, so the binary representaiton is 1 0 0 1 0 0 1.

38.   (C)

$f'(x) = 3x^2 - 6x = 3x(x - 2)$ and so $x = 2$ is the only critical point in $[1, 3]$. Now $f(1) = k - 2$, $f(2) = k - 4$, and $f(3) = k$. We must require $k = k - 4$ or $k = 4 - k$ and only the latter can be solved with $k = 2$.

39.   (D)

In general an n-gon must have $\binom{n}{2} - n = \dfrac{n(n - 3)}{2}$ diagonals. Note that $\binom{n}{2}$ counts the number of pairs of vertices and all but n of these pairs (sides) represent diagonals. Now to have 10 times as many diagonals requires $\dfrac{(n - 3)}{2} = 10$ and $n = 23$.

40. (A)

All three triangles are similar since they are right triangles sharing an acute angle. The dimensions of the small triangles are in ratio 3:4 as seen in the hypotenuses. Hence the areas must be in ratio $\left(\dfrac{3}{4}\right)^2 = \dfrac{9}{16}$.

41. (E)

Not considering the circular layout there are $6! = 720$ permutations. These can be grouped into 6 cyclic permutations per group each representing equivalent circular arrangements. So we get $\dfrac{6!}{6} = 120$.

42. (D)

The average value is defined as the area under the curve (in this case a quarter circle of radius 2) divided by the base interval length. We get $\dfrac{\pi 2^2}{8} = \dfrac{\pi}{2}$. The integration approach to the area is much harder than this approach.

43. (D)

It is well known that $F(x)$ converges to the average of its left and right hand limits at all points. Here,

$$F(4) = \frac{F(4^-) + F(4^+)}{2} = \frac{0+4}{2} = 2.$$

44.   (A)

Of course many functions satisfy the coordinate criteria but all must have limit zero at $x = 0$. An example where this is the only limit is $f(x) = \sqrt{x}$ if x is rational but $f(x) = -\sqrt{x}$ if x is irrational. All points lie on the parabola $x = y^2$.

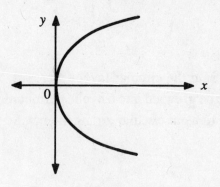

45.   (D)

Bounded sequences always contain convergent subsequences and the related sequence in (C) is always convergent. Any convergent subsequence contains infinitely many subsequences all converging to the same limit. Since $\{x^n\}$ is divergent we must have different limits for $\min\limits_{k \leq n} x_k$ and $\max\limits_{k \leq n} x_k$.

46.   (E)

"$\bar{r}$ implies $\bar{s}$" is the negation of "r implies s" and is equivalent to its converse which is not generally true. The contrapositive of "$\bar{p}$ implies $\bar{q}$ and $\bar{r}$" is "q or r implies p" and these are equivalent. So q implies p as q satisfies "q or r" and hence I. is true. Also r implies p and, via the transitivity property, since p implies q we must have "r implies q" and III. is true.

47. (C)

I. follows as true since in general $|ab| = |a||b|$.

II. is also true since $|x| \neq |y|$ implies that $|x + y| > 0$.

III. is not generally true. The triangle inequality states that

$|x + y| \leq |x| + |y|$ in general but $|x - y| \geq \dfrac{1}{(|x|+|y|)}$

fails to imply that $|x - y| \geq \dfrac{1}{|x + y|} \geq \dfrac{1}{(|x|+|y|)}$.

For example, $x = \dfrac{4}{5}$ and $y = -\dfrac{3}{5}$ finds $|x - y| < \dfrac{1}{|x + y|}$.

Similarly, $|x - y| \geq \dfrac{1}{4}$ fails to imply $|x - y| \geq \dfrac{1}{(|x|+|y|)}$

so IV. is false.

48. (E)

Let N represent the event "not one, two, or six" and let S represent the event "six." Then the probability is the sum of the probabilities of the sequences of events, $NN...NS$, where the number of N's varies as $0,1,2,...,k,....$ The sequence probabilities are $\left(\dfrac{1}{2}\right)^k\left(\dfrac{1}{6}\right)$ and the sum is geometric with value $\left(\dfrac{1}{6}\right)\left(1 - \dfrac{1}{2}\right) = \dfrac{1}{3}$.

49. (D)

Using $F(x,y,z) = x^2z - 2yz^2 + xy$ we find

$$\frac{\partial x}{\partial z} = -\frac{F_z}{F_x} = -\frac{[x^2 - 4yz]}{[2xz + y]}.$$

At $(1,1,1)$ the value is $-\dfrac{(-3)}{3} = 1$.

50.   (C)

The general idea is that inverses of products are products of inverses in the reverse order.

51.   (E)

A left ideal is a subring with the additional property that for each $r \in R$ and $h \in H$ we have $rh \in H$ so $RH \subseteq H$. Since $eH = H$ we have $H \subseteq RH$ so $RH = H$. For any subring, $HH = H$.

52.   (C)

This is a fundamental result of real analysis. The example with $C_n = \left[0, \frac{1}{n}\right]$ yields singleton $S = \{0\}$ which is a counterexample to (D). Boundedness is necessary or $C_n = [n, \infty)$ implies $S = 0$.

53.   (E)

Only 10 values of $X(I)$ are examined since $J = 11$ initiates a return. $M = 0$ is replaced only when $X(J) > 0$ so negative entries in the array are not further processed. Whenever a greater positive value of $X(J)$ occurs, M takes this value. Hence the last statement is strongest as minimums or maximums in general may be negative and a strictly positive array is not required as in (C).

54.   (D)

Simplest is a conditional probability approach on the second ball drawn when two colors are permitted (20 balls) out of the remaining 29 balls following the first draw.

55.   (D)

By inspection, the sum of the coefficients is zero so 1 is a root. Synthetic division implies the quadratic quotient is $x^2 - 2x + 3$ with roots

$$\frac{(2 \pm \sqrt{-8})}{2} = 1 \pm \sqrt{2}\,i \,.$$

56.   (E)

The main theoretical point is that the coefficient of $(x-2)^n$ is $\frac{f^{(n)}(2)}{n!}$ and here, with $n = 5$, we get

$$\frac{1}{32 \cdot 6} = \frac{f^{(5)}(2)}{5!} \text{ so } f^{(5)}(2) = \frac{120}{32 \cdot 6} = \frac{5}{8} \,.$$

57.   (A)

Since our function is "even" we know that $f(-7) = f(7)$.

58.   (D)

$$\left| 2(AB)^{-1} \right| = \frac{2^4}{|AB|} = \frac{2^4}{(|A||B|)} = \frac{2^4}{6} = \frac{8}{3} \,.$$

59.   (B)

Using modular artithmetic, we find that

$$7x + 3y \equiv 0 \pmod{13} \text{ and } 8x + ky \equiv 0 \pmod{13},$$

so by subtraction

$$x + (k - 3)y \equiv 0 \pmod{13} \,.$$

Multiplying by 6, we have

$$6x + 6(k - 3)y \equiv 0 \pmod{13} \,.$$

Adding $7x + 3y \equiv 0 \pmod{13}$ gives

$$13x + 6(k-3)y + 3y \equiv 0 \pmod{13}$$

$$\Rightarrow 13x + [6(k-3)+3]y \equiv 0 \pmod{13} .$$

$$\Rightarrow (6k-15)y \equiv 0 \pmod{13}$$

$$\Rightarrow (6k-2)y \equiv 0 \pmod{13}$$

Since y can vary, we require
$$(6k-2) \equiv 0 \pmod{13}$$
and by inspection of the choices, we find that $k = 9$ works, since

$$6 \cdot 9 - 2 = 54 - 2 = 52 = 13 \cdot 4 \equiv 0 \pmod{13} .$$

60. (A)

The approximating form is $y_{n+1} = y_n + y'(x_n)\Delta x$.
In this case
$$\Delta x = 0.1, x_0 = y_0 = 1 \quad \text{and} \quad y' = \frac{(x+y)}{x} .$$

Then
$$y_1 = 1 + (2)(0.1)$$

$$= 1.2 .$$

So
$$y_2 = 1.2 + \left[\frac{(1.1+1.2)}{1.1}\right](0.1)$$

$$= \frac{6}{5} + \frac{23}{100}$$

$$= \frac{155}{110}$$

$$= \frac{31}{22} .$$

61. (B)

Since 1440 has prime factorization $2^5 \cdot 3^2 \cdot 5^1$, the number of divisors is $(6)(3)(2) = 36$. This follows by a simple counting scheme in that divisors of 1440 must have from 0 to 5 factors that are 2, 0 to 2 factors that are 3, and 0 or 1 factors which are 5. The divisor, 1, corresponds to the case when no prime factors are chosen.

62. (D)

The smallest intersection that is nonempty will contain one point, x, and so we only need count the number of subsets of S that contain x. Each such set will be the union of $\{x\}$ with any subset containing any remaining elements. There are $2^9 = 512$ such subsets. So, the answer is (D).

63. (D)

Linear combinations provide all solutions in the form $c_1 f(x) + c_2 g(x)$ where c_1, c_2 are constants.

64. (C)

The characteristic polynomial of A is $|\lambda I - A| = \lambda^2 - 5\lambda - 2$. The Cayley-Hamilton Theorem implies that $A^2 - 5A - 2I = 0$.

65. (A)

The translation $(x, y) \rightarrow (x, y + 1)$ works for both I and II. The rotation through one radian maps $(\cos n, \sin n)$ into $(\cos (n + 1), \sin (n + 1))$ leaving the point $(1,0)$ out of the image. No point can map onto the image since n radians cannot equal $2k\pi$ radians as π is irrational.

66.   (B)

An eigenvalue, λ, must satisfy the equation $|A - \lambda I| = 0$. We see that $A - (-2I)$ has all rows equal (all 3's) and so its determinant is immediately zero.

GRE

MATH TEST

TEST V

THE GRADUATE RECORD EXAMINATION

MATH TEST

ANSWER SHEET

1. Ⓐ Ⓑ Ⓒ Ⓓ Ⓔ
2. Ⓐ Ⓑ Ⓒ Ⓓ Ⓔ
3. Ⓐ Ⓑ Ⓒ Ⓓ Ⓔ
4. Ⓐ Ⓑ Ⓒ Ⓓ Ⓔ
5. Ⓐ Ⓑ Ⓒ Ⓓ Ⓔ
6. Ⓐ Ⓑ Ⓒ Ⓓ Ⓔ
7. Ⓐ Ⓑ Ⓒ Ⓓ Ⓔ
8. Ⓐ Ⓑ Ⓒ Ⓓ Ⓔ
9. Ⓐ Ⓑ Ⓒ Ⓓ Ⓔ
10. Ⓐ Ⓑ Ⓒ Ⓓ Ⓔ
11. Ⓐ Ⓑ Ⓒ Ⓓ Ⓔ
12. Ⓐ Ⓑ Ⓒ Ⓓ Ⓔ
13. Ⓐ Ⓑ Ⓒ Ⓓ Ⓔ
14. Ⓐ Ⓑ Ⓒ Ⓓ Ⓔ
15. Ⓐ Ⓑ Ⓒ Ⓓ Ⓔ
16. Ⓐ Ⓑ Ⓒ Ⓓ Ⓔ
17. Ⓐ Ⓑ Ⓒ Ⓓ Ⓔ
18. Ⓐ Ⓑ Ⓒ Ⓓ Ⓔ
19. Ⓐ Ⓑ Ⓒ Ⓓ Ⓔ
20. Ⓐ Ⓑ Ⓒ Ⓓ Ⓔ
21. Ⓐ Ⓑ Ⓒ Ⓓ Ⓔ
22. Ⓐ Ⓑ Ⓒ Ⓓ Ⓔ

23. Ⓐ Ⓑ Ⓒ Ⓓ Ⓔ
24. Ⓐ Ⓑ Ⓒ Ⓓ Ⓔ
25. Ⓐ Ⓑ Ⓒ Ⓓ Ⓔ
26. Ⓐ Ⓑ Ⓒ Ⓓ Ⓔ
27. Ⓐ Ⓑ Ⓒ Ⓓ Ⓔ
28. Ⓐ Ⓑ Ⓒ Ⓓ Ⓔ
29. Ⓐ Ⓑ Ⓒ Ⓓ Ⓔ
30. Ⓐ Ⓑ Ⓒ Ⓓ Ⓔ
31. Ⓐ Ⓑ Ⓒ Ⓓ Ⓔ
32. Ⓐ Ⓑ Ⓒ Ⓓ Ⓔ
33. Ⓐ Ⓑ Ⓒ Ⓓ Ⓔ
34. Ⓐ Ⓑ Ⓒ Ⓓ Ⓔ
35. Ⓐ Ⓑ Ⓒ Ⓓ Ⓔ
36. Ⓐ Ⓑ Ⓒ Ⓓ Ⓔ
37. Ⓐ Ⓑ Ⓒ Ⓓ Ⓔ
38. Ⓐ Ⓑ Ⓒ Ⓓ Ⓔ
39. Ⓐ Ⓑ Ⓒ Ⓓ Ⓔ
40. Ⓐ Ⓑ Ⓒ Ⓓ Ⓔ
41. Ⓐ Ⓑ Ⓒ Ⓓ Ⓔ
42. Ⓐ Ⓑ Ⓒ Ⓓ Ⓔ
43. Ⓐ Ⓑ Ⓒ Ⓓ Ⓔ
44. Ⓐ Ⓑ Ⓒ Ⓓ Ⓔ

45. Ⓐ Ⓑ Ⓒ Ⓓ Ⓔ
46. Ⓐ Ⓑ Ⓒ Ⓓ Ⓔ
47. Ⓐ Ⓑ Ⓒ Ⓓ Ⓔ
48. Ⓐ Ⓑ Ⓒ Ⓓ Ⓔ
49. Ⓐ Ⓑ Ⓒ Ⓓ Ⓔ
50. Ⓐ Ⓑ Ⓒ Ⓓ Ⓔ
51. Ⓐ Ⓑ Ⓒ Ⓓ Ⓔ
52. Ⓐ Ⓑ Ⓒ Ⓓ Ⓔ
53. Ⓐ Ⓑ Ⓒ Ⓓ Ⓔ
54. Ⓐ Ⓑ Ⓒ Ⓓ Ⓔ
55. Ⓐ Ⓑ Ⓒ Ⓓ Ⓔ
56. Ⓐ Ⓑ Ⓒ Ⓓ Ⓔ
57. Ⓐ Ⓑ Ⓒ Ⓓ Ⓔ
58. Ⓐ Ⓑ Ⓒ Ⓓ Ⓔ
59. Ⓐ Ⓑ Ⓒ Ⓓ Ⓔ
60. Ⓐ Ⓑ Ⓒ Ⓓ Ⓔ
61. Ⓐ Ⓑ Ⓒ Ⓓ Ⓔ
62. Ⓐ Ⓑ Ⓒ Ⓓ Ⓔ
63. Ⓐ Ⓑ Ⓒ Ⓓ Ⓔ
64. Ⓐ Ⓑ Ⓒ Ⓓ Ⓔ
65. Ⓐ Ⓑ Ⓒ Ⓓ Ⓔ
66. Ⓐ Ⓑ Ⓒ Ⓓ Ⓔ

GRE MATHEMATICS
TEST V

TIME: 2 hours and 50 minutes
66 Questions

DIRECTIONS: Choose the best answer for each question and mark the letter of your selection on the corresponding answer sheet.

1. $\lim\limits_{n \to \infty} \left(\prod\limits_{m=2}^{n} \left(1 - \frac{1}{m} \right) \right)$ is equal to

   (A) 1   (D) e^{-1}

   (B) e (E) 0

   (C) π

2. If $n = 2^{20}$, then what is the sum of all integer divisors d of n, $1 \le d \le n$?

   (A) $2^{22} + 1$ (D) $2^{21} + 1$

   (B) $2^{22} - 1$ (E) $2^{20} + 1$

   (C) $2^{21} - 1$

3. If $A = \begin{bmatrix} 1 & 2 \\ 3 & 4 \end{bmatrix}$ and A^{-1} is the inverse of A, what is the determinant of A^{-1} ?

(A) -2

(D) $-\dfrac{1}{2}$

(B) -5

(E) 2

(C) $\dfrac{1}{5}$

4. Which of the following complex numbers is equal to $(1+i)^{\frac{4}{3}}$?

(A) $2^{\frac{2}{3}}\left(-\dfrac{1}{2} + i\,\dfrac{\sqrt{3}}{2}\right)$

(D) $2^{\frac{2}{3}}\left(\sqrt{\dfrac{3}{2}} - i\,\dfrac{1}{2}\right)$

(B) $2^{\frac{2}{3}}\left(\dfrac{1}{2} + i\,\dfrac{\sqrt{3}}{2}\right)$

(E) $2^{\frac{2}{3}}\left(\sqrt{\dfrac{2}{3}} + i\,\dfrac{1}{\sqrt{3}}\right)$

(C) $2^{\frac{2}{3}}\left(\sqrt{\dfrac{3}{2}} + i\,\dfrac{1}{2}\right)$

5. What is the value of $5 \log_{15}(15x) - \log_{15} x^5$?

(A) 5

(D) $5 \log_{15} \dfrac{15}{x}$

(B) $105x^2$

(E) $5 \log_{15} 4x$

(C) 105

212

6. Find the value of $\displaystyle\lim_{x \to 0} \frac{1}{x} \int_0^x (1 + \sin t)^t \, dt$.

(A) 1

(D) $\dfrac{2}{3}$

(B) $\dfrac{3}{2}$

(E) e^{-1}

(C) e

7. What is the value of $\displaystyle\lim_{h \to 0} \frac{\sqrt{3 + h} - \sqrt{3}}{h}$?

(A) 0

(D) $\dfrac{\sqrt{3}}{6}$

(B) $\dfrac{\sqrt{3}}{3}$

(E) ∞

(C) Undefined

8. How many solutions are there of the equation

$$\cos^2 x = \cos x \text{ if } 0 \leq x \leq 2\pi ?$$

(A) No solutions

(D) 3

(B) 1

(E) 4

(C) 2

9. Given a set S of strictly negative real numbers, what is the greatest lower bound of the set $\{\, x \text{ real} \mid x \text{ is an upper bound of } S \,\}$?

(A) 0

(D) $-\infty$

(B) Infimum of s

(E) Does not exist

(C) supremum of s

10. The partial derivative $\dfrac{\partial}{\partial y}\left[\displaystyle\int_0^1 e^{y \sin x}\, dx\right]$ is equal to

(A) $\displaystyle\int_0^1 e^{y \sin x}\, dx$

(D) $\displaystyle\int_0^1 e^{y \sin x}(\sin y)\, dy$

(B) $\displaystyle\int_0^1 \cos x\, e^{y \sin x}\, dx$

(E) $\displaystyle\int_0^1 y \sin x\, e^{y \sin x}\, dx$

(C) $\displaystyle\int_0^1 \sin x\, e^{y \sin x}\, dx$

11. If $f(x,y) = \dfrac{2}{x^2} + 3xy$ for $x \neq 0$, and the gradient of f at (r, s) has length r, then which of the following equations is satisfied by r and s?

(A) $16 + 24\, r^3 s + 9 r^6 s^2 + 8\, r^8 = 0$

(B) $24 + 9\, r^3 s + r^6 s^2 + 8\, r^8 = 0$

(C) $16 - r^3 s + 9 r^6 s^2 + 8\, r^8 = 0$

(D) $16 - 24\, r^3 s + 9 r^6 s^2 + r^8 = 0$

(E) $16 - 24\, r^3 s + 9 r^6 s^2 + 8\, r^8 = 0$

12. Given $f(x) = \dfrac{x}{x-1}$, find an expression of $f(3x)$ in term of $f(x)$.

(A) $\dfrac{3f(x)}{3f(x) - 1}$

(D) $\dfrac{3f(x)}{2f(x) + 1}$

(B) $\dfrac{3f(x)}{3f(x) - 3}$

(E) $\dfrac{3f(x)}{2f(x) - 1}$

(C) $3f(x) - 1$

13. Let $S_n = -1 + 2\left(\dfrac{2}{3}\right) - 3\left(\dfrac{2}{3}\right)^2 + \ldots + (-1)^n n \left(\dfrac{2}{3}\right)^{n-1}$.

What is $\lim\limits_{n \to \infty} S_n$?

(A) $-\dfrac{9}{25}$

(D) $-\dfrac{25}{9}$

(B) $\dfrac{9}{25}$

(E) $\dfrac{5}{3}$

(C) $\dfrac{25}{9}$

14. If the domain of function $y = f(x)$ is $[0, 1]$, then what is the domain of function $f(x + \frac{1}{4}) + f(x - \frac{1}{4})$?

(A) $[0, 1]$

(D) $[\frac{1}{4}, \frac{3}{4}]$

(B) $(0, 1)$

(E) $(\frac{1}{4}, \frac{3}{4})$

(C) $[0, \frac{1}{2}]$

15. $\left[\sqrt{2}(1 - i) \right]^{48} =$

(A) 2^{24}

(D) -2^{48}

(B) -2^{24}

(E) $2^{24}(1 - i)$

(C) 2^{48}

16. The solution of differential equation $y\, dx + \sqrt{x^2 + 1}\, dy = 0$ is:

(A) $y\left(x + \sqrt{x^2 + 1}\right) = c$

(B) $y\left(1 + \sqrt{x^2 + 1}\right) = c$

(C) $xy + \sqrt{x^2 + 1} = c$

(D) $yx + \dfrac{y}{\sqrt{x^2 + 1}} = c$

(E) $yx + \dfrac{x}{\sqrt{x^2 + 1}} = c$

17. The length of the curve $x(t) = e^t \cos t$, $y(t) = -e^t \sin t$ for $0 \leq t \leq 1$ is

(A) $2(e-1)$

(D) $2e$

(B) $\sqrt{2}(e-1)$

(E) $\sqrt{2}$

(C) e

18. The normal line to the graph of $3x^2 + 4x^2y + xy^2 = 8$ at $(1, 1)$ intersects the x-axis at $x =$

(A) $\dfrac{3}{2}$

(D) $-\dfrac{2}{3}$

(B) $-\dfrac{3}{2}$

(E) $-\dfrac{2}{5}$

(C) $\dfrac{5}{2}$

19. Let $F(uv) = uv$ where $u = u(t)$ and $v = v(t)$. If $u(1) = 1$, $v(1) = 2$, $v'(1) = 1$ and $u'(1) = 2$, then $\dfrac{dF}{dt}$ at $t = 1$ is equal to

(A) 0

(D) 4

(B) 1

(E) 5

(C) 3

20. The number of points of discontinuity of the function

$$f(x) = \begin{cases} x+2 & \text{if } x \leq 0 \\ 1 & \text{if } 0 < x \leq 2 \\ x-6 & \text{if } 2 < x \leq 5 \\ (6-x)^2 & \text{if } 5 < x \end{cases}$$ is equal to

(A) 5

(B) 4

(C) 3

(D) 2

(E) 1

21. The solution set for the inequality $\dfrac{1}{x-2} < \dfrac{1}{x+3}$ is

(A) $(-3, -2)$

(B) $(-3, 2)$

(C) $(2, 3)$

(D) $(-2, 2)$

(E) $(0, 2)$

22. If $g\left(\dfrac{3+2x}{4}\right) = 1 - x$, for $-\infty < x < \infty$, then $g\left(\dfrac{7z-8}{4}\right)$ is equal to

(A) $-\dfrac{13+7z}{4}$

(B) $\dfrac{13}{2} - \dfrac{7z}{2}$

(C) $\dfrac{7-13z}{2}$

(D) $\dfrac{7+13z}{2}$

(E) $7z + 13$

23. If $f'(e^x) = 1 + x$, then $f(x) =$

(A) $1 + e^x + c$

(D) $x + \ln x + c$

(B) $1 + \ln x + c$

(E) $x \ln x + c$

(C) $\ln x + c$

24. The iterated integral $\int_0^1 \int_{\frac{y}{2}}^1 e^{x^2}\, dx\, dy$ can be expressed as

(A) $\int_0^1 \int_0^{2x} e^{x^2}\, dy\, dx$

(C) $\int_0^1 \int_0^{2y} e^{x^2}\, dx\, dy$

(B) $\int_{\frac{y}{2}}^1 \int_0^1 e^{x^2}\, dy\, dx$

(D) $\int_0^1 \int_0^{2y} e^{x^2}\, dy\, dx$

(E) $\int_0^1 \int_y^1 e^{x^2}\, dy\, dx + \int_0^1 \int_0^y e^{x^2}\, dx\, dy$

25. The series $\sum_{n=1}^{\infty} \frac{3^n}{n}(x-2)^n$ converges for x in the interval

(A) $\left(\frac{5}{3}, \frac{7}{3}\right)$

(D) $\left[\frac{5}{3}, \frac{7}{3}\right)$

(B) $\left(\frac{5}{3}, \frac{7}{3}\right]$

(E) $\left(0, \frac{7}{3}\right)$

(C) $\left[\frac{5}{3}, \frac{7}{3}\right]$

26. In R^3, an equation of the tangent plane to the surface $xz - yz^3 - yz^2 = 378$ at $(-3, 2, -6)$ is

(A) $2x + 60y + 65z = 516$

(B) $-2x + 60y + 65z + 516 = 0$

(C) $2x - 60y + 65z = 0$

(D) $x - 60y + z = 516$.

(E) $2x - 60y + 65z + 516 = 0$

27. If $\displaystyle\sum_{n=1}^{\infty} \frac{1}{n^2} = \frac{\pi^2}{6}$, then $\displaystyle\sum_{n=1}^{\infty} \frac{1}{(2n-1)^2}$ is equal to

(A) $\dfrac{\pi^2}{12}$

(D) $\dfrac{\pi^2}{7}$

(B) $\dfrac{\pi^2}{36}$

(E) $\dfrac{\pi^2}{8}$

(C) $\dfrac{2\pi^2}{9}$

28. The area of the triangle in R^3 with vertices at $A = (2, 1, 5)$, $B = (4, 0, 2)$ and $C = (-1, 0, -1)$ is

(A) $\dfrac{475}{2}$

(D) $\dfrac{\sqrt{475}}{2}$

(B) 475

(E) $\sqrt{\dfrac{475}{2}}$

(C) $\sqrt{475}$

29. The order of the permutation $\sigma = \begin{pmatrix} 1 & 2 & 3 & 4 & 5 \\ 4 & 2 & 5 & 3 & 1 \end{pmatrix}$ is

(A) 1   (D) 4

(B) 2   (E) 5

(C) 3

30. Let T be a linear transformation from R^3 to R^3. If u and v are two orthogonal vectors in R^3, which of the following pairs of vectors must be orthogonal to one another?

(A) ru and sv for all real r and s

(B) $u + v$ and $u - v$ (D) Tv and v

(C) Tu and u (E) Tu and Tv

31. If $x \varepsilon A \cap B$, which of the following is (are) true?

I. $x \varepsilon A$
II. $x \varepsilon B$
III. $x \varepsilon A' \cup B'$, where A' is the complement of A and B' is the complement of B

(A) I only   (B) II only

(C) I, II and III

(D) I and II only

(E) III only

32.   Let R be the set of real numbers. Define $a * b = a + b + ab$ for a, b in R. The solution of $5 * x * 3 = 7$ is

(A) $\dfrac{7}{15}$

(D) $\dfrac{3}{2}$

(B) $\dfrac{15}{7}$

(E) $-\dfrac{2}{3}$

(C) $\dfrac{2}{3}$

33.   If $(1 + 2x + 3x^2 + \ldots + (n+1) x^n \ldots)^2 = \sum\limits_{k=0}^{\infty} b_k x^k$ for $|x| < 1$ then b_k is

(A) $k (k + 1) (k + 2) (k + 3)$

(B) $\dfrac{k(k + 1) (k + 2)}{6}$

(C) $\dfrac{(k + 1)(k + 2) (k + 3)}{6}$

(D) $\dfrac{(k + 1) (k + 2)}{3}$

(E) $(k + 2) (k + 3)$

34. Suppose $g'(x)$ exists for all real x and $g(a) = g(b) = g(c) = 0$ where $a < b < c$. The minimum possible number of zeros for $g'(x)$ is

(A) 1   (D) 4

(B) 2   (E) 5

(C) 3

35. $\int_{0}^{\frac{\pi}{2}} \left| \sin x - \cos x \right| dx =$

(A) $2\sqrt{2} - 2$ (D) $2\sqrt{2}$

(B) 0 (E) $2 - 2\sqrt{2}$

(C) 1

36. Which of the following are groups?

I. All integers under subtraction
II. All non-zero real numbers under division
III. All even integers under addition
IV. All integers which are multiples of 13 under addition

(A) I and II only   (D) IV only

(B) II and III only   (E) III and IV only

(C) III only

37. $(1 + \sqrt{-1})^{8n} - (1 - \sqrt{-1})^{8n}$ is equal to

(A) 2^{4n}

(D) 0

(B) $(-1)^{n+1}\, 2^{4n}$

(E) $-e^{-2}$

(C) 2^{4n+1}

38. Given two vectors $\vec{U} = 2\vec{i} - 3\vec{j} + 5\vec{k}$, $\vec{V} = -\vec{i} + 4\vec{j} + 2\vec{k}$ then their vector product $\vec{U} \times \vec{V} =$

(A) $\vec{i} + \vec{j} + 7\vec{k}$

(D) $3\vec{i} + 4\vec{j} + 5\vec{k}$

(B) $-2\vec{i} - 12\vec{j} + 10\vec{k}$

(E) $3\vec{i} - 4\vec{j} - 5\vec{k}$

(C) $-26\vec{i} - 9\vec{j} + 5\vec{k}$

39. For what value(s) of p does the system of equations

$$px + y \quad = 1$$
$$x + py \quad = 2$$
$$y + pz = 3$$

have no solution?

(A) $0, 1$

(D) -2

(B) $1, -1$

(E) $0, 1, -1$

(C) -1

40. If the determinant of the matrix:

$$\begin{bmatrix} 1 & 0 & 0 & 0 & 0 \\ x & 2 & 0 & 0 & 0 \\ x^2 & x^3 & 3 & 0 & 0 \\ x^3 & x^4 & x^5 & 4 & 0 \\ x^4 & x^5 & x^6 & x^7 & 0 \end{bmatrix}$$

is zero, how many values of x are possible?

(A) 0

(D) 3

(B) 1

(E) ∞

(C) 2

41. The nth derivative of $f(x) = \dfrac{1}{1 - x^2}$ is

(A) $\dfrac{1}{(1 - x^2)^{n+1}}$

(C) $\dfrac{(-1)^n n!}{(1 - x^2)^{n+1}}$

(B) $\dfrac{x^n}{(1 - x^2)^{n+1}}$

(D) $\dfrac{n!}{(1 - x^2)^{n+1}}$

(E) $\dfrac{n!}{2}\left[\dfrac{1}{(1 - x)^{n+1}} + \dfrac{(-1)^n}{(1 + x)^{n+1}}\right]$

42. How many different partial derivatives of order k are possible for a function $f(x_1, \ldots, x_n)$ of n variables?

(A) 2^{n+k}

(B) $\dbinom{n + k - 1}{n}$

(C) $\begin{pmatrix} n + k - 1 \\ k \end{pmatrix}$ (D) $\begin{pmatrix} n + k \\ k \end{pmatrix}$

(E) $\begin{pmatrix} n + k \\ n - 1 \end{pmatrix}$

43. Let $T: C^\infty(R) \to C^\infty(R)$ be a linear map such that $T(e^{2x}) = \sin x$, $T(e^{3x}) = \cos 4x$ and $T(1) = e^{5x}$, where $C^\infty(R)$ is the vector space infinitely differentiable functions on the real numbers R. Then $T(4e^{2x} + 7e^{3x} - 5)$ is equal to

(A) $4 \sin x + 7 \cos 4x - 5e^{5x}$ (D) $7 \cos 4x - 5e^{5x}$

(B) $4 \sin x + 7 \cos 4x - 5$ (E) $\sin x + 7 \cos x - 5e^{5x}$

(C) $4 \sin x + 7 \cos 4x$

44. How many ways can 8 teachers be divided among 4 schools if each school must receive 2 teachers?

(A) 520   (D) 225

(B) 250   (E) 2^4

(C) 2520

45. Let C be the circle $| z | = 3$, described in counterclockwise orientation, and write

$$g(w) = \int_C^{1} \frac{2z^2 - 2 - z}{z - w} \, dz$$

Then $g(2)$ is equal to

(A) 1

(D) $4\pi i$

(B) $2\pi i$

(E) $8\pi i$

(C) 0

46. Given that

$$\ln 2 = 1 - \frac{1}{2} + \frac{1}{3} - \frac{1}{4} + \frac{1}{5} - \ldots$$

$$\text{then} \quad -2 + 1 - \frac{2}{3} + \frac{2}{4} - \frac{2}{5} + \frac{2}{6} - \ldots$$

is equal to

(A) $-2 \ln 2$

(D) $\ln 3$

(B) $-\ln 2$

(E) $-3 \ln 3$

(C) $2 \ln 2$

227

47. Let

$$A = \begin{bmatrix} 1 & 0 & 0 & 0 \\ -2 & 1 & 0 & 0 \\ -3 & -2 & 1 & 0 \\ -4 & -3 & -2 & 2 \end{bmatrix}$$

be a 3 x 3 matrix viewed as a linear transformation from R^4 to R^4. What is the dimension of the eigenspace corresponding to the eigenvalue $\lambda = 1$?

(A) 4

(D) 1

(B) 3

(E) 0

(C) 2

48. Let T be a linear transformation from a vector space V of dimension 11 <u>onto</u> a vector space W of dimension 7. What is the dimension of the null space of T?

(A) 0

(D) 4

(B) 2

(E) 5

(C) 3

49. In an $x - y$ plane, if $\vec{a} = (x, y)$, $\vec{b} = (x', y')$, then their scalor product $\vec{a} \cdot \vec{b} =$

(A) $xx' + yy'$

(B) $xx' - yy'$

(C) $xy - x'y'$

(D) $xy' + x'y$

(E) $xy' - x'y$

50. What is the mean of the random variable $\overline{X}$ whose distribution function is defined by

$$F(x) = \begin{cases} \dfrac{2}{\sqrt{\pi}} \displaystyle\int_0^x e^{-t^2} \, dt \, , & x > 0 \\ 0 & , \ x \leq 0 \end{cases}$$

(A) $\dfrac{2}{\pi}$

(B) $\dfrac{1}{\sqrt{\pi}}$

(C) $\sqrt{\dfrac{2}{\pi}}$

(D) 0

(E) Does not exist

51. If $A = \begin{pmatrix} 1 & 1 \\ 1 & 2 \end{pmatrix}$, a 2 x 2 matrix, which of the following is true?

(A) $A^2 - 3A = 0$

(B) $I - 3A = 0$

(C) $A^2 + I = 0$

(D) $A^2 - 3A + I = 0$

(E) None of the above

52. The equation of the tangent line to the graph of the equation
$$\begin{cases} x = t^3 - 4 \\ y = 2t^2 + 1 \end{cases} \text{ at } t = 2 \text{ is}$$

(A) $2x - 3y - 19 = 0$ (D) $3x - 2y + 6 = 0$

(B) $2x - 3y + 19 = 0$ (E) $3x + 2y - 6 = 0$

(C) $3x - 2y - 6 = 0$

53. If $f(0) = 1, f(2) = 3$ and $f'(2) = 5$, then $\int_0^1 xf''(2x)\, dx =$

(A) 0 (D) -1

(B) 1 (E) -2

(C) 2

54. Let P denote the product of any four consecutive integers. Then $1 + P$ is

(A) a multiple of 5   (D) a complete square

(B) a multiple of 4   (E) none of the above

(C) a prime number

55. The solution of the differential equation $y'' + 5y' + 6y = 0$ satisfying the initial conditions $y(0) = 0$ and $y'(0) = 1$ is

(A) $e^{2x} + e^{3x}$

(D) $e^{-2x} + e^{-3x}$

(B) $e^{2x} - e^{3x}$

(E) $e^{-2x} - e^{-3x}$

(C) $e^{-2x} + e^{3x}$

56. Which of the following functions is (are) analytic?

I. $\bar{z}$

II. $\bar{z} \sin z$

III. $z + \sin z$

IV. $z + \bar{z}$

V. $z e^z$

(A) I only

(D) IV only

(B) II and I only

(E) None of the above

(C) III and V only

57. For any positive integer n, $n^7 - n$ is divisible by...

(A) 4

(D) 14

(B) 6

(E) 18

(C) 7

58.   Consider the permutation $f = (1478)(265)(39)$ in S_9. $f^{-1} =$

    (A) $(1874)(256)(39)$ (D) $(1874)(265)(39)$

    (B) $(1874)(265)(39)$ (E) None of the above

    (C) $(1847)(256)(39)$

59.   For what value of c is the function

$$f(x) = \begin{cases} cxe^{-x^2}, & 0 < x < \infty \\ 0 & , \text{ elsewhere} \end{cases}$$

the probability density function of a random variable $\overline{X}$?

    (A) 1   (D) π

    (B) 2   (E) 2π

    (C) 3

60.   The negation of $\forall x \exists y \, (P(x,y) \wedge \neg Q(x,y))$ is

    (A) $\forall x \exists y \, (P(x,y) \rightarrow Q(x,y))$

    (B) $\forall x \exists y \, (Q(x,y) \rightarrow P(x,y))$

    (C) $\exists x \forall y \, (P(x,y) \rightarrow Q(x,y))$

    (D) $\exists x \forall y \, (Q(x,y) \rightarrow P(x,y))$

    (E) None of the above

61. If A is a countable subset of the interval $[0, 1]$, then the Lebesque measure of A is equal to

(A) $\dfrac{1}{2}$

(D) 3^{-1}

(B) 0

(E) None of the above

(C) $\dfrac{2}{3}$

62. What is the interval of convergence of the series

$$\sum_{n=0}^{\infty} (3-x)(6x-7)^n \ ?$$

(A) $[1, \dfrac{4}{3}]$

(D) $(1, \dfrac{4}{3})$

(B) $(1, \dfrac{4}{3}]$

(E) $(0, \dfrac{4}{3})$

(C) $[1, \dfrac{4}{3})$

63. Given

$$A = \begin{pmatrix} 1 & \dfrac{1}{2} & \dfrac{1}{3} & \dfrac{1}{4} \\ \dfrac{1}{2} & \dfrac{1}{3} & \dfrac{1}{4} & \dfrac{1}{5} \\ \dfrac{1}{3} & \dfrac{1}{4} & \dfrac{1}{5} & \dfrac{1}{6} \\ \dfrac{1}{4} & \dfrac{1}{5} & \dfrac{1}{6} & \dfrac{1}{7} \end{pmatrix}$$

with det $(A) \neq 0$, the system of equations

233

$$x_1 + \frac{1}{2}x_2 + \frac{1}{3}x_3 + \frac{1}{4}x_4 = 1$$

$$\frac{1}{2}x_1 + \frac{1}{3}x_2 + \frac{1}{4}x_3 + \frac{1}{5}x_4 = 2$$

$$\frac{1}{3}x_1 + \frac{1}{4}x_2 + \frac{1}{5}x_3 + \frac{1}{6}x_4 = 3$$

$$\frac{1}{4}x_1 + \frac{1}{5}x_2 + \frac{1}{6}x_3 + \frac{1}{7}x_4 = 4$$

has

(A) No solutions

(D) 3 solutions

(B) A unique solution

(E) Infinitely many solutions

(C) 2 solutions

64. Suppose $f(x) = x^4 + x^6 + \sin(x^2) + e^{x^3}$ and $f(x) = f_1(x) + f_2(x)$, where $f_1(x) = f_1(-x)$ and $f_2(-x) = -f_2(x)$. Then $f_2(x)$ is equal to

(A) $\frac{1}{2}\left(e^{x^3} - e^{-x^3}\right)$

(D) $\sin(x^2)$

(B) $\frac{1}{2}\left(e^{x^3} + e^{-x^3}\right)$

(E) $x^4 + x^6 + \sin(x^2) + e^{x^3}$

(C) $\frac{1}{2}\left(x^4 + x^6\right)$

65. If w is an nth root of unity other than one, then the sum $w + w^2 + \ldots + w^{n-1}$ is equal to

(A) 1

(D) 3

(B) 0

(E) -2

(C) -1

66. If $P(A) = 0.7$, $P(B) = 0.5$ and $P([A \cup B]') = 0.1$ then $P(A \mid B)$ is

(A) $\dfrac{3}{7}$

(D) $\dfrac{7}{9}$

(B) $\dfrac{3}{5}$

(E) 1

(C) $\dfrac{5}{7}$

GRE MATHEMATICS
TEST V

ANSWER KEY

1.	E	23.	E	45.	E
2.	C	24.	A	46.	A
3.	D	25.	D	47.	D
4.	B	26.	E	48.	D
5.	A	27.	E	49.	A
6.	A	28.	D	50.	B
7.	D	29.	D	51.	D
8.	E	30.	A	52.	B
9	C	31.	D	53.	C
10.	C	32.	E	54.	D
11.	E	33.	C	55.	E
12.	D	34.	B	56.	C
13.	A	35.	A	57.	C
14.	D	36.	E	58.	A
15.	C	37.	C	59.	B
16.	A	38.	D	60.	C
17.	B	39.	E	61.	B
18.	B	40.	E	62.	D
19.	E	41.	E	63.	B
20.	C	42.	C	64.	A
21.	B	43.	A	65.	C
22.	B	44.	C	66.	B

GRE MATHEMATICS
TEST V

DETAILED EXPLANATIONS
OF ANSWERS

1.   (E)

$$\text{Let } L = \lim_{n \to \infty} \left(\prod_{m=2}^{n} \left(1 - \frac{1}{m} \right) \right) = \lim_{n \to \infty} \left(\prod_{m=2}^{n} \left(\frac{m-1}{m} \right) \right)$$

Taking the natural logarithm of both sides we have

$$\ln L = \ln \lim_{n \to \infty} \left(\prod_{m=2}^{n} \frac{m-1}{m} \right) = \lim_{n \to \infty} \ln \left(\prod_{m=2}^{n} \left(\frac{m-1}{m} \right) \right)$$

We can interchange limit with ln because ln x is continuous. Using ln $(ab) = \ln a + \ln b$ we get

$$\ln L = \lim_{n \to \infty} \sum_{m=2}^{n} \left[\ln (m-1) - \ln m \right]$$

$$= \lim_{n \to \infty} (\ln 1 - \ln 2) + (\ln 2 - \ln 3) + \ldots + (\ln (n-1) - \ln n)$$

$$= \lim_{n \to \infty} (\ln 1 - \ln n)$$

$$= \lim_{n \to \infty} (-\ln n)$$

$$= -\infty ,$$

since ln $1 = 0$:

$$\Rightarrow L = \lim_{b \to \infty} e^{-b} = \lim_{b \to \infty} \frac{1}{e^{b}} = 0 .$$

So $L = 0$.

2.   (C)

All of the integer divisors of 2^{20} are of the form 2^k, $0 \leq k \leq 20$. Therefore, the sum of these divisors is

$$\sum_{k=0}^{20} 2^k = \frac{2^{21} - 1}{2 - 1} = 2^{21} - 1$$

using the fact that the sum of the geometric sequence

$$\sum_{k=0}^{m} r^k = \frac{r^{m+1} - 1}{r - 1}.$$

3.   (D)

The determinant of A is $\det(A) = 1.4 - 2.3 = 4 - 6 = -2$. Now $\det(A^{-1}) = [\det(A)]^{-1}$ using the fact that the determinant of a product is the product of their determinants.

$$\text{So } \det(A^{-1}) = (-2)^{-1} = -\frac{1}{2}.$$

4.   (B)

The polar form of a complex number $a + ib = re^{i\theta}$ where $r = \sqrt{a^2 + b^2}$ and $\theta = \tan^{-1}\left(\frac{b}{a}\right)$.

Therefore $1 + i = 2^{\frac{1}{2}} e^{i\frac{\pi}{4}}$ and, taking the 4/3 power, one obtains

$$(1 + i)^{\frac{4}{3}} = \left(2^{\frac{1}{2}} e^{i\frac{\pi}{4}}\right)^{\frac{4}{3}}$$

$$= \left(2^{\frac{1}{2}}\right)^{\frac{4}{3}} \left(e^{i\frac{\pi}{4}}\right)^{\frac{4}{3}}$$

$$= 2^{\frac{2}{3}} e^{i\frac{\pi}{3}}$$

$$= 2^{\frac{2}{3}} \left(\cos \frac{\pi}{3} + i \sin \frac{\pi}{3} \right)$$

$$= 2^{\frac{2}{3}} \left(\frac{1}{2} + \frac{i\sqrt{3}}{2} \right).$$

5. (A)

$$5 \log_{15} 15x - \log_{15} x^5 = 5 \left[\log_{15} 15 + \log_{15} x \right] - 5 \log_{15} x$$

$$= 5 \left[1 + \log_{15} x \right] - 5 \log_{15} x$$

$$= 5 + 5 \log_{15} x - 5 \log_{15} x$$

$$= 5$$

using the properties of log:

$$\log_a xy = \log_a x + \log_a y ,$$

$$\log_a x^n = n \log_a x \text{ and } \log_a a = 1$$

6. (A)
    By L'Hopital's rule,

$$\lim_{x \to 0} \frac{1}{x} \int_0^x (1 + \sin t)^t dt = \lim_{x \to 0} \frac{\displaystyle\int_0^x (1 + \sin t)^t dt}{x}$$

$$= \lim_{x \to 0} \frac{\dfrac{d}{dx} \displaystyle\int_0^x (1 + \sin t)^t dt}{\dfrac{dx}{dx}}$$

$$= \lim_{x \to 0} \frac{(1 + \sin x)^x}{1}$$

using the fundamental theorem of calculus:

$$\frac{d}{dx} \int_a^t f(t) \ dt = f(x).$$

Let
$$L = \lim_{x \to 0} (1 + \sin x)^x.$$

Taking ln of both sides, one gets

$$\ln L = \ln \lim_{x \to 0} (1 + \sin x)^x$$

$$= \ln \lim_{x \to 0} x \ \ln(1 + \sin x)$$

$$= \lim_{x \to 0} x \cdot \lim_{x \to 0} \ln(1 + \sin x)$$

$$= 0 \cdot \ln 1$$

$$= 0 \cdot 0$$

$$= 0$$

Therefore $L = e^0 = 1$.

7.   (D)

Let $f(x) = \sqrt{x}$. The derivative of f at 3 is

$$f'(3) = \frac{1}{2\sqrt{3}} = \frac{\sqrt{3}}{6}.$$

But

$$f'(3) = \lim_{h \to 0} . \ \frac{\sqrt{3 + h} - \sqrt{3}}{h},$$

by the definition of derivative. Therefore,

$$\lim_{h \to 0} . \ \frac{\sqrt{3 + h} - \sqrt{3}}{h} = f'(3) = \frac{\sqrt{3}}{6}.$$

8.   (E)

$\cos^2 x = \cos x$ or $\cos^2 x - \cos x = 0$ or $\cos x (\cos x - 1) = 0$ which implies $\cos x = 0$ or $\cos x - 1 = 0$. $\cos x = 0$ for $x = \dfrac{\pi}{2}$, $\dfrac{3\pi}{2}$ and $\cos x = 1$ for $x = 0$ and 2π.

9.   (C)

Let $B = \{ x \varepsilon R \mid x$ is an upper bound for $S \}$ where S is a set of strictly negative real numbers. B is non-empty since 0 is in B and every x in S is a lower bound of B. So B has an infimum in R; call it β. If $\gamma > \beta$, then γ is not a lower bound of B, so $\gamma \notin S$. It follows that $s \leq \beta$ for every s in S. Thus $\beta \in B$. If $\alpha < \beta$ then $\alpha \notin B$ since β is a lower bound of B. We have shown that $\beta \in B$ but $\alpha \notin B$ if $\alpha < \beta$. In other words, β is an upper bound of S, but α is not if $\alpha < \beta$. This means that $\beta = \sup S$.

10.   (C)

$$\frac{\partial}{\partial y} \left(\int_0^1 e^{y \sin x} dx \right) = \int_0^1 \frac{\partial}{\partial y} \left(e^{y \sin x} \right) dx$$

$$= \int_0^1 \sin x \, e^{y \sin x} \, dx \, ,$$

using the chain rule.

11.   (E)

The gradient of f, $\nabla f(x,y)$, is equal to $\left(\dfrac{\partial f}{\partial x}, \dfrac{\partial f}{\partial y} \right)$.

Differentiating $f(x,y) = \dfrac{2}{x^2} + 3xy$ with respect to x and y, respectively, we get

$$\frac{\partial f}{\partial x}(x,y) = -\frac{4}{x^3} + 3y \quad \text{and} \quad \frac{\partial f}{\partial y}(x,y) = 3x.$$

Now

$$r^2 = \|\nabla f(r,s)\|^2 = \left(\frac{\partial f}{\partial x}(r,s)\right)^2 + \left(\frac{\partial f}{\partial y}(r,s)\right)^2,$$

by the definition of the length of a vector

$$= \left(-\frac{4}{r^3} + 3s\right)^2 + (3r)^2$$

$$= \frac{16}{r^6} - 24\frac{s}{r^3} + 9s^2 + 9r^2$$

Multiplying both sides by r^6 we get

$$r^8 = 16 - 24r^3s + 9r^6s^2 + 9r^8.$$

That is,

$$16 - 24r^3s + 9r^6s^2 + 8r^8 = 0.$$

12. (D)

$$f(3x) = \frac{3x}{3x - 1}.$$

For (A), $\quad \dfrac{3f(x)}{3f(x) - 1} = \dfrac{\dfrac{3x}{x-1}}{\dfrac{3x}{x-1} - 1} = \dfrac{3x}{2x - 1}$

For (B), $\quad \dfrac{3f(x)}{3f(x) - 3} = \dfrac{\dfrac{3x}{x-1}}{\dfrac{3x}{x-1} - 3} = \dfrac{3x}{3} = x$

For (C), $\quad 3f(x) - 1 = \dfrac{3x}{x-1} - 1 = \dfrac{3x - x + 1}{x - 1} = \dfrac{2x - 1}{x - 1}$

For (D), $\dfrac{3f(x)}{2f(x)+1} = \dfrac{\dfrac{3x}{x-1}}{\dfrac{2x}{x-1}+1} = \dfrac{3x}{2x+x-1} = \dfrac{3x}{3x-1}$

For (E), $\dfrac{3f(x)}{2f(x)-1} = \dfrac{\dfrac{3x}{x-1}}{\dfrac{2x}{x-1}-1} = \dfrac{3x}{2x-x+1} = \dfrac{3x}{x+1}$

So, (D) is the right answer.

13.   (A)

The geometric series $\displaystyle\sum_{k=0}^{\infty}(-x)^k$ converges to $\dfrac{1}{1+x}$ for $|x|<1$.

Differentiating $\dfrac{1}{1+x} = \displaystyle\sum_{k=0}^{\infty}(-1)^k x^k$ one gets

$$-\dfrac{1}{(1+x^2)} = \sum_{k=1}^{\infty} k(-1)^k x^{k-1}.$$

Set $x = \dfrac{2}{3}$; then

$$-\dfrac{1}{\left(1+\dfrac{2}{3}\right)^2} = \sum_{k=1}^{\infty} k(-1)^k \left(\dfrac{2}{3}\right)^{k-1}$$

$$= \lim_{n\to\infty} \sum_{k=1}^{\infty} k(-1)^k \left(\dfrac{2}{3}\right)^{k-1}$$

or

$$-\dfrac{9}{25} = \lim_{n\to\infty}\left[-1+2\left(\dfrac{2}{3}\right)-3\left(\dfrac{2}{3}\right)^2+\ldots+(-1)^n n\left(\dfrac{2}{3}\right)^{n-1}\right] = \lim_{n\to\infty} S_n.$$

14.   (D)

Since the domain of $y = f(x)$ is $0 \le x \le 1$, the domain of

$$f\left(x+\dfrac{1}{4}\right)+f\left(x-\dfrac{1}{4}\right) \text{ is } \begin{cases} 0 \le x+\dfrac{1}{4} \le 1 \\ 0 \le x-\dfrac{1}{4} \le 1, \end{cases}$$

243

$$i.e., \quad \begin{cases} -\dfrac{1}{4} \le x \le \dfrac{3}{4} \\[2mm] \dfrac{1}{4} \le x \le \dfrac{5}{4} \end{cases}$$

So, the domain is $\left[\dfrac{1}{4}, \dfrac{3}{4} \right]$.

15. (C) $\qquad x + iy = z = re^{i\theta}$ where $r = \sqrt{x^2 + y^2}$

Using the polar form

$\tan^{-1}\left(\dfrac{y}{x}\right) = \theta$, we get $1 - i = \sqrt{2}\, e^{-i\frac{\pi}{4}}$. So

and

$$\left[\sqrt{2}(1 - i) \right]^{48} = \left[\sqrt{2} \cdot \sqrt{2} \cdot e^{-i\frac{\pi}{4}} \right]^{48}$$

$$= \left[2e^{-i\frac{\pi}{4}} \right]^{48}$$

$$= 2^{48}\, e^{-i12\pi}$$

$$= 2^{48}(\cos(-12\pi) + i\sin(-12\pi))$$

$$= 2^{48}.$$

16. (A)

$$y\,dx + \sqrt{x^2 + 1}\,dy = 0$$

$$\Rightarrow \frac{dx}{\sqrt{x^2 + 1}} + \frac{dy}{y} = 0$$

$$\Rightarrow \ln(x + \sqrt{x^2 + 1}) + \ln y = \ln C$$

$$\Rightarrow y(x + \sqrt{x^2 + 1}) = C.$$

17.   (B)

The length of the arc is

$$\int_0^1 \sqrt{\left(\frac{dx}{dt}\right)^2 + \left(\frac{dy}{dt}\right)^2}\ dt$$

Now differentiating $x(t) = e^t \cos t$ one obtains $\dfrac{dx}{dt} = e^t \cos t - e^t \sin t$,

using the product rule. Similarly $\dfrac{dy}{dt} = -e^t \sin t - e^t \cos t$.

So

$$\int_0^1 \sqrt{\left(\frac{dx}{dt}\right)^2 + \left(\frac{dy}{dt}\right)^2}\ dt$$

$$= \int_0^1 \sqrt{e^{2t}(\cos t - \sin t)^2 + e^{2t}(\cos t + \sin t)^2}\ dt$$

$$= \int_0^1 \sqrt{e^{2t}(\cos^2 t - 2\sin t \cos t + \sin^2 t + \cos^2 t + 2\sin t \cos t + \sin^2 t)}\ dt$$

$$= \int_0^1 \sqrt{2}\ e^t\ dt \ , \text{ after simplifying}$$

$$= \sqrt{2}\,(e - 1)\,.$$

18.   (B)

Differentiating $3x^2 + 4x^2y + xy^2 = 8$ with respect to x we get

$$6x + 8xy + 4x^2\frac{dy}{dx} + y^2 + 2xy\frac{dy}{dx} = 0\,.$$

So evaluating at $(1, 1)$ $\dfrac{dy}{dx} = -\dfrac{15}{6} = -\dfrac{5}{2}$. Thus the equation of the

normal line at $(1, 1)$ is $y - 1 = \dfrac{2}{5}(x - 1)$ (Slope of the normal line
is the negative reciprocal of the slope of tangent line). To find where
this line intersects the x–axis we set $y = 0$. So

$$-1 = \frac{2}{5}(x - 1) \Rightarrow -5 = 2x - 2 \Rightarrow 2x = -3 \Rightarrow x = -\frac{3}{2}\,.$$

19.   (E)
$$\frac{dF}{dt}(t) = \frac{du}{dt}(t)\, v(t) + u(t)\, \frac{dv}{dt}(t),$$

by the product rule. So

$$\frac{dF}{dt}(1) = \frac{du}{dt}(1) \cdot v(1) + u(1)\, \frac{dv}{dt}(1)$$
$$= 2 \cdot 2 + 1 \cdot 1$$
$$= 4 .$$

20.   (C)

The function

$$f(x) = \begin{cases} x + 2 & \text{if } x \leq 0 \\ 1 & \text{if } 0 < x \leq 2 \\ x - 6 & \text{if } 2 < x \leq 5 \\ (6 - x)^2 & \text{if } 5 < x \end{cases}$$

is continuous everywhere except at the three points $x = 0, 2$ and 5. So the number of discontinuities of f is 3.

21.   (B)
$$\frac{1}{x-2} < \frac{1}{x+3} \quad \text{or} \quad \frac{1}{x-2} - \frac{1}{x+3} < 0 , \text{ by adding } -\frac{1}{x+3}$$

to both sides or $\dfrac{x + 3 - x + 2}{(x-2)(x+3)} < 0$ that is, $\dfrac{5}{(x-2)(x+3)} < 0$

which implies

either $x - 2 > 0$ and $x + 3 < 0$ (1)
or $x - 2 < 0$ and $x + 3 > 0$ (2)

From relation (1) we have $x > 2$ and $x < -3$ which is impossible. From (2) we get $x < 2$ and $x > -3$. Thus the solution set is $(-3, 2)$.

22. (B)

Given that $g\left(\dfrac{3 + 2x}{4}\right) = 1 - x$, $-\infty < x < \infty$. Put $y = \dfrac{3 + 2x}{4}$

which implies $x = \dfrac{4y - 3}{2}$. So

$$g(y) = 1 - x$$

$$= 1 - \dfrac{(4y - 3)}{2}$$

$$= \dfrac{2 - 4y + 3}{2}$$

$$= \dfrac{5 - 4y}{2}$$

Thus, $g\left(\dfrac{7z - 8}{4}\right) = \dfrac{1}{2}\left[5 - 4\left(\dfrac{7z - 8}{4}\right)\right]$, by letting $y = \dfrac{7z - 8}{4}$

$$= \dfrac{1}{2}\,[5 - 7z + 8]$$

$$= \dfrac{1}{2}\,[13 - 7z]$$

$$= \dfrac{13}{2} - \dfrac{7z}{2}\,.$$

23. (E)

Let $e^x = u$, then $f'(u) = 1 + \ln u$.

So $f(u) = \displaystyle\int (1 + \ln u)\,du$

$$= u \ln u + C\,.$$

Therefore, $f(x) = x \ln x + C$.

24.   (A)

Let D be the region of the integration. Then

$$D = \left\{ (x,y): 0 \leq y \leq 1, \ \frac{y}{2} \leq x \leq 1 \right\}$$

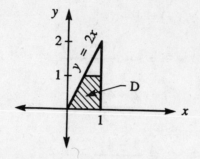

So the iterated integral $\displaystyle\int_0^1 \int_{\frac{y}{2}}^1 e^{x^2} \, dx \, dy$ can be written as

$$\int_0^1 \int_0^{2x} e^{x^2} \, dy \, dx = \int_0^1 \int_{\frac{y}{2}}^1 e^{x^2} \, dx \, dy \ .$$

25.   (D)

$$L = \lim_{n \to \infty} \frac{\left| \dfrac{3^{n+1}}{n+1} (x-2)^{n+1} \right|}{\left| \dfrac{3^n}{n} (x-2)^n \right|}$$

$$= \lim_{n \to \infty} |x-2| 3 \left(\frac{n}{n+1} \right)$$

$$= 3 \, |x-2|$$

By the ratio test, the series converges for

$$3|x-2| < 1 \Leftrightarrow |x-2| < \frac{1}{3}$$

$$\Leftrightarrow -\frac{1}{3} < x - 2 < \frac{1}{3}$$

$$\Leftrightarrow 2 - \frac{1}{3} < x < 2 + \frac{1}{3}$$

$$\Leftrightarrow \frac{5}{3} < x < \frac{7}{3} .$$

When $\quad x = \frac{5}{3}, \displaystyle\sum_{n=1}^{\infty} \frac{3^n}{n}\left(\frac{5}{3} - 2\right)^n = \sum_{n=1}^{\infty} \frac{(-1)^n}{n}$

which converges by the alternating series test . When

$$x = \frac{7}{3}, \sum_{n=1}^{\infty} \frac{3^n}{n}\left(\frac{7}{3} - 2\right)^n = \sum_{n=1}^{\infty} \frac{1}{n}$$

which is a divergent harmonic series. So the series

$$\sum_{n=1}^{\infty} \frac{3^n}{n}(x - 2)^n$$

converges for x in the interval $[\frac{5}{3}, \frac{7}{3})$.

26.   (E)

The equation of the tangent plane is

$$\nabla f(-3, 2, -6) \cdot (x + 3, y - 2, z + 6) = 0$$

where ∇f is the gradient of f and $f(x, y, z) = xz - yz^3 - yz^2 - 378$. Now differentiating f with respect to x, y and z respectively, we get

$$\frac{\partial f}{\partial x} = z$$

$$\frac{\partial f}{\partial y} = -z^3 - z^2$$

$$\frac{\partial f}{\partial z} = -3yz^2 - 2yz + x$$

Evaluating these derivatives at $(-3, 2, -6)$ one sees that $\nabla f(-3, 2, -6) = (-6, 180, -195)$. Therefore, the equation of the tangent plane is $(-6, 180, -195) \cdot (x + 3, y - 2, z + 6) = 0$ that is, $-6x - 18 + 180y - 360 - 195z - 1170 = 0$ or $-6x + 180y - 195z - 1548 = 0$. Dividing throughout by -3, we have $2x - 60y + 65z + 516 = 0$.

27.   (E)

Notice that

$$\sum_{n=1}^{\infty} \frac{1}{n^2} = \sum_{n=1}^{\infty} \frac{1}{(2n-1)^2} + \sum_{n=1}^{\infty} \frac{1}{(2n)^2}$$

("odd terms" + "even terms"). So

$$\sum_{n=1}^{\infty} \frac{1}{(2n-1)^2} = \sum_{n=1}^{\infty} \frac{1}{n^2} - \frac{1}{4} \sum_{n=1}^{\infty} \frac{1}{n^2}$$

$$= \frac{3}{4} \sum_{n=1}^{\infty} \frac{1}{n^2}$$

Therefore,

$$\sum_{n=1}^{\infty} \frac{1}{(2n-1)^2} = \frac{3}{4} \cdot \frac{\pi^2}{6} = \frac{\pi^2}{8}$$

28.   (D)

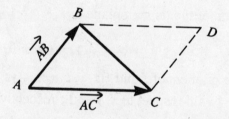

The area of triangle $\triangle ABC$ is 1/2 of the area of the parallelogram $ABDC$, which is equal to $\frac{1}{2}\|\overrightarrow{AB} \times \overrightarrow{AC}\|$, i.e., 1/2 (the magnitude of the cross product of the vectors $\overrightarrow{AB}$ and $\overrightarrow{AC}$). Now

$$\overrightarrow{AB} = B - A = (4,0,2) - (2,1,5)$$

$$= (2,-1,-3)$$

and

$$\overrightarrow{AC} = C - A = (-1,0,-1) - (2,1,5)$$

$$= (-3,-1,-6)$$

250

So

$$\vec{AB} \times \vec{AC} = \det \begin{pmatrix} \vec{i} & \vec{j} & \vec{k} \\ 2 & -1 & -3 \\ -3 & -1 & -6 \end{pmatrix}$$

$$= 3\vec{i} - (-21)\vec{j} + (-5)\vec{k}$$

Therefore,

$$\|\vec{AB} \times \vec{AC}\| = \sqrt{3^2 + 21^2 + 5^2}$$

$$= \sqrt{9 + 441 + 25}$$

$$= \sqrt{475} .$$

Hence the area of the triangle is $\dfrac{\sqrt{475}}{2}$.

29.   (D)

The order of a permutation σ is the least positive integer n such that σ^n = identity. Now

$$\sigma^9 = \begin{pmatrix} 1 & 2 & 3 & 4 & 5 \\ 4 & 2 & 5 & 3 & 1 \end{pmatrix} \begin{pmatrix} 1 & 2 & 3 & 4 & 5 \\ 4 & 2 & 5 & 3 & 1 \end{pmatrix} = \begin{pmatrix} 1 & 2 & 3 & 4 & 5 \\ 3 & 2 & 1 & 5 & 4 \end{pmatrix}$$

Similarly

$$\sigma^3 = \begin{pmatrix} 1 & 2 & 3 & 4 & 5 \\ 4 & 2 & 5 & 3 & 1 \end{pmatrix} \begin{pmatrix} 1 & 2 & 3 & 4 & 5 \\ 3 & 2 & 1 & 5 & 4 \end{pmatrix} = \begin{pmatrix} 1 & 2 & 3 & 4 & 5 \\ 5 & 2 & 4 & 1 & 3 \end{pmatrix}$$

and

$$\sigma^4 = \begin{pmatrix} 1 & 2 & 3 & 4 & 5 \\ 4 & 2 & 5 & 3 & 1 \end{pmatrix} \begin{pmatrix} 1 & 2 & 3 & 4 & 5 \\ 5 & 2 & 4 & 1 & 3 \end{pmatrix} = \begin{pmatrix} 1 & 2 & 3 & 4 & 5 \\ 1 & 2 & 3 & 4 & 5 \end{pmatrix}.$$

Therefore the order of σ is 4.

30. (A)

If $\vec{u}$ and $\vec{v}$ are orthogonal vectors, then their dot product is zero, that is $r\vec{u} \cdot s\vec{v} = 0$ and therfore $r\vec{u} \cdot s\vec{v} = (rs)(\vec{u} \cdot \vec{v}) = 0$ for all real r and s.

31. (D)

$x \,\varepsilon\, A \cap B$ then $x \,\varepsilon\, A$ and $x \,\varepsilon\, B$.

32. (E)

First observe that R is an abelian group under the $*$ operation with identity element 0 and inverse of every $a \neq -1$ in R given by $-\dfrac{a}{1+a}$. Therefore

$$7 = 5 * x * 3$$
$$= x * 5 * 3 \quad \text{by using the abelian property}$$
$$= x * (5 + 3 + 15) \quad \text{by using the definition of } *.$$
$$= x * (23) .$$

Thus

$$7 * \left(-\frac{23}{24}\right) = x * 23 * \left(-\frac{23}{24}\right)$$

$$= x * 0 \quad \text{as} \quad 23 * \left(-\frac{23}{24}\right) = 23 - \frac{23}{24} - \frac{23 \cdot 23}{24} = 0$$

$$= x .$$

Hence

$$x = 7 * \left(-\frac{23}{24}\right) = 7 - \frac{23}{24} - 7 \cdot \frac{23}{24}$$

$$= \frac{168 - 23 - 161}{24}$$

by simplifying

$$= -\frac{16}{24} = -\frac{2}{3} .$$

33. (C)

$$\frac{1}{1-x} = 1 + x + x^2 + \ldots + x^k \ldots \quad \text{for } |x| < 1.$$

Differentiating both sides we get

$$\frac{1}{(1-x)^2} = 1 + 2x + 3x^2 + \ldots + kx^{k-1} + (k+1)x^k + \ldots \quad \text{for } |x| < 1.$$

Differentiating two more times we obtain

$$\frac{2}{(1-x)^3} = 2 + 3 \cdot 2x + \ldots + (k+1)kx^{k-1} + (k+2)(k+1)x^k + \ldots$$

and

$$\frac{6}{(1-x)^4} = 3 \cdot 2 + 4 \cdot 3 \cdot 2x + \ldots + (k+3)(k+2)(k+1)x^k + \ldots$$

or

$$\frac{1}{(1-x)^4} = \frac{3 \cdot 2}{6} + \frac{4 \cdot 3 \cdot 2}{6}x + \ldots$$

$$+ \frac{(k+3)(k+2)(k+1)}{6}x^k + \ldots$$

by dividing by 6. Now

$$(1 + 2x + 3x^2 + \ldots + (n+1)x^n + \ldots)^2$$

$$= \left[\frac{1}{(1-x)^2} \right]^2$$

$$= \frac{1}{(1-x)^4}$$

$$= \sum_{k=0}^{\infty} \frac{(k+3)(k+2)(k+1)}{6} x^k$$

Therefore

$$b_k = \frac{(k+3)(k+2)(k+1)}{6}.$$

34. (B)

   g is continuous since $g'(x)$ exists for all real x. By the mean value theorem, there exist x_1 and x_2, $a < x_1 < b < x_2 < c$ such that

$$g'(x_1) = \frac{g(b) - g(a)}{b - a}$$

and

$$g'(x_2) = \frac{g(c) - g(b)}{c - b}.$$

But $g(a) = g(b) = g(c) = 0$, therefore $g'(x_1) = 0 = g'(x_2)$ and hence the minimum possible zeros for $g'(x)$ is 2.

35.   (A)

   Notice that

$$\text{if } 0 \leq x \leq \frac{\pi}{4}, \text{ then } \sin x - \cos x \leq 0,$$

$$\text{if } \frac{\pi}{4} \leq x \leq \frac{\pi}{2}, \text{ then } \sin x - \cos x \geq 0,$$

$$\int_0^{\frac{\pi}{2}} |\sin x - \cos x|\, dx = \int_0^{\frac{\pi}{4}} (\cos x - \sin x)\, dx +$$

$$\int_{\frac{\pi}{4}}^{\frac{\pi}{2}} (\sin x - \cos x)\, dx$$

$$= 2\sqrt{2} - 2.$$

36.   (E)

   I. The set of integers under subtraction is not a group because $a - (b - c) \neq (a - b) - c$, that is associativity fails.

   II. The set of non-zero real numbers under division is not a group.

   III. The set of even integers under addition is a group.

   IV. The set of all integer multiples of 13 is group under addtion.

37. (C)

$$\vec{u} \times \vec{v} = \begin{vmatrix} \vec{i} & \vec{j} & \vec{k} \\ 2 & -3 & 5 \\ -1 & 4 & 2 \end{vmatrix} = -6\vec{i} + 8\vec{k} - 5\vec{j} - 3\vec{k} - 20\vec{i} - 4\vec{j}$$

$$= -26\vec{i} - 9\vec{j} + 5\vec{k}.$$

38. (D)

Matrix multiplication is defined whenever the number of columns of the first is equal to the number of rows of the second. Thus only TS and ST are defined.

39. (E)

The system of equations

$$px + y \quad\quad = 1$$
$$x + py \quad\quad = 2$$
$$y + pz = 3$$

has no solutions if and only if the determinant of the coefficient matrix is zero. Thus

$$\det \begin{pmatrix} p & 1 & 0 \\ 1 & p & 0 \\ 0 & 1 & p \end{pmatrix} = p(p^2 - 0) - 1(p - 0) + 0(1 - 0)$$

$$= p(p^2 - 1)$$

$$= p(p + 1)(p - 1)$$

which is zero when $p = 0, 1$ or -1.

40. **(E)**

The determinant of the given matrix is always zero for any value of x, because the determinant of a lower triangular matrix is the product of its diagonal elements, which in this case is $1 \cdot 2 \cdot 3 \cdot 4 \cdot 0 = 0$.

41. **(E)**

By partial fractions decomposition

$$f(x) = \frac{1}{1 - x^2} = \frac{1}{2}\left[\frac{1}{1 - x} + \frac{1}{1 + x}\right].$$

The nth derivative of $\dfrac{1}{1 - x}$ is $\dfrac{n!}{(1 - x)^{n+1}}$ and the nth derivative

of $\dfrac{1}{1 + x}$ is $\dfrac{(-1)^n\, n!}{(1 + x)^{n+1}}$. Therefore

$$f^{(n)}(x) = \frac{n!}{2}\left[\frac{1}{(1 - x)^{n+1}} + \frac{(-1)^n}{(1 + x)^{n+1}}\right].$$

42. **(C)**

The number of different partial derivatives of order k is equal to the number of distinct nonnegative integer-valued vectors $(\alpha_1, \alpha_2, \ldots, \alpha_n)$ satisfying $\alpha_1 + \alpha_2 + \ldots + \alpha_n = k$. There are

$$\binom{k + n = 1}{k}$$

such vectors. Thus the number of different partial derivatives of order k is

$$\binom{k + n - 1}{k}$$

43. (A)
$$T(4e^{2x} + 7e^{3x} - 5) = 4T(e^{2x}) + 7T(e^{3x}) - 5T(1) \text{ by linearity}$$
$$= 4\sin x + 7\cos 4x - 5e^{5x}.$$

44. (C)

First school has $\binom{8}{2}$ choices, second school has $\binom{6}{2}$ choices, third school has $\binom{4}{2}$ choices and last school has to accept the remaining 2. Therefore 8 teachers can be divided into 4 schools in

$$\binom{8}{2}\binom{6}{2}\binom{4}{2}\binom{2}{2} = 2520$$

ways if each school must receive 2 teachers.

45. (E)

The Cauchy integral formula states that

$$f(z_0) = \frac{1}{2\pi i} \int_C \frac{f(z)}{z - z_0} dz$$

where z_0 is an interior point of C. In the case at hand $f(z) = 2z^2 - z - 2$ which is analytic and $z_0 = 2$ which lies inside the circle $|z| = 3$. Observe that $f(2) = 4$. Therefore

$$g(2) - \int_C \frac{f(z)}{z - 2} dz = 2\pi i \, f(2) = 8\pi i.$$

46. (A)

Factoring out -2 in $-2 + 1 - \frac{2}{3} + \frac{2}{4} - \frac{2}{5} + \frac{2}{6} \dots$ one gets

$$-2 + 1 - \frac{2}{3} + \frac{2}{4} - \frac{2}{5} + \frac{2}{6} - \dots$$

$$= -2\left(1 - \frac{1}{2} + \frac{1}{3} - \frac{1}{4} + \frac{1}{5} - \frac{1}{6} + \dots\right)$$

$$= -2\ln 2.$$

47.   (D)

The dimension of the eigenspace corresponding to the eigenvalue $\lambda = 1$ is the number of linearly independent solutions of the homogeneous equations $(A - I)\,\overline{X} = 0$. This is equal to

$$\begin{pmatrix} 0 & 0 & 0 & 0 \\ -2 & 0 & 0 & 0 \\ -3 & -2 & 0 & 0 \\ -4 & -3 & -2 & 1 \end{pmatrix} \begin{pmatrix} x \\ y \\ z \\ w \end{pmatrix} = \begin{pmatrix} 0 \\ 0 \\ 0 \\ 0 \end{pmatrix}.$$

That is, using matrix multiplication this reduces to

$$0 = 0$$

$$-2x = 0$$

$$-3x - 2y = 0$$

$$-4x - 3y - 2z + w = 0.$$

Now $-zx = 0$ implies $x = 0$ and $-3x - 2y = 0$ and $x = 0$ implies $y = 0$. Substituting $x = 0$ and $y = 0$, in the fourth equation we have $w = 2z$. Thus there is only one solution

$$\begin{pmatrix} 0 \\ 0 \\ 2 \\ 1 \end{pmatrix}.$$

Therefore the dimension of the eigenspace is 1.

48.   (D)

Since T is onto, the dimension of the range space of T is equal to the dimension of W, which is 7. By the rank-nullity theorem we have dim V = dim of the null space + dim of range space. Therefore the dimension of the null space of T is equal to $11 - 7 = 4$.

49.   (A)

$$\vec{u} \cdot \vec{v} = (x, y) \cdot (x', y')$$

$$= xx' + yy'.$$

50.   (B)

Differentiating

$$F(x) = \begin{cases} \dfrac{2}{\sqrt{\pi}} \displaystyle\int_0^x e^{-t^2} \, dt \, , & x > 0 \\[2ex] 0 & , \quad x \le 0 \end{cases}$$

with respect to x we get the density function

$$f(x) = F'(x) = \frac{2}{\sqrt{\pi}} e^{-x^2}$$

for $x > 0$ and 0 for $x < 0$. The mean is

$$E(\overline{X}) = \int_{-\infty}^{\infty} x f(x) \, dx$$

$$= \frac{1}{\sqrt{\pi}} \int_0^{\infty} 2x e^{-x^2} \, dx$$

$$\int_0^{\infty} 2x e^{-x^2} \, dx = \lim_{b \to \infty} \int_0^b 2x e^{-x^2} \, dx$$

$$= \lim_{b \to \infty} 1 - e^{-b^2} = 1$$

Therefore the mean is $\dfrac{1}{\sqrt{\pi}}$.

51.   (D)

The characteristic polynomial of A is given by

$$P_A(x) = \det(A - xI) = \det \begin{bmatrix} 1-x & 1 \\ 1 & 2-x \end{bmatrix}$$

$$= (1-x)(2-x) - 1$$

$$= 2 - 3x + x^2 - 1$$

$$= x^2 - 3x + 1.$$

By the Cayley-Hamilton theorem $P_A(A) = 0$; that is $A^2 - 3A + I = 0$.

52.   (B)

When $t = 2, x = 2^3 - 4 = 4, y = 2 \cdot 2^2 + 1 = 9$. The slope of the tangent line is $\dfrac{dy}{dx}$.

$$\frac{dy}{dx} = \frac{dy}{dt} \cdot \frac{dt}{dx} = \frac{4}{3t}.$$

So $\dfrac{dy}{dx}\bigg|_{t=2} = \dfrac{2}{3}$, this equation is $y - 9 = \dfrac{2}{3}(x - 4)$

or $2x - 3y + 19 = 0$.

53.   (C)

$$\int_0^1 x f''(2x)\, dx = \frac{1}{2}\int_0^1 x\, d\left[f'(2x)\right]$$

$$= \frac{1}{2}\left[xf'(2x)\bigg|_0^1 - \int_0^1 f'(2x)\, dx\right]$$

$$= \frac{1}{2}\left[5 - \frac{1}{2}f(2x)\bigg|_0^1\right]$$

$$= \frac{1}{2}\left[5 - \frac{1}{2}f(2) + \frac{1}{2}f(0)\right]$$

$$= 2$$

54.   **(D)**

Let four consecutive integers be $n, n + 1, n + 2,$ and $n + 3$, then

$$n(n + 1)\,(n + 2)\,(n + 3) + 1 \;= n^4 + 6n^3 + 11n^2 + 6n + 1$$

$$= n^4 + 2n^2\,(3n + 1) + (9n^2 + 6n + 1)$$

$$= n^4 + 2n^2\,(3n + 1) + (3n + 1)^2$$

$$= (n^2 + 3n + 1)^2.$$

55.   **(E)**

The auxiliary equation is $r^2 + 5r + 6 = 0$ whose solutions are $r = -2$ and -3. Thus the solution of the differential equation is $y(x) = c_1\,e^{-2x} + c_2 e^{-3x}$. Using the initial conditions we get $c_1 + c_2 = 0$ and $-2c_1 - 3c_2 = 1$, whose solution is $c_1 = 1$ and $c_2 = -1$. Hence the solution of the differential equation satisfying the initial conditions is given by $y(x) = +e^{-2x} - e^{-3x}$.

56.   **(C)**

$z + \sin z$ and ze^z are analytic functions.

57.   **(C)**

We know that if p is a prime number, then $n^p \equiv n \pmod{p}$ for any positive integer n. i.e., $n^p - n \equiv 0 \pmod{p}$. In this problem, 7 is prime, so the answer is (C).

58. (A)

$$f = (1478)(265)(39) = \begin{pmatrix} 1 & 2 & 3 & 4 & 5 & 6 & 7 & 8 & 9 \\ 4 & 6 & 9 & 7 & 2 & 5 & 8 & 1 & 3 \end{pmatrix}$$

$$\therefore f^{-1} = \begin{pmatrix} 1 & 2 & 3 & 4 & 5 & 6 & 7 & 8 & 9 \\ 8 & 5 & 9 & 1 & 6 & 2 & 4 & 7 & 3 \end{pmatrix}$$

$$= (1874)(256)(39) .$$

59. (B)

If f is a probability density function then

$$\int_{-\infty}^{\infty} f(x) \, dx = 1 .$$

So

$$c \int_{0}^{\infty} x e^{-x^2} dx = 1 . \text{ Now } \int_{0}^{\infty} x e^{-x^2} dx = \frac{1}{2} \int_{0}^{\infty} 2x \, e^{-x^2} dx .$$

Let $u = x^2$ then $du = 2x \, dx$ and

$$\int_{0}^{\infty} x e^{-x^2} dx = \frac{1}{2} \int_{0}^{+\infty} e^{-u} \, du = \frac{1}{2} .$$

Therefore $\dfrac{c}{2} = 1$ which implies $c = 2$.

60. (C)

$$\neg \, [\forall x \, \exists \, y(P(x,y) \wedge \neg \, Q(x,y)]$$

$$= \exists \, x \, \forall \, y(\neg \, P(x,y) \vee Q(x,y))$$

$$= \exists \, x \, \forall \, y(P(x,y) \rightarrow Q(x,y)) .$$

61. (B)

The Lebesque measure of a countable set is always zero.

62. (D)

The ratio test gives

$$L = \lim_{n \to \infty} \left| \frac{(3-x)(6x-7)^{n+1}}{(3-x)(6x-7)^{n}} \right|$$

$$= |6x - 7|.$$

So the series converges for $|6x-7| < 1$, that is $-1 < 6x - 7 < 1$. Then dividing by 6 we have $1 < x < \frac{4}{3}$. Now we check the end points. When $x = 1$ the series

$$\sum_{n=0}^{\infty} (3-1)(6-7)^{n} = \sum_{n=0}^{\infty} 2(-1)^{n}$$

diverges by the nth term test. When $x = \frac{4}{3}$, the series

$$\sum_{n=0}^{\infty} (3 - \frac{4}{3})(6 \cdot \frac{4}{3} - 7)^{n} = \sum_{n=0}^{\infty} \frac{5}{3} (1)^{n}$$

which diverges again by the nth term test. Thus, the interval of convergence is $(1, \frac{4}{3})$.

63. (B)

Since the coefficient matrix A has non-zero determinant, the system has a unique solution.

64. **(A)**

$$f(x) = f_1(x) + f_2(x) \quad \text{where} \quad f_1(x) = \frac{1}{2}\left[f(x) + f(-x)\right]$$

$$\text{and } f_2(x) = \frac{1}{2}\left[f(x) - f(-x)\right].$$

Thus for the given function $f(x) = x^4 + x^6 + \sin(x^2) + e^{x^3}$. We have

$$f_2(x) = \frac{1}{2}\left[x^4 + x^6 + \sin(x^2) + e^{x^3} - x^4 - x^6 - \sin((-x)^2) - e^{-x^3}\right]$$

$$= \frac{1}{2}\left(e^{x^3} - e^{-x^3}\right).$$

65. **(C)**

The sum of the geometric sequence $1 + w + w^2 + \ldots + w^{n-1} = \frac{1-w^n}{1-w}$ and hence using the fact that w is nth root of unity, $w^n = 1$, we have $1 + w + w^2 + \ldots + w^{n-1} = 0$. Therefore $w + w^2 + \ldots + w^{n-1} = -1$.

66. **(B)**

$$P(A \cup B) = 1 - P([A \cup B]')$$

$$= 1 - 0.1$$

$$= 0.9$$

Now $\quad P(A \cup B) = P(A) + P(B) - P(A \cap B)$ and hence

$$P(A \cap B) = P(A) + P(B) - P(A \cup B)$$

$$= 0.7 + 0.5 - 0.9$$

$$= 0.3.$$

Therefore $\quad P(A|B) = \dfrac{P(A \cap B)}{P(B)} = \dfrac{0.3}{0.5} = \dfrac{3}{5}.$

GRE

MATH TEST

TEST VI

THE GRADUATE RECORD EXAMINATION

MATH TEST

ANSWER SHEET

1. Ⓐ Ⓑ Ⓒ Ⓓ Ⓔ
2. Ⓐ Ⓑ Ⓒ Ⓓ Ⓔ
3. Ⓐ Ⓑ Ⓒ Ⓓ Ⓔ
4. Ⓐ Ⓑ Ⓒ Ⓓ Ⓔ
5. Ⓐ Ⓑ Ⓒ Ⓓ Ⓔ
6. Ⓐ Ⓑ Ⓒ Ⓓ Ⓔ
7. Ⓐ Ⓑ Ⓒ Ⓓ Ⓔ
8. Ⓐ Ⓑ Ⓒ Ⓓ Ⓔ
9. Ⓐ Ⓑ Ⓒ Ⓓ Ⓔ
10. Ⓐ Ⓑ Ⓒ Ⓓ Ⓔ
11. Ⓐ Ⓑ Ⓒ Ⓓ Ⓔ
12. Ⓐ Ⓑ Ⓒ Ⓓ Ⓔ
13. Ⓐ Ⓑ Ⓒ Ⓓ Ⓔ
14. Ⓐ Ⓑ Ⓒ Ⓓ Ⓔ
15. Ⓐ Ⓑ Ⓒ Ⓓ Ⓔ
16. Ⓐ Ⓑ Ⓒ Ⓓ Ⓔ
17. Ⓐ Ⓑ Ⓒ Ⓓ Ⓔ
18. Ⓐ Ⓑ Ⓒ Ⓓ Ⓔ
19. Ⓐ Ⓑ Ⓒ Ⓓ Ⓔ
20. Ⓐ Ⓑ Ⓒ Ⓓ Ⓔ
21. Ⓐ Ⓑ Ⓒ Ⓓ Ⓔ
22. Ⓐ Ⓑ Ⓒ Ⓓ Ⓔ

23. Ⓐ Ⓑ Ⓒ Ⓓ Ⓔ
24. Ⓐ Ⓑ Ⓒ Ⓓ Ⓔ
25. Ⓐ Ⓑ Ⓒ Ⓓ Ⓔ
26. Ⓐ Ⓑ Ⓒ Ⓓ Ⓔ
27. Ⓐ Ⓑ Ⓒ Ⓓ Ⓔ
28. Ⓐ Ⓑ Ⓒ Ⓓ Ⓔ
29. Ⓐ Ⓑ Ⓒ Ⓓ Ⓔ
30. Ⓐ Ⓑ Ⓒ Ⓓ Ⓔ
31. Ⓐ Ⓑ Ⓒ Ⓓ Ⓔ
32. Ⓐ Ⓑ Ⓒ Ⓓ Ⓔ
33. Ⓐ Ⓑ Ⓒ Ⓓ Ⓔ
34. Ⓐ Ⓑ Ⓒ Ⓓ Ⓔ
35. Ⓐ Ⓑ Ⓒ Ⓓ Ⓔ
36. Ⓐ Ⓑ Ⓒ Ⓓ Ⓔ
37. Ⓐ Ⓑ Ⓒ Ⓓ Ⓔ
38. Ⓐ Ⓑ Ⓒ Ⓓ Ⓔ
39. Ⓐ Ⓑ Ⓒ Ⓓ Ⓔ
40. Ⓐ Ⓑ Ⓒ Ⓓ Ⓔ
41. Ⓐ Ⓑ Ⓒ Ⓓ Ⓔ
42. Ⓐ Ⓑ Ⓒ Ⓓ Ⓔ
43. Ⓐ Ⓑ Ⓒ Ⓓ Ⓔ
44. Ⓐ Ⓑ Ⓒ Ⓓ Ⓔ

45. Ⓐ Ⓑ Ⓒ Ⓓ Ⓔ
46. Ⓐ Ⓑ Ⓒ Ⓓ Ⓔ
47. Ⓐ Ⓑ Ⓒ Ⓓ Ⓔ
48. Ⓐ Ⓑ Ⓒ Ⓓ Ⓔ
49. Ⓐ Ⓑ Ⓒ Ⓓ Ⓔ
50. Ⓐ Ⓑ Ⓒ Ⓓ Ⓔ
51. Ⓐ Ⓑ Ⓒ Ⓓ Ⓔ
52. Ⓐ Ⓑ Ⓒ Ⓓ Ⓔ
53. Ⓐ Ⓑ Ⓒ Ⓓ Ⓔ
54. Ⓐ Ⓑ Ⓒ Ⓓ Ⓔ
55. Ⓐ Ⓑ Ⓒ Ⓓ Ⓔ
56. Ⓐ Ⓑ Ⓒ Ⓓ Ⓔ
57. Ⓐ Ⓑ Ⓒ Ⓓ Ⓔ
58. Ⓐ Ⓑ Ⓒ Ⓓ Ⓔ
59. Ⓐ Ⓑ Ⓒ Ⓓ Ⓔ
60. Ⓐ Ⓑ Ⓒ Ⓓ Ⓔ
61. Ⓐ Ⓑ Ⓒ Ⓓ Ⓔ
62. Ⓐ Ⓑ Ⓒ Ⓓ Ⓔ
63. Ⓐ Ⓑ Ⓒ Ⓓ Ⓔ
64. Ⓐ Ⓑ Ⓒ Ⓓ Ⓔ
65. Ⓐ Ⓑ Ⓒ Ⓓ Ⓔ
66. Ⓐ Ⓑ Ⓒ Ⓓ Ⓔ

GRE MATHEMATICS
TEST VI

TIME: 2 hours and 50 minutes
66 Questions

DIRECTIONS: Choose the best answer for each question and mark the letter of your selection on the corresponding answer sheet.

1. Let $f(x) = \left(\dfrac{\sin x}{x} \right)^{(1/x^2)}$. Evaluate $\lim\limits_{x \to 0^+} f(x)$.

    (A) $-1/6$ (D) $\ln (1/6)$

    (B) 0 (E) 1

    (C) $e^{-1/6}$

2. Suppose $\vec{a}$ and $\vec{b}$ are vectors in R^2 and further, that $\vec{a}$ and $\vec{b}$ are linearly independent.

    Let $\vec{c} = \dfrac{\vec{a} \cdot \vec{b}}{\|\vec{a}\|} \, \vec{a} - \vec{b}.$

    (A) $\vec{a}$ and $\vec{c}$ are linearly dependent.

    (B) $\vec{a}$ and $\vec{c}$ are orthogonal.

    (C) $\vec{b}$ and $\vec{c}$ are linearly dependent.

(D) $\vec{b}$ and $\vec{c}$ are orthogonal.

(E) $\{\vec{a}, \vec{b}, \vec{c}\}$ form a linearly independent set.

3. Let $A = \bigcap_{n=0}^{\infty} A_n$, where A_n are the intervals given by

$$\left(1 - \frac{1}{2^n}, 2 + \frac{1}{2^n}\right).$$

Then the set A is the interval

(A) $(1, 2)$ (D) $(0, 3)$

(B) $(1/2, 3/2)$ (E) None of the above

(C) $[1, 2]$

4. The sum of the infinite series $\displaystyle\sum_{n=1}^{\infty} \frac{1}{4n^2 - 1}$ is

(A) $\dfrac{1}{2}$ (D) $\dfrac{3}{4}$

(B) $\dfrac{1}{4}$ (E) 1

(C) $\dfrac{3}{2}$

5. Suppose $f(x) = \sum_{n=1}^{\infty} e^{-n \sin x} / n^2$. For what values of x does the series converge?

(A) $x > 0$

(B) $x \in (n\pi, (n+1)\pi), n = 0, \pm 1, \ldots$

(C) $x \in [n\pi, (n+1)\pi], n = 0, \pm 1, \ldots$

(D) $x \in (2n\pi, (2n+1)\pi), n = 0, \pm 1, \ldots$

(E) $x \in [2n\pi, (2n+1)\pi], n = 0, \pm 1, \ldots$

6. Let V_5 be the multiplicative group of invertible elements of Z_5. Let $v \in V_5$. How many roots does the equation $v^4 = \bar{1}$ have in V_5?

(A) 1   (D) 4

(B) 2   (E) 5

(C) 3

7. Suppose $u(x, y)$ is harmonic in a domain D and $v(x, y)$ is an harmonic conjugate of u. Let $f(z) = u(x, y) + iv(x, y)$. Which statements are true?

I. $g(z) = v - iu$ is analytic in D.
II. $f'(z) = u_x + iv_y$.
III. $v(x, y) + x + y$ satisfies Laplace's equation in D.

(A) I only

(D) I and II only

(B) II only

(E) I and III only

(C) III only

8.   Let $f(x) = x^x$ with $0 < x < 1$. Determine the minimum value of f on the interval.

(A) 1/2

(D) 1/4

(B) 1/e

(E) 0

(C) 1/π

9.   Which curve in Figure 1 cannot be a mapping of the unit circle $|z| = 1$ under the transformation $w = (az + b)/(cz + d)$ where a, b, c and d are real, and $ad - bc \neq 0$?

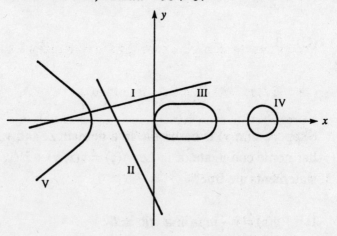

Figure 1:

(A) I only   (D) III and V only

(B) I and II only   (E) IV only

(C) I, II, and III only

10. Let $p(\lambda)$ be the characteristic polynomial for an $(n \times n)$ matrix
     A. Suppose that $\lambda = 0$ is a root of $p(\lambda)$. Which statements are
     always false?

     I.   A has n linearly independent eigenvectors.
     II.   det $[p(A)] = 0$.
     III. A is invertible.

     (A) I only   (D) I and II only

     (B) II only   (E) I and III only

     (C) III

11. Determine the complex roots of the equation $e^{3z} + i = 0$.

     (A) $(i/3)(-\pi/2 + 2n\pi)$, n an integer.

     (B) $(i/3)(\pi/2 + 2n\pi)$, n an integer.

     (C) $(i/3)(\pi/2 + n\pi)$, n an integer.

     (D) $(i/2)(\pi/2 + 2n\pi)$, n an integer.

     (E) $(i/3)(\pi + 2n\pi)$, n an integer.

12.   Determine the Laurent series for $f(z) = 1/(z-2)$ which converges in the annulus $1 < |z-3| < \infty$.

(A) $\displaystyle\sum_{n=0}^{\infty} (z-3)^n$

(D) $\displaystyle\sum_{n=0}^{\infty} (-1)^n (z-3)^{-n}$

(B) $\displaystyle\sum_{n=0}^{\infty} (z-3)^{-n}$

(E) $\displaystyle\sum_{n=1}^{\infty} (-1)^n (z-3)^{-n}$

(C) $\displaystyle\sum_{n=0}^{\infty} (-1)^n (z-3)^{-n-1}$

13.   Which of the following could be the equation for the curve in Figure 2?

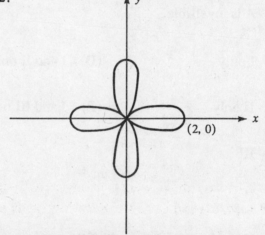

Figure 2:

(A) $r = 1 - 2 \sin 2\theta$

(D) $r = 2 \sin 4\theta$

(B) $r = 1 + 2 \sin 2\theta$

(E) $r = 2 \cos 4\theta$

(C) $r = 4 \cos 2\theta$

14.   Suppose $\phi'(x)$ exists and $\phi' \neq 0$ on $[\alpha, \beta]$. Further, suppose there exists a $\gamma \varepsilon [\alpha, \beta]$ such that $\phi(\gamma) = 0$. Let γ_0 in $[\alpha, \beta]$ be chosen arbitrarily. Let γ_1 be the point at which the tangent line to $\phi(x)$ at $(\gamma_0, \phi(\gamma_0))$ crosses the x-axis. For each $n \geq 0$, let γ_n be the x-intercept of the line tangent to ϕ at $(\gamma_{n-1}, \phi(\gamma_{n-1}))$. Which formula describes this method for approximateing the root of $\phi(x)$?

(A) $\gamma_{n+1} = \gamma_n - \phi''(\gamma_n)/\phi(\gamma_{n+1})$

(B) $\gamma_{n+1} = \gamma_n - \phi(\gamma_n)(\gamma_n - \gamma_{n-1})/(\phi(\gamma_n - \gamma_{n-1}))$

(C) $\gamma_{n+1} = \gamma_n + \phi(\gamma_n)/\phi'(\gamma_n)$

(D) $\gamma_{n+1} = \gamma_n - \phi'(\gamma_n)/\phi(\gamma_n)$

(E) $\gamma_{n+1} = \gamma_n - \phi(\gamma_n)/\phi'(\gamma_n)$

15.   Let $P(S)$ denote the power set of any set S. Suppose $A = \{a, b, c\}$, $B = \{d, e\}$, and $C = P(A) \times B$. How many elements are in $P(C)$?

(A) 8   (D) 2^{16}

(B) 32   (E) 16

(C) 2^{10}

272

16. What is the indicial equation for the ordinary differential equation $x^2 y'' + 4xy' + 4y = 0$?

(A) $r^2 + 2r + 4$

(D) $r^2 + 3r + 4$

(B) $r^2 + 4r + 4$

(E) $r^2 + 4xr + 4$

(C) $r^2 + r + 1$

17. Which elements of the modular ring Z_9 are not invertible?

(A) $\bar{0}, \bar{3}, \bar{6}$

(D) $\bar{0}, \bar{2}$

(B) $\bar{0}, \bar{4}, \bar{8}$

(E) $\bar{0}, \bar{7}$

(C) $\bar{0}, \bar{3}$

18. A witness to a robbery told the police that the license number of the car contained three digits, the first of which was a 9, followed by three letters, the last of which was an A. The witness cannot remember the second and third digit, nor the first and second letter, but is positive that all the numbers were different and that the first two letters were the same, but different from the last letter. How many possible license plates match the description given by the witness?

(A) 1872

(D) 729

(B) 2600

(E) 1800

(C) 2106

19.   A warm object is placed into a special refrigerator. The rate of
        change of the temperature of the object is proportional (with
        proportionality constant k) to the difference between its tem-
        perature and the ambient temperature in the refrigerator. Sup-
        pose the ambient temperature is 0 degrees, and further, that
        after one hour, the object's temperature is half its initial value.
        What is the value of k?

        (A) ln 2   (D) 2

        (B) 1/2   (E) None of the above

        (C) e^2

20.   Let G be a group with m elements g satisfying $g^2 = e$ where e
        is the group identity. How many elements of order 2 are there
        in G?

        (A) $m + 1$ (D) 1

        (B) m (E) None of the above

        (C) $m - 1$

21.   Which functions have unique fixed points on the stated inter-
        vals?

        I. $f(x) = e^{-x}, x \in [1/3, 1]$
        II. $g(x) = \pi + 1/2 \sin x, x \in [0, 2\pi]$
        III. $h(x) = x^3 - 1, x \in [1, 2]$

(A) I only

(D) II and III

(B) I and II only

(E) None of the above

(C) I, II, and III

22. Let P and Q be logical propositions. Which of the following forms are tautologies?

I. $(P \vee Q) \wedge \neg (P \wedge Q)$
II. $(P \wedge \neg P) \Rightarrow Q$
III. $(P \vee Q) \Rightarrow \neg (Q \wedge P)$

(A) I and II only

(D) II

(B) I and III only

(E) III

(C) II and III only

23. In R^3, let $\alpha_1 = (1, 0, 1)$, $\alpha_2 = (0, 1, -2)$ and $\alpha_3 = (-1, -1, 0)$. If $f(\alpha)$ is a linear functional in R^3 such that $f(\alpha_1) = 1$, $f(\alpha_2) = -1$ and $f(\alpha_3) = 3$, and if $\alpha = (a, b, c)$, the $f(\alpha)$ can be expressed as

(A) $-4a - 7b + 3c$

(D) $3a - 6b - 2c$

(B) $4a - 7b - 3c$

(E) $4a - 7b + 3c$

(C) $3a - 6b - 3c$

24. Let $U = \{0, 1, c\}$ be a ring with three elements (1 is the unity). Which statements are true?

I. $1 + 1 + 1 = 0$
II. $1 + 1 = c$
III. $c^2 = 1$

(A) I only

(D) II and III only

(B) II only

(E) I, II, and III

(C) I and II only

25. Which equation describes the plane passing through the points $(2, -1, -2)$, $(-1, -2, -3)$, and $(4, 1, 0)$?

(A) $2x + y - 3z = 9$

(D) $x + 2y + z = 9$

(B) $x + 2y - 3z = 7$

(E) $x + 2y - 3z = 11$

(C) $3x + 2y - z = 5$

26. Let $\beta = \begin{pmatrix} 1 & 2 & 3 & 4 & 5 \\ 3 & 1 & 2 & 5 & 4 \end{pmatrix}$ be an element of the symmetric group S_5. What is the order of β?

(A) 2

(D) 5

(B) 3

(E) 6

(C) 4

276

27. If $A = \begin{pmatrix} 3 & 1 \\ -1 & -1 \end{pmatrix}$ and $I = \begin{pmatrix} 1 & 0 \\ 0 & 1 \end{pmatrix}$, which matrix polynomial vanishes?

(A) $A^2 - 2A - 4I$

(D) $A^2 - 2A - 2I$

(B) $A^2 - 2A + 4I$

(E) $A^2 - A + 2I$

(C) $A^2 + A + 2I$

28. Let the binary operation o be defined on all integers by $a \circ b = a + 2b + ab$. Which statemets are false?

I.   o is associative.
II. o is commutative.
III. For every a, there is an inverse a^{-1} such that $a \circ a^{-1} = 1$.

(A) I only

(D) I, II, and III

(B) II only

(E) None of the above

(C) I and II only

29. A random variable X has mean μ, variance σ^2, and an unknown density function. Determine the constant c so that $P(|X - \mu| \geq c) \leq P_0$, where P_0 is a given constant probability.

(A) σ

(B) $\sigma/\sqrt{P_0}$

(C) $P_0\sigma$

(D) σ/P_0

(E) σ^2/P_0^2

30. A coin is biased so that a tail is twice as likely to occur as a head. What is the expected number of tails if the coin is tossed twice?

(A) 4/3

(D) 1/2

(B) 8/9

(E) 2

(C) 4/9

31. Which of the following matrices is orthogonal?

(A) $\begin{pmatrix} 0 & 1 \\ -1 & 0 \end{pmatrix}$

(D) $\begin{pmatrix} 2 & 1 \\ 0 & 1 \end{pmatrix}$

(B) $\begin{pmatrix} 1 & 2 \\ 0 & 1 \end{pmatrix}$

(E) $\begin{pmatrix} 1 & -1 \\ 1 & -1 \end{pmatrix}$

(C) $\begin{pmatrix} 1 & 0 \\ 1 & 0 \end{pmatrix}$

32. Evaluate $\lim\limits_{x\to 0} \dfrac{\int_{-x}^{0} \sin t^3 \, dt}{x^4}$.

(A) $-1/2$

(B) $1/2$

(C) 1/4

(D) − 1/4

(E) $\pi/2$

33. Which of the following subsets of C [−1, 1] are not vector spaces?

(A) $\{f(x) \in C$ [−1, 1] : $f(−1) = f(1)\}$

(B) $\{f(x) \in C$ [−1, 1] : $f(x) = 0$ if $x \in$ [−1/2, 1/2]$\}$

(C) $\{f(x) \in C$ [−1, 1] : $f(1) = 1\}$

(D) $\{f(x) \in C$ [−1, 1] : $f(1) = 0\}$

(E) $\{f(x) \in C$ [−1, 1] : $\int_{-1}^{1} f(x) \, dx = 0\}$

34. A real, symmetric matrix is called positive definite if $x^T Ax > 0$ for all x in R^n. Which of the following is positive definite?

(A) $\begin{pmatrix} 4 & 2 \\ 2 & 1 \end{pmatrix}$

(D) $\begin{pmatrix} 0 & 1 \\ 1 & 0 \end{pmatrix}$

(B) $\begin{pmatrix} 0 & 1 \\ 1 & -1 \end{pmatrix}$

(E) $\begin{pmatrix} 1 & -2 \\ -2 & 0 \end{pmatrix}$

(C) $\begin{pmatrix} 2 & 0 \\ 0 & -2 \end{pmatrix}$

35. Let A and B be $n \times n$ symmetric matrices. Which of the following is a necessary and sufficient condition for AB to be symmetric?

(A) BA is skew-symmetric

(B) A and B are nonsingular

(C) $|AB| = |BA|$

(D) A and B commute

(E) B is Hermitian

36. Evaluate $\lim_{x \to \infty} \sqrt{x^2 + 2x} - x$.

(A) 0   (D) 2

(B) 1   (E) ∞

(C) $\sqrt{2}$

37. Let $f(x) = \sin^{-1} x + \cos^{-1} x$, where $-\pi/2 \leq \sin^{-1} x \leq \pi/2$ and $0 \leq \cos^{-1} x \leq \pi$. Which statements are true?

I. $f'(x) \leq 0$ for all x

II. $f(1/2) = \pi/2$

III. $f(x)$ is an even function

(A) I only

(D) II and III only

(B) II only

(E) I, II, and III

(C) III only

38. Consider the following boundary value problem for $y(x)$:

$$d^2y/dx^2 + \lambda^2 y = 0, \ y(0) = 0, \ y'(1) = 0,$$

where $y' = dy/dx$ and λ is a parameter. For what values of *lambda* does this boundary value problem have nontrivial solutions?

(A) $n\pi, \ n = 1, 2, \ldots$

(B) $\pm n\pi, \ n = 1, 2, \ldots$

(C) $\dfrac{2n + 1}{2} \pi, \ n = 0, 1, 2, \ldots$

(D) $\pm \dfrac{2n + 1}{2} \pi, \ n = 0, 1, 2, \ldots$

(E) $\dfrac{2n - 1}{2} \pi, \ n = 0, 1, 2, \ldots$

39. If $f(x)$ is everywhere differentiable on the closed interval $[a, b]$, then

(A) $f'(x)$ is Riuemann integrable

(B) $f''(x)$ exists

(C) $f'(x)$ is continuous

(D) $f(x)$ may be unbounded

(E) $f(x)$ is uniformly continuous on the interval

40. Which function is not periodic?

(A) $\sin(e^{\sin x})$

(D) $\cos[\cos(e^x)]$

(B) $\tan h[\cos(\sin x)]$

(E) $\ln[1/(2 + \cos x)]$

(C) $\sqrt{\left|\tan\left(\frac{1}{2}\cos x\right)\right|}$

41. Let $a_n = \left(\dfrac{n+2}{n+1}\right)^{2n+3}$. Determine $\lim\limits_{n \to \infty} a_n$.

(A) 1

(D) e^3

(B) e

(E) 0

(C) e^2

42. Determine the maximum value of $|A|$ where

$$A = \begin{pmatrix} 1 & 1 & x \\ 1 & -1 & x^2 \\ -1 & 0 & 1 \end{pmatrix}$$

(A) $-5/4$ (D) $1/2$

(B) $-1/2$ (E) $3/4$

(C) 0

43.   Consider the flow of heat in a thin, uniform bar of length L. The
      temperature distribution $u(x, t)$ in the bar obeys the partial
      differential equation

$$u_t = ku_{xx},$$

where k is a constant. Suppose the temperature of the bar at
$x=0$ is fixed at 0 degrees, while the temperature at $x=L$ is fixed
at 1 degree. At time $t = 0$, the temperature distribution is
$u(x, 0) = f(x)$. What is the average temperature in the bar in the
limit as $t \to \infty$?

(A) 0 (C) 5

(B) $\dfrac{1}{10} \displaystyle\int_0^L f(x)\, dx$ (D) 10

(E) $\displaystyle\sum_{n=1}^{\infty} A_n \cos(n\pi x/L)\exp(-kn^2\pi^2 t/L)$

44.   The differential equation

$$dP/dt = P(1 - P)(P - 2),$$

possesses the three equilibrium solutions $P_1 = 0, P_2 = 1$, and P_3
$= 2$. Which of these are stable?

283

(A) P_1 and P_2 only   (D) P_2 only

(B) P_2 and P_3 only   (E) P_3 only

(C) P_1 only

45.   Let $f(z) = 1/(z^2 + 1)$. Evaluate $\oint_\Gamma f(z)\, dz$ where Γ is the curve shown in Figure 3.

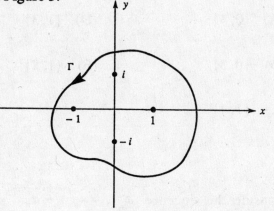

Figure 3:

(A) 0   (D) 2π

(B) π (E) $2\pi i$

(C) πi

46.   Determine an harmonic conjugate $v(x, y)$ for the harmonic function $u(x, y) = y + 3xy^2 - x^3$.

(A) $-y + 3xy^2 - x^3$ (B) $x + 3xy^2 - x^3$

284

(C) $y^3 - 3x^2y - x$ (D) $y^3 - 3x^2y + x$

(E) $y^3 - 3x^2y + x$

47.   Let $A = \begin{pmatrix} 2 & 1 \\ -1 & x \end{pmatrix}$. For what values of x does A possess a repeated eigenvalue?

(A) $\{0, 4\}$ (D) $\{1, 3\}$

(B) $\{0, 3\}$ (E) $\{1, 2\}$

(C) $\{1, 4\}$

48.   Consider the sequence $a_{n+1} = \sqrt{b + a_n}$ where $a_1 = 1$. What is the smallest positive value of b such that b is divisible by 7 and that the limit of the sequence is an integer?

(A) 7   (D) 84

(B) 42   (E) 98

(C) 49

49.   What is the volume of the body of revolution formed by rotating the curve $y = e^{-x}, 0 \le x \le \infty$ about the x-axis?

(A) $\pi/2$ (B) $1/2$

(C) π (D) 1

(E) 2π

50. Suppose $\int_0^\infty f(x)\, dx$ exists. Which statements are false?

I. $\lim_{x\to\infty} f(x) = 0$

II. $\int_0^\infty |f(x)|\, dx$ exists

III. $\int_0^\infty [f(x)]^2\, dx$ exists

(A) I only   (D) II and III only

(B) II only   (E) I, II, and III

(C) I and II only

51. Suppose $f(z)$ is a nonconstant entire function. Which statement is always true?

(A) $\lim_{z\to\infty} f(z) = 0$

(B) $\lim_{z\to 0} f(z) = 0$

(C) $f'(z)$ may not be entire

(D) $\oint f(z)\, dz = 2\pi i$ for every simple closed curve in the complex plane

(E) None of the above

52. If $y = x$ is a solution of the differential equation

$$y'' + xy - y = 0,$$

another, linearly-independent solution is given by

(A) x^2

(B) $x^2 \int^x e^{-t^2}/t^2\, dt$

(C) $x \int^x e^{-t^2}/t^2\, dt$

(D) $x \int^x e^{-t^2}\, dt$

(E) $x \int^x e^{-t^2}/t^2\, dt$

53. Which of the following could be the equation for the curve shown in Figure 4?

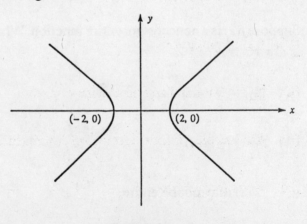

Figure 4:

(A) $x^2/4 + y^2 = 1$ (D) $y^2 - x^2/2 = 1$

(B) $x^2/2 - y^2 = 1$ (E) $x^2/4 - y^2 = 1$

(C) $x^2/2 + y^2 = 1$

54. If $z = i^i$, then z can assume the real value

(A) -1 (D) $e^{2\pi}$

(B) 1 (E) $\pi/2$

(C) $e^{3\pi/2}$

55. Let $f(x)$ be a real-valued function defined on $[a, b]$. Which of the following conditions is not sufficient to ensure that $\int_a^b f(x)\, dx$ exists?

(A) $f(x)$ is monotonic

(B) $f(x)$ is continuous

(C) $f(x)$ is bounded and piecewise smooth

(D) $f(x)$ has only a finite number of discontinuities

(E) None of the above

56. Let $f(x)$ be a function defined for all real x such that the coordinates of each point of its graph satisfy $|y| = x^2$. The total number of points at which $f(x)$ must be differentiable is

(A) none

(D) 4

(B) 1

(E) infinite

(C) 2

57. Let $f(x) = x^{1/\ln x}$, $x > 0$, and $x \neq 1$. If $f(x)$ is continuous at $x = 1$, then $f(1)$ is

(A) 0

(D) e

(B) 1

(E) 4

(C) 2

58. The series $\displaystyle\sum_{n=2}^{\infty} \frac{(x + 2)^n}{n^3 3^{n+1}}$ has the inverval of convergence

(A) $-3 < x < 3$

(D) $-5 \leq x \leq 1$

(B) $-3 \leq x \leq 3$

(E) $-5 \leq x \leq 3$

(C) $-5 \leq x < 1$

59. For the algorithm described below, what is the complete output

sequence if the input value is 13?

```
procedure test;
variable x : real;
begin{test}
    input(x);
    repeat
        if x mod 2 = 0 then x := x/2
            else x := 3 * x + 1;
        output(x);
    until x = 1;
end.{test}
```

(A)   13, 40, 20, 10, 5, 16, 8, 4, 2, 1

(B)   13, 40, 20, 10, 5, 1

(C)   40, 20, 10, 5, 18, 8, 4, 2, 1

(D)   13, 39, 40, 20, 10, 5, 1

(E)   40, 20, 10, 5, 20, 10, 8, 4, 2, 1

60.   Which of the following sets in R^2 are compact?

(A) $\{x, y \mid x \geq 0, y \geq 0\}$

(B) $\{x, y \mid 1 \leq x \leq 2, 0 \leq y \leq 1\}$

(C) $\{x, y \mid 1 \leq x \leq 2, y = 0\}$

290

(D) $\{x, y \mid x^2 + y^2 \le 2\} \cap \{x, y \mid x^2 + y^2 > 1\}$

(E) $\{x, y \mid |x + y| < 1\}$

61. If $6x + 5y$ is a multiple of 13, what must b be so that $8x + by$ is also a multiple of 13?

(A) 0   (D) 9

(B) 5   (E) 11

(C) 7

62. Which statements about fields are always true?

I.   Every field contains at least one finite subfield.
II.   The transcendental real numbers form a field.
III.   Every field is an integral domain.

(A) I only   (D) I and II

(B) II only   (E) I and III

(C) III only

63. Inside the registers of a microprocessor, two numbers are ANDed by forming the logical AND of their respective binary digits. What is the result of ANDing 27 and 52?

(A) 16   (D) 79

(B) 22   (E) 127

(C) 63

64.   Which of the following could be a density function of a
      continuous random variable X?

(A) $f(x) = \dfrac{1}{1 + x^2}$

(B) $f(x) = \begin{cases} 0, & x < 0 \\ 2e^{-2x}, & x \geq 0 \end{cases}$

(C) $f(x) = \begin{cases} 0, & x < 1 \\ 1, & 1 \leq x \leq 2 \\ 0, & x > 2 \end{cases}$

(D) $f(x) = \begin{cases} 0, & x < 2 \\ 1/x^2, & x \geq 2 \end{cases}$

(E) $f(x) = \begin{cases} 0, & x \text{ rational} \\ 1, & x \text{ irrational} \end{cases}$

65.   Which of the following is the contrapositive of the statement
      $P \wedge Q \Rightarrow \neg R \wedge S$?

(A) $\neg R \wedge S \Rightarrow P \wedge Q$ (B) $P \wedge Q \Rightarrow R \vee \neg S$

(C) $R \vee \neg S \Rightarrow \neg P \vee \neg Q$

(D) $\neg P \vee \neg Q \Rightarrow R \vee \neg S$

(E) $P \vee Q \Rightarrow \neg R \vee S$

66. Suppose $A = \begin{pmatrix} 5 & -2 \\ 6 & -2 \end{pmatrix}$. Which matrix below can be used to diagonalize A?

(A) $\begin{pmatrix} 2 & 1 \\ 3 & 2 \end{pmatrix}$

(D) $\begin{pmatrix} 1 & 0 \\ 0 & 2 \end{pmatrix}$

(B) $\begin{pmatrix} 6 & -2 \\ 5 & -2 \end{pmatrix}$

(E) $\begin{pmatrix} 2 & 3 \\ 1 & 2 \end{pmatrix}$

(C) $\begin{pmatrix} 2 & 0 \\ 0 & 1 \end{pmatrix}$

GRE MATHEMATICS
TEST VI

ANSWER KEY

1.	C	23.	B	45.	A
2.	B	24.	E	46.	C
3.	C	25.	A	47.	A
4.	A	26.	E	48.	B
5.	E	27.	D	49.	A
6.	D	28.	D	50.	E
7.	E	29.	B	51.	E
8.	B	30.	A	52.	B
9	D	31.	A	53.	E
10.	C	32.	C	54.	C
11.	A	33.	C	55.	D
12.	C	34.	A	56.	B
13.	E	35.	D	57.	D
14.	E	36.	B	58.	D
15.	D	37.	E	59.	C
16.	D	38.	D	60.	B
17.	A	39.	E	61.	E
18.	E	40.	D	62.	C
19.	A	41.	C	63.	A
20.	C	42.	A	64.	B
21.	B	43.	C	65.	C
22.	D	44.	D	66.	A

GRE MATHEMATICS
TEST VI

DETAILED EXPLANATIONS
OF ANSWERS

1.   (C)

Note that the limit takes on the indeterminate form 1^∞. Thus, we apply L'Hopital's rule several times to the logarithm of $f(x)$:

$$\ln f(x) = \frac{\ln \frac{\sin x}{x}}{x^2} \sim \frac{x \cos x - \sin x}{2x^2 \sin x} \sim -\frac{\sin x}{4 \sin x + 2x \cos x}$$

$$\sim -\frac{\cos x}{6 \cos x - 2x \sin x} \sim -\frac{1}{6}.$$

Thus, $\ln f(x) \to -1/6$ or $f(x) \to -e^{-1/6}$.

2.   (B)

A direct calculation shows that $\vec{a} \cdot \vec{c} = 0$, which implies that $\vec{a}$ and $\vec{c}$ are orthogonal. The other answers are all false.

3.   (C)

Note that the intervals are nested, i.e., $A_{n+1} \subset A_n$. The limiting interval is therefore $(1, 2)$. However, the endpoints of this interval are in every A_n. Consequently, the intersection of the nested intervals is $[1, 2]$.

4.　　(A)

By partial fraction decomposition,

$$\frac{1}{4n^2 - 1} = \frac{1}{2}\left(\frac{1}{2n - 1} - \frac{1}{2n + 1}\right).$$

The partial sums of the series form a telescoping sum, so that

$$\sum_{n=1}^{m} \frac{1}{4n^2 - 1} = \frac{1}{2}\left[\begin{array}{c}(-1 + 1) + \left(1 - \frac{1}{3}\right) + \left(\frac{1}{3} - \frac{1}{5}\right) \\ +\ldots+ \left(\frac{1}{2m - 1} - \frac{1}{2m + 1}\right)\end{array}\right]$$

$$= \frac{1}{2}\left(1 - \frac{1}{2m + 1}\right),$$

and the partial sums $\rightarrow \dfrac{1}{2}$ as $m \rightarrow \infty$.

5.　　(E)

Applying the ratio test, it can be shown that

$$\left|\frac{a_{n+1}}{a_n}\right| \rightarrow e^{-\sin x}.$$

Convergence therefore follows when $\sin x > 0$. This holds whenever $2n\pi < x < (2n+1)\pi$ for any integer n. At the endpoints of these intervals, $\sin x = 0$, and each term of the series is $1/n^2$. In that case, the series also converges. Thus, the closed intervals given by (E) represent the allowable values for x.

6.　　(D)

Note that $V_5 = \{1, 2, 3, 4\}$. Since $1^4 = 1$, $2^4 = 16 = \bar{1}$, $4^2 = 16 = \bar{1}$, and $3^2 = 9 = \bar{4}$, it follows that every element of V_5 is a solution to the given equation.

7.   (E)

Note first that $-if(z) = g(z)$. Since $f(z)$ is analytic, so is $g(z)$; thus I is true. However, $f'(z) = u_x + iv_x$, and so II is false. Finally, since $v(x, y)$ is harmonic, it satisfies Laplace's equation. The second partials of $(x + y)$ vanish, and so III is true.

8.   (B)

Taking logarithmic derivatives, we find that $f'(x) = x^x(\ln x + 1)$. This vanishes when $x = 1/e$. Since $f(x) \to 1$ as $x \to 0$ or 1, the minimum of $f(x)$ occurs at $1/e$.

9.   (D)

The indicated mapping is a linear fractional transformation which always maps circles (and straight lines) into circles and straight lines. The ellipse (III) and hyperbola (V) cannot be images of a circle under a linear fractional transformation.

10.   (C)

Let $A = \begin{pmatrix} 1 & 0 \\ 0 & 0 \end{pmatrix}$. This matrix has eigenvalues $\{0, 1\}$ and eigenvectors $(1, 0)^T$ and $(0, 1)^T$. These eigenvectors are clearly linearly independent. Thus, I is *sometimes* true. By the Cayley-Hamilton theorem, every square matrix A satisfies its characteristic polynomial. Thus $p(A)$ is the zero matrix and II is *always* true. Finally, if $\lambda = 0$ is an eigenvalue of A, the $\det (A - \lambda I) = \det (A) = 0$, which implies that A is singular and therefore not invertible. III is *never* true.

11.　　(A)

Rewrite the equation as

$$e^{3z} = -i = e^{i(-\pi/2 + 2n\pi)}, \; n \text{ an integer,}$$

which implies that

$$z = (i/3)(\pi/2 + 2n\pi).$$

12.　　(C)

Observe that

$$\frac{1}{z-2} = \frac{1}{1+z-3} = \frac{1}{z-3} \cdot \frac{1}{1 - \dfrac{-1}{z-3}},$$

and expanding this last term in a geometric series yields the Laurent series given by (C).

13.　　(E)

The four petals in the figure indicate that the equation must contain an argument proportional to 4θ. Of the two possibilities, only (E) intersects the point $(2, 0)$, which is on the x–axis.

14.　　(E)

The algorithm described in Newton's method whose correct formula is given by (E).

15.　　(D)

$P(A)$ contains $2^3 = 8$ elements and B contains 2 elements, so that

C contains 16 elements. $P(C)$ therefore contains 2^{16} elements.

16.   (D)

The differential equation is of the Cauchy-Euler type. The indicial equation is found by making the substitution $y = x^r$ which yields

$$r(r-1)\, x^2 x^{-2} + 4rxx^{-1} + 4x^r = 0.$$

Then we cancel out the common factor x^r from each term.

17.   (A)

The non-invertible elements are those whose squares are equal to the additive identity. Since $3^2 = 9 = 0 \bmod 9$ and $6^2 = 36 = 0 \bmod 9$, the correct answer is (A).

18.   (E)

There are 9 possibilities for the second digit and 8 possibilities for the third digit. In addition, there are 25 possibilities for the double set of letters. Thus, there are $9 \cdot 8 \cdot 25 = 1800$ possible license plates which match the stated description.

19.   (A)

Let T be the temperature and t be time. From the problem statement, the rate of change of temperature, which is the derivative dT/dt is proportional to the difference between the object's temperature T and the ambient temperature which is zero. Thus, $dT/dt = -kT$, where $k > 0$ (the object must cool–thus the negative sign). The solution to this differential equation is $T = T_0 e^{-kt}$ where T_0 is the initial temperature. When $t = 1$, $T = T_0/2$, or $T_0/2 = T_0 e^{-k}$. Solving for k, we obtain $k = \ln 2$.

20.   (C)

An element g is of order 2 if $g^2 = e$ but $g \neq e$. Since e is one of the m elements satisfying the indicated relation, there must be exactly $m - 1$ elements of order 2 in the group.

21.   (B)

The function $f(x)$ has a unique fixed point when it maps $[a, b]$ into $[a, b]$ and $|f'(x)| \leq k \leq 1$. The functions in I and II satisfy these conditions. However, III violates the bound on the derivative.

22.   (D)

A tautology is a logical form which is always true, regardless of the truth value of its components. In II, $(P \wedge \neg P)$ is always false. Theorems with a false hypothesis are always true, independent of the truth value of the conclusion. In the other hand, in I, if P and Q are both false, the statement is false, while if P and Q are both true, the statement is true. Thus I cannot be a tautology. Similarly, in III, if P and Q are both false, the statement is true, while if P and Q are both true, the statement is false. Thus, II is the only tautology.

23.   (B)

A linear functional in R^3 must have the form $f(\alpha) = ax + by + cz$ where $\alpha = (a, b, c)$ and $x, y,$ and z are real constants. Using the information given in the problem statement, a system of three equations for $x, y,$ and z are obtained, with solution $x = 4, y = -7,$ and $z = -3$. Thus, the correct form of the functional is given by (B).

24.   (E)

The three elements of U form an abelian group under addition. The only possible value for $1 + 1$ is c, so II holds. By the same token, $c + 1 = 0$ and, using II, I is also true. Finally, by constructing the multiplicative table for U, $c^2 = c \cdot c = 1$ must also hold. Thus, all three statements are true.

25.   (A)

The cross product of any two (non-parallel) vectors in the plane must be normal to the plane. Two such vectors are those joining the given points, namely $\vec{v} = (3, -2, 1)$ and $\vec{w} = (-2, -2, -2)$. Thus, $\vec{v} \times \vec{w} = (8, 4, -12)$. If $P_0 = (x_0, y_0, z_0)$ is a point in the plane, then the equation of the plane is given by

$$A(x - x_0) + B(y - y_0) + C(z - z_0) = 0 \, ,$$

where (A, B, C) is normal to the plane. Using our computed results for the normal, and any of the three given points for P_0 we obtain (A) as the equation for the plane.

26.   (E)

Since $1 \mapsto 3 \mapsto 2 \mapsto 1$ and $5 \mapsto 4 \mapsto 5$, it is straightforward to show that $\beta^7 = \beta$. Thus β^6 is the identity, and so the order of β is six.

27.   (D)

The characteristic polynomial of A is found from the equation $|A - \lambda I| = 0$:

$$\begin{vmatrix} 3 - \lambda & 1 \\ -1 & -1 - \lambda \end{vmatrix} = 0 \, .$$

This determinant evaluates to the polynomial $\lambda^2 - 2\lambda - 2 = 0$. This polynomial also annihilates A, i.e., $A^2 - 2A - 2I = 0$.

28.   (D)

First, note that $(a \circ b) - (b \circ a) = b - a$, so the operation is not commutative. Further, $[a \circ (b \circ c)] - [(a \circ b) \circ c] = 2c - ac$. Thus the operator is not associative. Finally, it is easy to show that inverses in general do not exist. Let $a = 2$. Then $a^{-1} = -1/4$ satisfies the equation, but is not an integer. All three statements are false.

29.   (B)

First, note that

$$P(|x - \mu| \geq c) = 1 - P(-c + \mu \leq x \leq c + \mu).$$

By Chebyshev's theorem, $P(\mu - k\sigma < x < \mu + k\sigma) \geq 1 - 1/k^2$. Letting $k = \sigma/c$, we find that

$$1 - P(-c + \mu \leq x \leq c + \mu) \leq \sigma^2/c^2.$$

Setting the right half of this inequality equal to P_0 yields $c = \sigma/\sqrt{P_0}$.

30.   (A)

The probability of a head on a single toss is $1/3$ and of a tail is $2/3$. For two tosses, the outcomes are $\{HH, TH, HT, TT\}$. If X is the number of tails, then $P(X=0) = P(HH) = 1/9, P(X=1) = P(HT) + P(TH) = 4/9$, and $P(X=2) = P(TT) = 4/9$. The probability distribution is then

$$f(x) = \begin{cases} 1/9, & \text{if } x = 0; \\ 4/9, & \text{if } x = 1; \\ 4/9, & \text{if } x = 2, \end{cases}$$

and

$$E(X) = \sum_{i=1}^{3} x_i f(x_i) = 4/3.$$

31.   (A)

A matrix is orthogonal if $AA^T = I$. We can verify that

$$\begin{pmatrix} 0 & 1 \\ -1 & 0 \end{pmatrix} \cdot \begin{pmatrix} 0 & -1 \\ 1 & 0 \end{pmatrix} = \begin{pmatrix} 1 & 0 \\ 0 & 1 \end{pmatrix},$$

so that (A) is the correct choice.

32.   (C)

Using L'Hopital's rule, we find that

$$\frac{\int_{-x}^{0} \sin t^3 \, dt}{x^4} \rightarrow - \frac{\int_{0}^{-x} \sin t^3 \, dt}{x^4} \rightarrow \frac{\sin x^3}{4x^3} \rightarrow 1/4,$$

since $\sin x / x \rightarrow 1$.

33.   (C)

Every vector space possesses a zero element. In the case of $C[-1, 1]$, the zero element is simply the function $f(x) = 0$. Since every subset of $C[-1, 1]$ that is a vector space must also contain this function, it is clear that the set in (C), which excludes the zero element, cannot be a vector space.

34.   (A)
Let $x^T = (x_1, x_2)$. For the martix in (A),

$$x^T A x = 4x_1^2 + 4x_1 x_2 + x_2^2 = (2x_1 + x_2)^2 \geq 0,$$

with equality only if x_1 and x_2 are both zero.

35.   (D)
Since A and B are symmetric, we have that $(AB)^T = B^T A^T = BA$. Thus AB is symmetric if and only if $AB = BA$, i.e., that A and B commute.

36.   (B)
Note that

$$\sqrt{x^2 + 2x} - x \cdot \frac{\sqrt{x^2 + 2x} + x}{\sqrt{x^2 + 2x} + x} = \frac{2}{\sqrt{1 + 2/x} + 1},$$

and the last quantity evidently tends to 1 as $x \to \infty$.

37.   (E)
Using the sum-of-angles identity, note that

$$\sin[f(x)] = x^2 + \cos(\sin^{-1} x) \sin(\cos^{-1} x)$$

$$= x^2 + (\sqrt{1 - x^2})^2 = 1.$$

Thus, $f(x) = \pi/2$ for every value of x. I, II, and III are all true for constant functions.

38.   (D)

The general solution to the differential equation is $y(x) = c_1 \sin |\lambda x| + c_2 \cos |\lambda| x$ where c_1 and c_2 are arbitrary constants. Now, $y(0) = 0$ implies that $c_2 = 0$. In addition, $y'(1) = 0$ implies that $\cos |\lambda| = 0$. Thus, $|\lambda| = \pi/2 + n\pi$ for every integer n, or

$$\lambda = \pm \frac{2n + 1}{2} \pi, \ n = 0, 1, 2, \ldots$$

39.   (E)

If $f(x)$ is everywhere differentiable, it is continuous, and since the interval is closed and bounded, $f(x)$ is uniformly continuous. Note that the existence of $f'(x)$ implies nothing about the continuity of the derivative nor the existence of the second derivative. In fact, $f'(x)$ may exist, but not be Riemann-integrable.

40.   (D)

A function is periodic if $f(x + T) = f(x)$ for every x and some $T > 0$. For all the indicated functions, the innermost (first evaluated) function in the compositions is periodic, except for (D), which is not periodic. For example $\lim_{x \to -\infty} \cos[\cos(e^x)] = \cos(1)$, a constant, which cannot happen for a nonconstant periodic function.

41.   (C)

First, note that

$$\left(\frac{n + 2}{n + 1} \right)^{2n+3} = \left(1 + \frac{1}{n + 1} \right)^{2(n+1)+1}.$$

Since $[1 + 1/(n + 1)]^{n+1} \to e$, the right term above converges to e^2.

42.   (A)

Evaluating the determinant yields the polynomial $|A| = -x^2 - x - 2$. By setting the first derivative to zero, we find that an extreme value is achieved at $x = -1/2$. This must be a maximum since the second derivative is a negative constant. Finally, note that for this value of x, $|A| = -5/4$.

43.   (C)

As $t \to \infty$ the temperature approaches a steady state because there are no sources of heat and the boundary conditions are time-independent. Under this condition, the governing equation reduces to $u_{xx} = 0$, which is in fact an ordinary differential equation. The solution to the heat equation in this limit is easily seen to be $u = 10x/L$, obtained by integrating the ODE and applying the boundary conditions. The average value of u is then found from the mean value theorem for integrals to be 5.

44.   (D)

First, let $P = \hat{P}_i$, where $i = 1, 2, 3$. Now, substituting this change on dependent variable into the differential equation, and linearizing gives the result that $\hat{P}_1$ and $\hat{P}_3$ become unbounded, but the $\hat{P}_2$ decays to zero. Thus, P_2' is the only stable equilibrium point.

45.   (A)

By the residue theorem, $\oint_\Gamma f(z)\, dz = 2\pi i \sum \text{Res}[f(z)]$. Evaluating the residues at each singularity of $f(z)$, we find that $\text{Res}[f(z)]_{z=i} = -i/2$ and $\text{Res}[f(z)]_{z=-i} = i/2$. Since the sum of the residues vanishes, the integral evaluates to zero.

46.   (C)

By the Cauchy Riemann equations, $u_x = v_y$ and $u_y = -v_x$. Thus, $v_y = 3y^2 - 3x^2$ so that $v(x, y) = y^3 - 3x^2 y + f(x)$. From this, $v_x = -6xy + f'(x)$ which must equal $-u_y$. This last condition implies that $f(x) = -x$. Consequently, $v(x, y) = y^3 - 3x^2 y - x$.

47.   (A)

Evaluating the expression $| A - \lambda I | = 0$ yields the following polynomial for λ :

$$\lambda^2 - (2 + x)\lambda + 2x + 1 = 0,$$

which has the solution

$$\lambda = \frac{2 + x \pm \sqrt{(2 + x)^2 - 4(2x + 1)}}{2}.$$

There will be a double eigenvalue when the discriminant is zero, that is when

$$(2 + x)^2 - 4(2x + 1) = 0.$$

The roots to this last equation are at $x = 0$ and $x = 4$.

48.   (B)

Since the sequence converges, let $a = \lim\limits_{n \to \infty} a_n$. Then $a = \sqrt{b + a}$. Because the sequence is monotone increasing, a must be positive. Solving for a, we find that

$$a = \frac{1 + \sqrt{1 + 4b}}{2}.$$

For a to be an integer, $1 + 4b$ must be an odd perfect square. Examining the odd perfect squares from 9 upward, the first value of b to occur which is a multiple of 7 is 42.

49.   (A)

Using the disk method, the infintesimal volume dV of a disk centered at x is $dV = \pi[r(x)]^2dx$, where $r(x) = e^{-x}$. Thus,

$$V = \int_0^\infty dV = \int_0^\infty \pi e^{-2x} dx = \pi/2 .$$

50.   (E)

Counterexamples exist for all three statements. For example, the

Fresnel integral $\int_0^\infty \sin(x^2) \, dx$, converges, but $\sin(x^2)$ does not coverge at all as $x \to \infty$. Thus, I may be false. By the same token, the integral just mentioned is not absolutely integrable, so II is also false. In fact, the Fresnel integral is not a square integrable either, and III is false as well.

51.   (E)

Since $f(z)$ is entire, it is analytic everywhere in the complex plane. Thus $f'(z)$ is also entire. In addition, $f(z)$ has a singularity at infinity, so that no limit exists as $z \to \infty$. Also, every contour integral vanishes because $f(z)$ is everywhere analytic. $f(z) = e^z$ does not vanish at the origin.

52.   (B)

Using the technique of reduction of order, a second linearly-independent solution has the form

$$y = x\left(\int^x\left[\frac{1}{s^2}\exp\left(-\int^s t\,dt\right)\right]\right).$$

This evaluates to $y = x\int^x e^{-t^2}/t^2\,dt$.

53.   (E)

The curves are recognized as a pair of hyperbola. The general equation for this conic section is $\pm x^2/a^2 \mp y^2/b^2 = 1$. Since the hyperbolas have vertices at $(\pm 2, 0)$, it must hold that $a^2 = 4$. The only equation with the correct form is (E).

54.   (C)

Note that

$$i^i = e^{(i\pi/2 + 2n\pi i)i} = e^{-\pi/2 + 2n\pi},$$

where n is any integer. For $n = 1$, $i^i = e^{3\pi/2}$.

55.   (D)

Monotonicity and continuity (or a closed and bounded interval) are sufficient conditions for integrability. In addition, all bounded and piecewise smooth functions are also integrable. However, consider the function

$$f(x) = \begin{cases} 0, & \text{if } x = 0 \\ 1/x, & \text{if } 0 < x \le 1. \end{cases}$$

This function is clearly not integrable, but has only one discontinuity.

56.   (B)

At worst, y can be discontinuous (hence not differentiable) at every point other than zero. For example, $y = x^2$ if x is rational and $y = -x^2$ if x is irrational. However, y is differentiable at the origin. To see this, examine the difference quotient at $x = 0$:

$$-x \leq (y - 0)/(x - 0) \leq x.$$

As $x \to 0$, the difference quotient goes to 0 as well, showing that y' exists at the origin.

57.   (D)

Take the logarithm of $f(x)$:

$$\ln f(x) = \frac{1}{\ln x} \cdot \ln x = 1,$$

so that $f(x) = e$ for $x \neq 1$. Clearly $f(1) = e$ also.

58.   (D)

Applying the ratio test, we obtain

$$\lim_{n \to \infty} \left| \frac{a_{n+1}}{a_n} \right| = \frac{|x + 2|}{3}.$$

Since the limit must be less than unity for convergence, we have that $|x + 2| < 3$ or $-5 < x < 2$. At the right and left end of the interval, the series converges by the comparison test.

59.   (C)

Note that this algorithm implements the formula

$$a_{n+1} = \begin{cases} a_n/2, & \text{if } a_n \text{ is even;} \\ 3a_n + 1, & \text{if } a_n \text{ is odd.} \end{cases}$$

Since the first value output is made *after* the input is changed, the first output values must be 40. The remaining output values are obtained by applying the above formula until the output value 1 is produced at which point the algorithm terminates.

60.   (B)

In R^2, sets are compact if and only if they are both closed and bounded. (A) is closed but unbounded. (E) is open. (C) and (D) are bounded, but neither open nor closed. (B) is both closed and bounded.

61.   (E)

In Z_{13}, we have two simultaneous equations

$$\bar{6}x + \bar{5}y = \bar{0} \text{ and } \bar{8}x + by = \bar{0}.$$

Eliminating x, we find that the remaining equation for y is satisfied only if

$$\bar{3}b = \bar{7}.$$

Since $33 = 7 \mod 13$, $b = 11$.

62.   (C)

That every field is also an integral domain follows from the definition of a field. However, not every field has a finite subfield. For example, the rational numbers possess no finite subfield. The transcendental real numbers are not a field because 0 (the additive identity) is not in the set.

63.   (A)

Note that $27 = 2^4 + 2^3 + 2^1 + 2^0 = (011011)_2$ and $52 = 2^5 + 2^4 + 2^2$ $= (110100)_2$. The result digit is 1 if and only if both respective digits are 1. The result is therefore $(010000)_2 = 2^4 = 16$.

64.   (B)

Every density function must integrate to unity. (E) is not integrable, while (A), (C), and (D) integrate to something other than 1. (B), in fact, is an example of an exponential distribution.

65.   (C)

The contraposition of an implication is that the negation of the conclusion implies the negation of the hypothesis. Thus,

$$\neg(\neg R \wedge S) = R \vee \neg S \Rightarrow \neg(P \wedge Q) = \neg P \vee \neg Q.$$

66.   (A)

First, note that the eigenvalues of A are $\lambda_1 = 2$ and $\lambda_2 = 1$. Corresponding eigenvectors are $x^T_1 = (2, 3)$ and $x^T_2 = (1, 2)$. These eigenvalues form the columns of a matrix S which can be used to diagonalize A. The similarity matrix is therefore given by (A).

REA's Problem Solvers

REA's Test Preps
The Best in Test Preparations

The REA "Test Preps" are far more comprehensive than any other test series. They contain more tests with much more extensive explanations than others on the market. Each book provides several complete practice exams, based on the most recent tests given in the particular field. Every type of question likely to be given on the exams is included. Each individual test is followed by a complete answer key. **The answers are accompanied by full and detailed explanations.** By studying each test and the pertinent explanations, students will become well-prepared for the actual exam.

REA has published 20 Test Preparation volumes in several series. They include:

Advanced Placement Exams
Biology
Calculus AB & Calculus BC
Chemistry
English Literature & Composition
European History
United States History

College Board Achievement Tests
American History
Biology
Chemistry
English Composition
French
German
Spanish
Literature
Mathematics Level I & II

Graduate Record Exams
Biology
Chemistry
Computer Science
Economics
Engineering
General
Literature in English
Mathematics
Physics
Psychology

FE - Fundamentals of Engineering Exam
GMAT - Graduate Management Admission Test
MCAT - Medical College Admission Test
NTE - National Teachers Exam
SAT - Scholastic Aptitude Test
LSAT - Law School Admission Test
TOEFL - Test of English as a Foreign Language

HANDBOOK of
**MATHEMATICAL,
SCIENTIFIC, &
ENGINEERING**
FORMULAS, FUNCTIONS,
GRAPHS, TABLES,
& TRANSFORMS

RESEARCH & EDUCATION ASSOCIATION

HANDBOOK AND GUIDE FOR
COMPARING and SELECTING
COMPUTER LANGUAGES

BASIC	PL/1
FORTRAN	APL
PASCAL	ALGOL-60
COBOL	C

- This book is the first of its kind ever produced in computer science.

- It examines and highlights the differences and similarities among the eight most widely used computer languages.

- A practical guide for selecting the most appropriate programming language for any given task.

- Sample programs in all eight languages are written and compared side-by-side. Their merits are analyzed and evaluated.

- Comprehensive glossary of computer terms.

Available at your local bookstore or order directly from us by sending in coupon below.

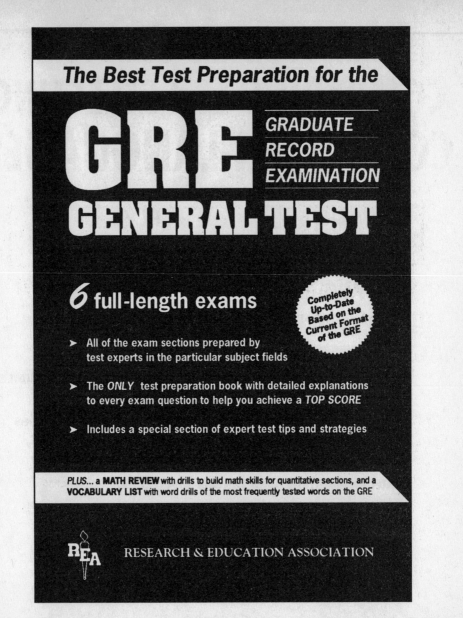